W9-CMK-664

THE WOMAN
IN AMERICA

DISCARDED
FROM
UNIVERSITY OF DAYTON
ROESCH LIBRARY

THE DAEDALUS LIBRARY

Each of these volumes is available as a Beacon Press Paperback.

A New Europe? Edited by Stephen R. Graubard
The Professions in America, Edited by Kenneth S. Lynn
The Woman in America, Edited by Robert Jay Lifton
Science and Culture, Edited by Gerald Holton
Utopias and Utopian Thought, Edited by Frank E. Manuel
The Contemporary University: U.S.A., Edited by Robert S. Morison
The Negro American, Edited by Talcott Parsons and Kenneth B. Clark

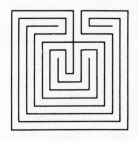

THE WOMAN
IN AMERICA

EDITED BY ROBERT JAY LIFTON

BEACON PRESS   BOSTON

WOMEN'S STUDIES PROGRAM
UNIVERSITY OF DAYTON
ST. JOSEPH   414

Copyright © 1964, 1965 by the
American Academy of Arts and Sciences

First published as a Beacon Paperback in 1967 by
arrangement with Houghton Mifflin Company

Beacon Press books are published under the auspices
of the Unitarian Universalist Association

All rights reserved including the right to reproduce
this book or parts thereof in any form

Most of the essays in this book first appeared
in the Spring 1964 issue of *Daedalus,* the Journal
of the American Academy of Arts and Sciences

Published simultaneously in Canada by Saunders of Toronto, Ltd.

Printed in the United States of America

International Standard Book Number: 0-8070-4197-1

Third printing, March 1971

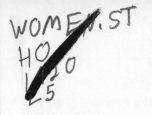

WOMEN.ST
HO
L 5

CONTENTS

Contents

INTRODUCTION

THE FOLLOWING dialogue (whose participants are of undisclosed gender) did *not* take place at the original conference from which most of this book evolved.

INERTIA: No matter what people say these days, I still think there is much to the idea of "eternal woman." I agree with the man who said some time ago: "It is a great consolation to reflect that, among all the bewildering changes to which the world is subject, the character of woman cannot be altered."

FLUX: False consolation, my dear Inertia. Women are, in fact, changing much more rapidly than our ideas about them. The question is whether we can at least make an effort to catch up by casting off precisely the shibboleths you express.

INERTIA: Well, the principle that "anatomy is destiny" was good enough for both Napoleon and Freud. *They* held to the idea of the biological basis of woman's nature. It seems to me that we should hold to it too.

FLUX: I couldn't disagree with you more. There is, in fact, no such thing as woman's nature. Woman, like man, is a product of human history.

INERTIA: Come now, Flux. You can't mean that. Take the American woman, for example. Whatever her special history, she is, deep down, like all other women—concerned with love, marriage, family, and so on.

FLUX: Wrong again. She seems to me to be different from other women in every way. And, in case you haven't heard, she is interested in quite a few things besides love, marriage, and family.

INERTIA: Well, let's look at the matter another way. Women in America have been given extraordinary opportunities to express themselves—whether in work or in social or family life. But has this made them any happier or given them real fulfillment?

FLUX: Frankly, I don't think that American society has been as generous to its women as people think it has. Women are still discriminated against in most professions, and there are so many ways in which our institutions place great limitation upon their freedom. America has a long way to go before it can claim to have created large numbers of truly emancipated women.

INERTIA: I doubt whether any society ever "creates" its women, but let that pass. Consider for a moment the intellectual woman in America. Now she has certainly involved herself in a lot of areas that we used to think were limited to men. But I get the impression that these involvements have only caused her confusion and a feeling of being pulled in all directions.

FLUX: Well, give her time. Offered the chance, there's no telling what kind of things she might be capable of doing. She may, in fact, turn into a totally new kind of woman.

INERTIA: I'll tell you what your trouble is, Flux. You are too restless. And that is exactly the trouble with those American women you have been talking about. If they would just settle down and be women, everyone would be better off.

FLUX: Inertia, my friend, no one settles down any more. These days it just isn't done. The only way for American women to be women is to go on changing indefinitely. . . .

Happily, the tone of the dialogue at our conference—held in October, 1963, at the House of the American Academy of Arts and Sciences—was a bit different. Neither Inertia nor Flux, in the caricatured versions I have presented here, could be heard. But the issues raised in this little exchange were very much present, since they are pertinent to any approach to the woman in America or elsewhere. By restating the Inertia-Flux controversy in somewhat more illuminating terms, we come to five questions which dominated the *Dædalus* conference on women: What in woman may be said to be enduring, and what is subject to social and historical modification? To what extent is woman's psychological life determined by her anatomy and biology, and to what extent can we speak of a specific feminine psychology? What opportunities does American society hold out to its women, and are these appropriate to their needs? What are the special problems and potential of the highly educated woman? Are there ways in which women can make special contributions toward the particularly grave dilemmas which now confront the world?

Participants in the conference and authors contributing to this volume thus had no choice but to return to old questions. But to these old questions we attempted to add particularly contemporary dimensions. The essays included here vary enormously in approach —from descriptive elaboration, to comparative analysis, to radical proposal for action, to balanced contemplation. Yet I think they share two kinds of awareness: that of the commentator's special relationship to the very biological, evolutionary, and historical processes he or she describes; and that of the difficulty in, and necessity for, bringing together unique features of present experience with timeless universals. The volume has a clear psychological emphasis, but also has a good deal to say about general social and cultural issues. In particular, I think it makes some unusual forays into that difficult intellectual terrain that tries to combine psychology and history.

Whatever merit the volume may have is due in no small measure to the vision and energy of Stephen R. Graubard, who planned and chaired the original conference, edited the issue of *Dædalus* which contained most of these essays, and continued to guide all efforts right down to the time of publication. Helen Hill Miller offered valuable advice, and a grant from the Edgar Stern Family Fund made both the book and the original issue of *Dædalus* possible.

It is customary at this point, in recognizing a book's limitations, to say something to the effect that it does not try to do any more than raise a few pertinent issues. But I think I would claim both a little more and a little less. We raise no issues that are entirely new. But we present a few ideas which seem to me sufficiently original and important to be heard and responded to.

ROBERT JAY LIFTON

Woodbridge, Conn.
March, 1965.

ERIK H. ERIKSON

Inner and Outer Space: Reflections on Womanhood

1.

THERE are a great number of practical reasons for an intensified
awareness of woman's position in the modern world: reasons concerning the availability of women for jobs in which *they are needed*
and of their employability in jobs which *they need* in view of intensified industrial competition, international and national. But I
believe that there are deeper and darker reasons. The ubiquity of
nuclear threat, the breakthrough into outer space, and increasing
global communication are all bringing about a total change in the
sense of geographic space and of historical time, and thus they
necessitate a redefinition of the identity of the sexes within a new
image of man. I cannot go here into the alliances and oppositions
of the two sexes in previous styles of war and peace. This is a history as yet to be written and, indeed, discovered. But it is clear that
the danger of man-made poison dropping invisibly from outer space
into the marrow of the unborn in the wombs of women has suddenly brought one major male preoccupation, namely, the "solution"
of conflict by periodical and bigger and better wars to its own
limits. The question arises whether such a potential for annihilation
as now exists in the world should continue to exist without the representation of the mothers of the species in the councils of image-
making and of decision.

The frantic and diffused preoccupation with the differences between the sexes and the question as to what kind of woman, now
that equality assumes a new and world-wide importance, should be
mass manufactured in the future in place of the types now favored
by the mass media also reflect a widespread sense on the part of
both sexes that a great psychological counterforce has been neglected

1

in what has purported to be progress toward a technological millennium. The special dangers of the nuclear age clearly have brought male leadership close to the limit of its adaptive imagination. The dominant male identity is based on a fondness for "what works" and of what man can make, whether it helps to build or to destroy. For this very reason the all too obvious necessity to sacrifice some of the possible climaxes of technological triumph and of political hegemony for the sake of the mere preservation of mankind is not in itself an endeavor enhancing the male sense of identity. True, an American president felt impelled to say, and said with deep feeling: "A child is not a statistic"; yet the almost desperate urgency of his pleas made clear enough the need for a new kind of political and technological ethics. Maybe if women would only gain the determination to represent as image providers and law givers what they have always stood for privately in evolution and in history (realism of householding, responsibility of upbringing, resourcefulness in peacekeeping, and devotion to healing), they might well be mobilized to add an ethically restraining, because truly supranational, power to politics in the widest sense.

This, I think, many men and women hope openly and many more, secretly. But their hope collides with dominant trends in our technological civilization, and with deep inner resistances as well. Self-made man, in "granting" a relative emancipation to women, could offer only his self-made image as a model to be equaled; and much of the freedom thus won by women now seems to have been spent in gaining access to limited career competition, standardized consumership, and strenuous one-family homemaking. Thus woman, in many ways, has kept her place within the typologies and cosmologies which men have had the exclusive opportunity to cultivate and to idolize. In other words, even where equality is closer to realization it has not led to equivalence, and equal rights have by no means secured equal representation in the sense that the deepest concerns of women find expression in their public influence or, indeed, their actual role in the game of power. In view of the gigantic one-sidedness which is threatening to make man the slave of his triumphant technology, the now fashionable discussion, by women and by men, as to whether woman could and how she might become "fully human" in the traditional sense is really a cosmic parody, and for once one is nostalgic for gods with a sense of humor. The very question as to what it is to be "fully human" and who has the right to grant it to whom indicates that a discussion of the male and female elements in the potentialities of human nature must include rather fundamental issues.

An interdisciplinary symposium, therefore, cannot avoid exploring certain emotional reactions or resistances which hinder concerted discussion. We all have observed the fact that it seems almost impossible to discuss woman's nature or nurture without awaking the slogans (for and against) of the all too recent struggle for emancipation. Moralistic fervor outlives changed conditions, and feminist suspicion watches over any man's attempt to help define the uniqueness of womanhood. Yet it still seems to be amazingly hard for the vast majority of women to say clearly what they feel most deeply, and to find the right words for what to them is most acute and actual, without saying too much or too little, and without saying it with defiance or apology. Some who observe and think vividly and deeply do not seem to have the courage of their native intelligence, as if they were somehow afraid on some final confrontation to be found to have no "real" intelligence. Even successful academic competition has, in many, failed to correct this. Thus women are tempted quickly to go back to "their place" whenever they feel out of place. I would also think that a major problem exists in the relationship of leading women to each other and to their women followers. As far as I can judge, "leading" women are all too often inclined to lead in too volatile, moralistic, or sharp a manner (as if they agreed to the proposition that only exceptional and hard women can think) rather than to inform themselves of and to give voice to what the mass of undecided women are groping to say and are willing to stand by, and thus what use they may wish to make of an equal voice in world affairs. Here, maybe, countries in the stages of rapid development or urgent recovery are more fortunate, for immediate needs are more obvious, and free choices restricted.

On the other hand, the hesitance of many men to respond to the new "feminist" alarm, as well as the agitated response of others, may suggest explanations on many levels. No doubt there exists among men an honest sense of wishing to save at whatever cost a sexual polarity, a vital tension and an essential difference which they fear may be lost in too much sameness, equality, and equivalence, or at any rate in too much self-conscious talk. Beyond this, the defensiveness of men (and here we must include the best educated) has many facets. Where men desire, they want to awake desire, not empathize or ask for empathy. Where they do not desire, they find it hard to empathize, especially where empathy makes it necessary

3

to see the other in yourself and yourself in the other, and where therefore the horror of diffused delineations is apt to kill both joy in otherness and sympathy for sameness. It also stands to reason that where dominant identities depend on being dominant, it is hard to grant real equality to the dominated. And, finally, where one feels exposed, threatened, or cornered, it is difficult to be judicious.

For all of this there are age-old psychological reasons, upon only a very few of which will I be able to throw light with my essay. But even a limited report, in the present climate, calls for an acknowledgment from the onset that ambivalences and ambiguities of ancient standing are apt to be temporarily aggravated rather than alleviated by attempts to share partial insight in these matters.

2.

There is another general consideration which must precede the discussion of a subject which is so incompletely formulated and which always retains an intense actuality. Every discussant will and must begin where he feels his own field has succeeded or failed to do justice to the issue as he sees it, that is, where he feels he is coming from and going within his own advancing discipline. But since the intricacies of his discipline and of his position in it cannot be intimately known to all discussants, he is apt to be confronted with the remark which a Vermont farmer made to a driver who asked him for directions: "Man, if I wanted to go where you want to go, I wouldn't start here."

Here is where I am, and where I intend to go. In my preface to the book which grew out of the Youth issue of *Dædalus*,[1] I pointed out that that extraordinary symposium failed to develop fully— although Bruno Bettelheim made a determined start—the problem of the identity of female youth. This is a severe theoretical handicap. For the student of development and practitioner of psychoanalysis, the stage of life crucial for the understanding of womanhood is the step from youth to maturity, the state when the young woman relinquishes the care received from the parental family and the extended care of institutions of education, in order to commit herself to the love of a stranger and to the care to be given to his and her offspring. In the *Dædalus* issue on Youth, I suggested that the mental and emotional ability to receive and to give *Fidelity* marks the conclusion of adolescence, while adulthood begins with the ability to receive and give *Love* and *Care*. If the terms here capitalized sound shockingly virtuous in a way reminiscent of moralistic values, I offer no apology: to me, they represent human strengths which are not a matter of moral or esthetic choice, but of stark necessity in individual development and social evolution. For the strength of the generations (and by this I mean a basic disposition *underlying* all varieties of human value systems) depends on the process by which the youths of the two sexes find their respective identities, fuse them in love and marriage, revitalize their respective traditions, and together create and "bring up" the next generation. Here whatever sexual differences and dispositions have developed in earlier life become polarized with finality because they must become part of the whole process of production and procreation which marks adulthood. But how, then, does a woman's identity formation differ by dint of the fact that her somatic design harbors an "inner space" destined to bear the offspring of chosen men and, with it, a biological, psychological, and ethical commitment to take care of human infancy? Is not the disposition for this commitment (whether it be realized in actual motherhood or not) the core problem of *female* fidelity?

The psychoanalytic psychology of women, however, does not "start here." In line with its originological orientation, i.e. the endeavor to infer the meaning of an issue from its origins, it begins with the earliest experiences of differentiation, largely reconstructed from women patients necessarily at odds with their womanhood and with the permanent inequality to which it seemed to doom them. However, since the psychoanalytic method could be developed only in work with acutely suffering individuals, whether adults or children, it was necessary to accept clinical observation as the original starting point for investigating what the little girl, when becoming aware of sex-differences, can *know* as observable fact, can *feel* because it causes intense pleasure or unpleasant tension, or may *infer* or *intuit* with the cognitive and imaginative means at her disposal. Here it would be as unfair as it would be easy to extract quotations from psychoanalysts who were much too circumspect not to offer at least on the margins of their discourses extensive modifications of Freud's position. Nevertheless, I think it is fair to say that the psychoanalytic view of womanhood has been strongly influenced by the fact that the first and basic observations were made by clinicians whose task it was to understand suffering and to offer a remedy; and that they by necessity had to understand the female psyche with male means of empathy, and to offer what the ethos of enlightenment dictated, namely, the "acceptance of reality." It is in line with this historical position that they saw, in the reconstructed lives of little girls, primarily an attempt to observe what could be seen and grasped (namely, what was there in boys and hardly there in girls) and to base on this observation "infantile sexual theories" of vast consequence.

From this point of view, the most obvious fact, namely that children of both sexes sooner or later "know" the penis to be missing in one sex, leaving in its place a woundlike aperture, has led to generalizations concerning women's nature and nurture. From an adaptive point of view, however, it does not seem reasonable to assume that observation and empathy, except in moments of acute or transitory disturbance, would so exclusively focus on what is *not* there. The female child under all but extreme urban conditions is disposed to observe evidence in older girls and women and in female animals of the fact that an inner-bodily space—with productive as well as dangerous potentials—does exist. Here one thinks not only of pregnancy and childbirth, but also of lactation, and of all the richly convex parts of the female anatomy which suggest fullness, warmth, and generosity. One wonders, for example, whether girls are quite as upset by observed symptoms of pregnancy or of menstruation as are (certain) boys, or whether they absorb such observation in the rudiments of a female identity—unless, of course, they are "protected" from the opportunity of comprehending the ubiquity and the meaning of these natural phenomena. Now, no doubt, at various stages of childhood observed data will be interpreted with the cognitive means then available, will be perceived in analogy with the organs then most intensely experienced, and will be endowed with the impulses then prevailing. Dreams, myths, and cults attest to the fact that the vagina has and retains (for both sexes) connotations of a devouring mouth as well as an eliminating sphincter, in addition to being a bleeding wound. However, the cumulative experience of being and becoming a man or a woman cannot, I believe, be entirely dependent upon fearful analogies and phantasies. Sensory reality and logical conclusion are given form by kinesthetic experience and by series of memories which "make sense"; and in this total actuality the existence of a *productive inner-bodily space* safely set in the center of female form and carriage has a reality superior to that of the missing organ.

This whole controversy has, I am sure, little to do with the starting point of most participants in this symposium. If I nevertheless start from here, it is because I believe that a future formulation of sex-differences must at least include post-Freudian insights in order not to succumb to the repressions and denials of pre-Freudian days.

3.

Let me present here an observation which makes my point wordlessly. Since it has already been presented on a number of other occasions, I should admit that I am the kind of clinical worker in whose mind a few observations linger for a long time. Such observations are marked by a combination of being surprised by the unexpected and yet somehow confirmed by something long awaited. For this same reason, I am apt to present such observations to various audiences, hoping each time that understanding may be deepened.

It was in the observation of preadolescent children that I was enabled to observe sex-differences in a nonclinical setting. The children were Californian boys and girls, aged ten, eleven, and twelve years, who twice a year came to be measured, interviewed, and tested in the "Guidance Study" of the University of California. It speaks for the feminine genius of the director of the study, Jean Walker Macfarlane, that for over more than two decades the children (and their parents) not only came with regularity, but confided their thoughts with little reservation and, in fact, with much "zest"— to use Jean Macfarlane's favorite word. That means they were confident of being appreciated as growing individuals and eager to reveal and to demonstrate what (so they had been convincingly told) was useful to know and might be helpful to others. Since this psychoanalyst, before joining the California study, had made it his business to interpret play-behavior—a nonverbal approach which had helped him to understand better what his small patients were not able to communicate in words—it was decided that he would test his clinical hypotheses by securing a number of play-constructions from each child. Over a span of two years, I saw 150 boys and 150 girls three times and presented them, one at a time, with the task of constructing a "scene" with toys on a table. The toys were rather ordinary: a family; some uniformed figures (policeman, aviator, Indian, monk, etc.); wild and domestic animals; furniture; automobiles. But I also provided a variety of blocks. The children were asked to imagine that the table was a moving picture studio; the toys, actors and props; and they themselves, moving picture directors. They were to arrange on the table "an exciting scene from an imaginary moving picture," and then tell the plot. This was recorded, the scene photographed, and the child complimented. It may be necessary to add that no "interpretation" was given.

The observer then compared the individual constructions with about ten years of data in the files to see whether it provided some key to the major determinants of the child's inner development. On the whole this proved helpful, but that is not the point to be made here. The experiment also made possible a comparison of all play constructions with each other.

A few of the children went about the task with the somewhat contemptuous attitude of one doing something which was not exactly worth the effort of a young person already in his teens, but almost all of these bright and willing youngsters in somber jeans and gay dresses were drawn to the challenge by that eagerness to serve and to please which characterized the whole population of the study. And once they were "involved," certain properties of the task took over and guided them.

It soon became evident that among these properties the spatial one was dominant. Only half of the scenes were "exciting," and only a handful had anything to do with moving pictures. In fact, the stories told at the end were for the most part brief and in no way comparable to the thematic richness evidenced in verbal tests. But the care and (one is tempted to say) esthetic responsibility with which the children selected blocks and toys and then arranged them according to an apparently deeply held sense of spatial propriety was astounding. At the end, it seemed to be a sudden feeling of "now it's right" which made them come to a sense of completion and, as if awakening from a wordless experience, turn to me and say, "I am ready now,"—meaning: to tell you what this is all about.

I, myself, was most interested in defining the tools and developing the art of observing not only imaginative themes but also spatial configurations in relation to stages of the life cycle, and, of course, in checking psychoanalytic assumptions concerning the sources and forms of neurotic tension in prepuberty. Sex-differences thus were not the initial focus of my interest in spatial behavior. I concentrated my attention on how these constructions-in-progress moved forward to the edge of the table or back to the wall behind it; how they rose to shaky heights or remained close to the table surface; how they were spread over the available space or constricted to a portion of the space. That all of this "says" something about the constructor is the open secret of all "projective techniques." This, too, cannot be discussed here. But soon I realized that in evaluating a child's play-construction, I had to take into consideration the fact that girls and boys used space differently, and that certain configurations occurred strikingly often in the constructions of one sex and rarely in those of the other.

The differences themselves were so simple that at first they seemed a matter of course. History in the meantime has offered a slogan for it: the girls emphasized inner and the boys outer space.

This difference I was soon able to state in such simple configurational terms that other observers, when shown photographs of the constructions without knowing the sex of the constructor (nor, indeed, having any idea of my thoughts concerning the possible meaning of the differences), could sort the photographs according to the configurations most dominant in them, and this significantly in the statistical sense. These independent ratings showed that considerably more than two thirds of what I subsequently called male configurations occurred in scenes constructed by boys, and more than two thirds of the "female" configurations in the constructions of girls. I will here omit the finer points which still characterized the atypical scenes as clearly built by a boy or by a girl. This, then, is typical: the girl's scene is an *interior* scene, represented either as a configuration of furniture without any surrounding walls, or by a *simple enclosure* built with blocks. In the girl's scene, people and animals are mostly *within* such an interior or enclosure, and they are primarily people or animals in a *static* (sitting, standing) position. Girls' enclosures consist of *low walls*, i.e. only one block high, except for an occasional elaborate *doorway*. These interiors of houses with or without walls were, for the most part, expressly *peaceful*. Often, a little girl was playing the piano. In a number of cases, however, the *interior was intruded* by animals or dangerous men. Yet the idea of an intruding creature did not necessarily lead to the defensive erection of walls or the closing of doors. Rather the majority of these intrusions have an element of humor and of pleasurable excitement.

Boys' scenes are either houses with *elaborate walls* or *façades with protrusions* such as cones or cylinders representing ornaments or cannons. There are *high towers;* and there are *exterior scenes.* In boys' constructions more people and animals are *outside* enclosures or buildings, and there are more *automotive objects* and *animals moving* along streets and intersections. There are elaborate automotive *accidents,* but also traffic channeled or arrested by the *policeman.* While high structures are prevalent in the configurations of the boys, there is also much play with the danger of collapse or *downfall; ruins* were exclusively boys' constructions.

The male and female spaces, then, were dominated, respectively, by height and downfall and by strong motion and its channelization or arrest; and by static interiors which were open or simply enclosed, and peaceful or intruded upon. It may come as a surprise to some, and seem a matter of course to others, that here sexual differences in the organization of a play space seem to parallel the morphology of genital differentiation itself: in the male, an *external* organ, *erectible* and *intrusive* in character, serving the channelization of *mobile* sperm cells; *internal* organs in the female, with vestibular *access*, leading to *statically expectant* ova. The question is, what *is* really surprising about this, and what only too obvious, and in either case, what does it tell us about the two sexes?

4.

Since I first presented these data a decade and a half ago to workers in different fields, some standard interpretations have not yielded an iota. There are, of course, derisive reactions which take it for granted that a psychoanalyst would want to read the bad old symbols into this kind of data. And indeed, Freud did note more than half a century ago that "a house is the only regularly occurring symbol of the (whole) human body in dreams." But there is quite a methodological step (not to be specified here) from the occurrence of a symbol in dreams and a configuration created in actual space. Nevertheless, the purely psychoanalytic or somatic explanation has been advanced that the scenes reflect the preadolescent's preoccupation with his own sexual organs.

The purely "social" interpretation, on the other hand, denies the necessity to see anything symbolic or, indeed, somatic in these configurations. It takes it for granted that boys love the outdoors and girls the indoors, or at any rate that they see their respective roles assigned to the indoors of houses and to the great outdoors of adventure, to tranquil feminine love for family and children and to high masculine aspiration.

One cannot help agreeing with both interpretations—up to a point. Of course, whatever social role is associated with one's physique will be expressed thematically in any playful or artistic representation. And, of course, under conditions of special tension or preoccupation with one part of the body, that body part may be recognizable in play-configurations. The spokesmen for the anatomical and for the social interpretations are thus both right if they insist that neither possibility may be ignored. But this does not make either exclusively right.

A pure interpretation in terms of social role leaves many questions unanswered. If the boys thought primarily of their present or anticipated roles, why, for example, is the policeman their favorite toy, traffic stopped dead a frequent scene? If vigorous activity outdoors is a determinant of the boys' scenes, why did they not arrange *any* sports fields on the play table? (One tomboyish girl did.) Why did the girls' love for home life not result in an increase in high walls and closed doors as guarantors of intimacy and security? And could the role of playing the piano in the bosom of their families really be considered representative of what these girls (some of them passionate horseback riders and all future automobilists) wanted to do most or, indeed, thought they should pretend they wanted to do most? Thus the boys' *caution outdoors* and the girls' *goodness indoors* in response to the explicit instruction to construct an *exciting movie scene* suggested dynamic dimensions and acute conflicts not explained by a theory of mere compliance with cultural and conscious roles.

I would suggest an altogether more inclusive interpretation, according to which a profound difference exists between the sexes in the experience of the groundplan of the human body. I could point to a number of diverse observations of spontaneous play and of test responses, all of which converge on the fact that there are, indeed, early as well as persistent sexual differences in the preferred treatment of space. The emphasis here is on predisposition and predeliction, rather than on exclusive ability, for both sexes (if otherwise matched in maturation or intelligence) learn readily to imitate the spatial mode of the other sex. Nothing in our interpretation, then, is meant to claim that either sex is doomed to one spatial mode or another; rather, it is suggested that in contexts which are not imitative or competitive, these modes "come more naturally" for natural reasons which must claim our interest. The spatial phenomenon observed here would then express two principles of arranging space which correspond to the male and female principles in body construction. These may receive special emphasis in pre-puberty, and maybe in some other stages of life as well, but they are relevant throughout life to the elaboration of sex-roles in cultural space-times. Such an interpretation cannot be "proven," of course, by the

11

one observation offered here. The question is whether it is in line with observations of spatial behavior in other media and at other ages; whether it can be made a plausible part of a developmental theory; and whether, indeed, it gives to other sex-differences closely related to male and female structure and function a more convincing order. On the other hand, it would not be contradicted by the fact that other media of observation employed to test male and female performance might reveal few or no sexual differences in areas of the mind which have the function of securing verbal or cognitive agreement on matters dominated by the mathematical nature of the universe and the verbal agreement of cultural traditions. Such agreement, in fact, may have as its very function the *correction* of what differentiates the experience of the sexes, even as it also corrects the idiosyncrasies separating other classes of men.

The play-constructing children in Berkeley, California, will lead us into a number of spatial considerations, especially concerning feminine development and outlook. Here I will say little about men; their accomplishments in the conquest of geographic space and of scientific fields and in the dissemination of ideas speak loudly for themselves and confirm traditional values of masculinity. Yet the play-constructing boys in Berkeley may give us pause: on the world scene, do we not see a supremely gifted yet somewhat boyish mankind playing with history and technology, and this following a male pattern as embarrassingly simple (if technologically complex) as the play-constructions of the preadolescent? Do we not see the themes of the toy microcosm dominating an expanding human space: height, penetration, and speed; collision, explosion—and cosmic super-police? In the meantime, women have found their identities in the care suggested in their bodies and in the needs of their issue, and seem to have taken it for granted that the outer world space belongs to the men.

5.

Many of the original conclusions of psychoanalysis concerning womanhood hinge on the so-called genital trauma, i.e. the little girl's sudden comprehension of the fact that she does not and never will have a penis. The assumed prevalence of envy in women; the assumption that the future baby is a substitute for the penis; the interpretation that the girl turns from the mother to the father because she finds that the mother not only cheated her out of a penis but has been cheated herself; and finally the woman's disposition to abandon (male) activity and aggressivity for the sake of a "passive-masochistic" orientation: all of these depend on "the trauma," and all have been built into elaborate explanations of femininity. They all exist; and their psychic truth can be shown by psychoanalysis, although it must always be suspected that a special method bares truths especially true under the circumstances created by the method, here the venting in free association of hidden resentments and repressed traumata. These truths, however, assume the character of very partial truths within a theory of feminine development which would assume the early relevance of the productive interior and would thus allow for a shift of theoretical emphasis from the loss of an external organ to a sense of vital inner potential; from a hateful contempt of the mother to a solidarity with her and other women; from a "passive" renunciation of male activity to the purposeful and competent activity of one endowed with ovaries and a uterus; and from a masochistic pleasure in pain to an ability to stand (and to understand) pain as a meaningful aspect of human experience in general, and of the feminine role in particular. And so it is, in the "fully feminine" woman, as such outstanding writers as Helena Deutsch have recognized even though their nomenclature was tied to the psychopathological term "masochism" (a word which is derived from the name of an Austrian man and novelist who described the perversion of being sexually aroused and satisfied by having pain inflicted on him, even as the tendency to inflict it has been named after the Marquis de Sade).

When this is seen, much now dispersed data will, I believe, fall into line. However, a clinician must ask himself in passing what kind of thinking may have permitted such a nomenclature to arise and to be assented to by outstanding woman clinicians. This thinking is, I believe, to be found not only in the psychopathological beginnings of psychoanalysis, but also in the original analytic-atomistic method employed by it. In science, our capacity to think atomistically corresponds to the nature of matter to a high degree and thus leads to the mastery over matter. But when we apply atomistic thinking to man, we break him down into isolated fragments rather than into constituent elements. In fact, when we look at man in a morbid state, he is already fragmented; so that in psychopathology an atomizing mind meets a phenomenon of fragmentation and is apt to mistake fragments for atoms. In psychoanalysis we repeat for our own encouragement (and as an argument against others) that human nature can best be studied in a state of partial breakdown or, at any rate, of marked conflict because—so we say—a conflict delineates borderlines and clarifies the forces which collide on these borderlines. As Freud himself put it, we see a crystal's structure only when it cracks. But a crystal, on the one hand, and an organism or a personality, on the other, differ in the fact that one is inanimate and the other an organic whole which cannot be broken up without a withering of the parts. The ego (in the psychoanalytic sense of a guardian of inner continuity) is in a pathological state more or less inactivated; that is, it loses its capacity to organize personality and experience and to relate itself to other egos in mutual activation. To that extent its irrational defenses are "easier to study" in a state of conflict and isolation than is the ego of a person in vivid interaction with other persons. Yet we cannot assume that we can entirely reconstruct the ego's normal functions from an understanding of its dysfunctions, nor that we can understand all vital conflict as neurotic conflict. This, then, would characterize a post-Freudian position: the complexes and conflicts unearthed by psychoanalysis in its first breakthrough to human nature are recognized as existing; they do threaten to dominate the developmental and accidental crises of life. But the freshness and wholeness of experience and the opportunities arising with a resolved crisis can, in an ongoing life, transcend trauma and defense. To illustrate this, let me briefly remark on the often repeated statement that the little girl at a given stage "turns to" her father, whereas in all preceding stages she had been attached to the mother. Actually, Freud insisted only that a theoretical libido was thus turning from one "object" to another, a theory which was, at one time, scientifically pleasing because it corresponded to a simple and (in principle) measurable transfer of energy. Developmentally seen, however, the girl turns to the father at a time when she is quite a different person from the one she was when primarily dependent on her mother. She has normally learned the nature of an "object relationship," once and for all, from the mother. The relationship to the father, then, is of a different kind, in that it happens when the girl has learned to trust (and does not need to retest) basic relationships. She autonomously develops a new form of love for a being who in turn is, or should be, ready to be responsive to the budding (and teasing) woman in her. The total process thus has many more aspects than can be condensed in the statement that the girl turns her libido from the mother to the father. Such transfer can, in fact, be reconstructed only where the ego has been inactivated in some of its capacity to reorganize experience in line with emotional, physical, and cognitive maturation; and only then can it be said that the girl turns to the father *because* she is disappointed in the mother over what the mother has seemingly refused to give her, namely, a penis. Now, no doubt, some unavoidable or excessive disappointment, and the expectation that a new relationship will make up for all the deficiencies of all the old ones, play an eminent role in all changes of attachment from an old to a new person or activity. But in any healthy change the fresh opportunities of the new relationship will outweigh the repetitious insistence on old disappointment. No doubt, also, new attachments prepare new disappointments. The increasing commitment to an inner-productive role will cause in the small woman such phantasies as must succumb to censorship and frustration; for example, in the insight that no daughter may give birth to her father's children. No doubt also the very importance of the promises and the limitations of the inner productive space exposes women to a sense of specific loneliness, to a fear of being left empty or deprived of treasures, of remaining unfulfilled and of drying up. This, no less than the strivings and disappointments of the little "oedipus" are fateful ingredients of the human individual and of the whole race. For this very reason it seems decisive not to misinterpret these feelings as totally due to a resentment of not being a boy or of having been mutilated.

It will now be clear why and in what way the children's play constructions evoked in me a response combining the "unexpected and yet awaited." What was unexpected was the domination of the whole space by the sex-differences—a dominance going far beyond the power of any "symbolism" or a "representation" of the morphology of sex organs. The data was "awaited," above all, as nonclinical and nonverbal support of pervasive clinical and developmental impressions concerning the importance of the "inner space" throughout the feminine life cycle. For, as pointed out, clinical observation suggests that in female experience an "inner space" is at the center of despair even as it is the very center of potential fulfillment. Emptiness is the female form of perdition—known at times to men of the inner life (whom we will discuss later), but standard experience for all women. To be left, for her, means to be left empty, to be drained of the blood of the body, the warmth of the heart, the sap of life. How a woman thus can be hurt in depth is a wonder to many a man, and it can arouse both his empathic horror and his refusal to understand. Such hurt can be re-experienced in each menstruation; it is crying to heaven in the mourning over a child; and it becomes a permanent scar in the menopause. Clinically, this "void" is so obvious that generations of clinicians must have had a special reason for not focusing on it. Maybe, even as primitive men banned it with phobic avoidances and magic rituals of purification, the enlightened men of a civilization pervaded by technological pride could meet it only with the interpretation that suffering woman wanted above all what man had, namely, exterior equipment and traditional access to "outer" space. Again, such envy exists and is aggravated in some cultures; but the explanation of it in male terms or the suggestion that it be borne with fatalism and compensated for by a redoubled enjoyment of the feminine equipment (duly certified and accepted as second rate) has not helped women to find their places in the modern world. For it can make of womanhood a ubiquitous compensation neurosis marked by a repetitious insistence on being "restored." Remarkably enough, the original focus of psychoanalysis on exterior anatomical inequality has led to an emphasis on vaginal response (denied by Kinsey), but has failed to assess a central fact in female sexuality, namely, the participation of the procreative recesses in the orgastic response.

6.

In briefly retracing our evolutionary steps, I will again call on a visual and nonverbal impression.

Recent motion pictures taken in Africa by Washburn and deVore* demonstrate vividly the morphology of basic baboon organization. The whole wandering troop in search of food over a certain territory is so organized as to keep within a safe inner space the females who bear future offspring within their bodies or carry their growing young. They are protectively surrounded by powerful males who, in turn, keep their eyes on the horizon, guiding the troop toward available food and guarding it from potential danger. In peacetime, the strong males also protect the "inner circle" of pregnant and nursing females against the encroachments of the relatively weaker and definitely more importunate males. Once danger is spotted, the whole wandering configuration stops and consolidates into an inner space of safety and an outer space of combat. In the

* Three films taken in Kenya, 1959: "Baboon Behavior," "Baboon Social Organization," and "Baboon Ecology."

center sit the pregnant females and mothers with their newborns. At the periphery are the males best equipped to fight or scare off predators.

I was impressed with these movies not only for their beauty and ingenuity, but because here I could see in the Bush configurations analogous to those in the Berkeley play structures. The baboon pictures, however, can lead us one step further. Whatever the morphological differences between the female and the male baboons' bony structures, postures, and behaviors, they are adapted to their respective tasks of harboring and defending the concentric circles, from the procreative womb to the limits of the "productive" and defensible territory. Thus morphological trends "fit" given necessities and are therefore elaborated by basic social organization. And it deserves emphasis that, even among the baboons, the greatest warriors display a chivalry which permits the female baboons, for example, to have weaker shoulders and lesser fighting equipment.

Whether, when, and in what respects, then, a female in any setting is "weaker" is (already on a purely biological level) a matter to be decided not on the basis of comparative tests of isolated muscles, capacities, or traits but on that of the functional fitness of each item as part of an organism which, in turn, fits into an ecology of divided function.

Human society and technology has, of course, transcended evolutionary arrangement, making room for cultural triumphs and for high individual diversity as well as for physical and psychological maladaptation on a large scale. But when we speak of biologically given strengths and weaknesses in the human female, we may yet have to accept as one measure of all difference the biological rockbottom of sexual differentiation. In this, the woman's productive inner space may well remain one principal criterion, whether she chooses to build her life partially or wholly around it or not. At any rate, many of the testable items on the long list of "inborn" differences between human males and females can be shown to have a meaningful function within an ecology which is built, as any mammalian ecology must be, around the fact that the human foetus must be carried inside the womb for a given number of months; and that the infant must be suckled or, at any rate, raised within a maternal world best staffed at first by the mother (and this for the sake of her own awakened motherliness as well as for the newborn's needs), with a gradual addition of other women. Here years of specialized womanhours of work are involved. It makes sense, then, that the little girl, the bearer of ova and of maternal powers, tends to survive her birth more surely and is a tougher creature, to be plagued, to be sure, by many small ailments, but more resistant to some man-killing diseases (for example, of the heart) and with a longer life expectancy. It also makes sense that she is able earlier than boys to concentrate on details immediate in time and space, and has throughout a finer discrimination for things seen, touched, and heard. To these she reacts more vividly, more personally, and with greater compassion. More easily touched and touchable, however, she is said also to recover faster, ready to react again and elsewhere. That all of this is essential to the "biological" task of reacting to the differential needs of others, especially infants, will not appear to be a farfetched interpretation; nor will it, in this context, seem a deplorable inequality that in the employment of larger muscles she shows less vigor, speed, and coordination. The little girl also learns to be more easily content within a limited circle of activities and shows less resistance to control and less impulsivity of the kind that later leads boys and men to "delinquency." All of these and more certified "differences" could be shown to have corollaries in our play constructions.

Now it is clear that much of the basic schema suggested here as female also exists in some form in all men and decisively so in men of special giftedness—or weakness. The inner life which characterizes some artistic and creative men certainly also compensates for their being biologically men by helping them to specialize in that inwardness and sensitive indwelling (the German *Innigkeit*) usually ascribed to women. E. E. Cummings describes as a poet's task the ability to leave the "measurable doing world" for the "immeasurable inner world of living." They are prone to cyclic swings of mood while they carry conceived ideas to fruition and toward the act of disciplined creation. The point is that in women the basic schema exists within a *total optimum configuration* such as cultures have every reason to nurture in the majority of women, and this for the sake of collective survival as well as individual fulfillment. It makes little sense, then, when discussing basic sex-differences to quote the deviations and accomplishments (or both) of exceptional men or women without an inclusive account of their many-sided personalities, their special conflicts and their complex life histories. On the other hand, one should also emphasize (and especially so in a post-Puritan civilization which continues to decree predestination by mercilessly typing individuals) that successive stages of life offer

18

growing and maturing individuals ample leeway for free variation in essential sameness.

For example, woman's life too contains an adolescent stage which I have come to call a psychosocial moratorium, a sanctioned period of delay of adult functioning. The maturing girl and the young woman, in contrast to the little girl and the mature woman, can thus be relatively freer from the tyranny of the inner space. In fact, she may venture into "outer space" with a bearing and a curiosity which often appears hermaphroditic if not outright "masculine." A special ambulatory dimension is thus added to the inventory of her spatial behavior. If she overdoes this she is said to be "running around"; and many societies counteract such danger with special rules of virginal restraint. Where the mores permit, however, the young girl tries out a variety of possible identifications with the phallic-ambulatory male, even as she experiments with the experience of being his counterpart and principal attraction—a seeming contradiction which will eventually be transformed into a polarity and into a sexual and personal style. In all this, the call of the inner space is expressed only in persistent and *selective attractiveness*, for whether the young woman draws others to herself with magnetic inwardness, with challenging outwardness, or with a dramatic alternation of both, she selectively invites what seeks her.

Young women often ask, whether they can "have an identity" before they know whom they will marry and for whom they will make a home. Granted that something in the young woman's identity must keep itself open for the peculiarities of the man to be joined and of the children to be brought up, I think that much of a young woman's identity is already defined in her kind of attractiveness and in the selectivity of her search for the man (or men) by whom she wishes to be sought. This, of course, is only the psychosexual aspect of her identity; and she may go far in postponing its closure while training herself as a worker and a citizen and while developing as a person within the role-possibilities of her time. The singular loveliness and brilliance which young women display in an array of activities obviously removed from the future function of childbearing is one of those esthetic experiences (for herself and for others) which almost seem to transcend all goals and purposes and therefore come to symbolize the self-containment of pure being —wherefore young women, in the arts of the ages, have served as the visible representation of ideals and ideas, and as the creative man's muse, anima, and enigma. One is almost reluctant, therefore, to assign an ulterior meaning to what seems so meaningful in itself, and to suggest that the inner space is tacitly present in it all. But a true moratorium must have a term and a conclusion: womanhood arrives when attractiveness and experience have succeeded in selecting what is to be admitted to the custody of the inner space "for keeps."

Thus only a total configurational approach—somatic, historical, individual—can help us to see the differences of functioning and experiencing in context rather than in isolated and senseless comparison. Woman, then, is not "more passive" than man simply because her central biological function forces her or permits her to be active in a manner tuned to inner-bodily processes, or because she may be gifted with a certain intimacy and contained intensity of feeling, or because she may choose to dwell in the protected inner circle within which maternal care can flourish. Nor is she "more masochistic" because she must accept inner periodicities (Benedek) in addition to the pain of childbirth, which is explained in the Bible as the eternal penalty for Eve's delinquent behavior and interpreted by writers as recent as de Beauvoir as "a hostile element within her own body." Taken together with the phenomena of sexual life and motherhood, it is obvious that woman's knowledge of pain makes her a "dolorosa" in a deeper sense than one who is addicted to small pains. She is, rather, one who "takes pains" to understand and alleviate suffering, and who can train others in the forbearance necessary to stand unavoidable pain. She is a "masochist," then, only when she exploits pain perversely or vindictively, which means that she steps out of, rather than deeper into, her female function. By the same token, a woman is pathologically passive only when she becomes too passive within a sphere of efficacy and personal integration which includes her disposition for female activity.

One argument, however, is hard to counter. Woman, through the ages (at any rate, the patriarchal ones), has lent herself to a variety of roles conducive to an exploitation of masochistic potentials: she has let herself be incarcerated and immobilized, enslaved and infantilized, prostituted and exploited, deriving from it at best what in psychopathology we call "secondary gains" of devious dominance. This fact, however, could be satisfactorily explained only within a new kind of biocultural history which (and this is one of my main points) would first have to overcome the prejudiced opinion that woman must be, or will be, what she is or has been under particular historical conditions.

7.

Am I saying, then, that "anatomy *is* destiny"? Yes, it is destiny, insofar as it determines the potentials of physiological functioning, and its limitations. But anatomy also, to an extent, codetermines personality configurations. The modalities of woman's commitment and involvement, for better *and* for worse, also reflect the ground-plan of her body. We may mention only woman's capacity on many levels of existence to (actively) include, to accept, to "have and hold"—but also to hold on, and to hold in. She may be protective with high selectivity, and overprotective without discrimination. That she must protect means that she must rely on protection—and she may demand overprotection. She too has her organ of intrusion, the nipple which nurses; and her wish to succor can, indeed, become intrusive and oppressive. It is, in fact, of such exaggerations and deviations that many men and also women think when the unique potentials of womanhood are discussed.

In all of this, however, the problem is not whether a woman is "more so" than a man, but how much she varies within womanhood, and what she makes of it within the leeway of her stage of life and of her historical and economic opportunities. For a human being, in addition to having a body, is *some*body; which means he is an indivisible personality *and* a defined member of a group. In this sense Napoleon's dictum that *History is destiny,* which was, I believe, to be counterpointed by Freud's dictum that destiny lies in anatomy (and one often must know what a man tried to counter-point with his most one-sided dicta) is equally valid. In other words: anatomy, history, and personality are our *combined destiny.*

Men, of course, have shared and taken care of some of the concerns for which women stand: each sex can transcend itself to feel and to represent the concerns of the other. For even as real women harbor a legitimate as well as a compensatory masculinity, so real men can partake of motherliness—if permitted to do so by powerful mores.

In search of an observation which bridges biology and history, an extreme historical example comes to mind in which women elevated their procreative function to a style of life when their men seemed totally defeated.

This story was highlighted for me on two occasions when I participated in conferences in the Caribbean and learned of family patterns prevailing throughout the islands. Churchmen have had reason to deplore, and anthropologists to explore, the pattern of Caribbean family life, obviously an outgrowth of the slavery days of plantation America, which extended from the northeast coast of Brazil through the Caribbean half-circle into the southeast of the present United States. Plantations, of course, were agricultural factories owned and operated by gentlemen whose cultural and economic identity had its roots in a supraregional upper class. They were worked by slaves, that is, by men who, being mere equipment, were put to use when and where necessary, and who often had to relinquish all chance of becoming the masters of their families and communities. Thus the women were left with the offspring of a variety of men who could give neither provision nor protection, nor provide any identity except that of a subordinate species. The family system which ensued is described in the literature in terms of circumscriptions: the rendering of "sexual services" between persons who cannot be called anything more definite than "lovers"; "maximum instability" in the sexual lives of young girls, who often "relinquish" the care of their offspring to their mothers; and mothers and grandmothers who determine the "standardized mode of co-activity" which is the minimum requirement for calling a group of individuals a family. These are, then, called "household groups"—single dwellings occupied by people sharing a common food supply. These households are "matrifocal," a word understating the grandiose role of the all-powerful grandmother figure, who will encourage her daughters to leave their infants with her, or at any rate to stay with her as long as they continue to bear children. Motherhood thus became community life; and where churchmen could find little or no morality, and casual observers little or no order at all, the mothers and grandmothers had to become fathers and grandfathers, in the sense that they exerted the only continuous influence resulting in an ever newly improvised set of rules for the economic obligations of the men who had fathered the children. They upheld the rules of incestuous avoidance. Above all, so it seems to me, they provided the only superidentity which was left open after the enslavement of the men, namely, that of the worthwhileness of a human infant irrespective of his parentage. It is well known how many little white gentlemen benefited from the extended fervor of the nurturant Negro woman—southern mammies, creole das, or Brazilian babas. This phenomenal caring is, of course, being played down by the racists as mere servitude, while the predominance of personal warmth in Caribbean women is decried by moralists as African sensualism or idolized as true femininity by refugees from "Continental" womanhood. One may, however, see at the roots of this maternalism a grandiose gesture of human adaptation which has given the area of the Caribbean (now searching for a political and economic pattern to do justice to its cultural unity) both the promise of a positive maternal identity and the threat of a negative male one: for the fact that identity relied on the mere worth of being born has undoubtedly weakened economic aspiration in many men.

That this has been an important historical issue can be seen in the life of Simón Bolívar. This "liberator of South America" originated in the coastal region of Venezuela, which is one anchorpoint of the great Caribbean half circle. When in 1827 Bolívar liberated Caracas and entered it in triumph, he recognized the Negress Hipolita, his erstwhile wetnurse, in the crowd. He dismounted and "threw himself in the arms of the Negress who wept with joy." Two years earlier, he had written to his sister: "I enclose a letter to my mother Hipolita so that you give her all she wants and deal with her as if she were my mother; her milk fed my life, and I knew no other father than she" (translation not mine). Whatever personal reason can be found for Bolívar's attitude toward Hipolita (he had lost his mother when he was nine, etc.) is amply matched by the historical significance of the fact that he could play up this relationship as a propaganda item within that often contradictory ideology of race and origin which contributed to his charisma throughout the continent he conquered.

That continent does not concern us here. But as for the Caribbean area, the matrifocal theme explains much of a certain disbalance between extreme trustfulness and weakness of initiative which could be exploited by native dictators as well as by foreign capital and has now become the concern of the erstwhile colonial masters as well as of the emancipated leaders of various island groups. Knowing this, we may understand that the bearded group of men and boys who have taken over one of the islands represents a deliberately new type of man who insists on proving that the Caribbean male can earn his worth in production as well as in procreation without the imposition of "continental" leadership or ownership.

This transformation of a colorful island area into an inner space structured by woman is (historically speaking) an almost clinical example to be applied with caution. And yet it is only one story out of that unofficial history which is as yet to be written for all areas and eras: of how women have attempted to balance the official history of territories and domains, markets and empires; the history of women's quiet creativity in preserving and restoring what official history had torn apart. Some stirrings in contemporary historiography, such as attempts to describe closely the everyday atmosphere of a given locality in a given historical era, seem to bespeak a growing awareness of a need for, shall we say, an integrated history.

8.

We speak of anatomical, historical, and psychological facts; and yet, it must be clear that facts reliably ascertained by the methods of these three fields by the same token lose a most vital interconnection. Man is, at one and the same time, part of a somatic order of things, and part of a personal and of a social one. To avoid identifying these orders with established fields, we may call them Soma, Psyche, and Polis, and yet know that each can be hyphenated with the other to designate new fields of inquiry such as psycho-somatic and psycho-social. Each order guards a certain intactness and also offers a leeway of optional or at least workable choices; while man lives in all three and must work out their complementarities and contradictions.

Soma is the principle of the *organism*, living its *life cycle*. But the female Soma is not only comprised of what is within a woman's skin (and clothes). It includes a mediatorship in evolution, genetic as well as socio-genetic, by which she creates in each child the somatic (sensual, and sensory) basis for his physical, cultural, and individual identity. This mission, once a child is conceived, must be completed. It is woman's unique job. But no woman lives or needs to live only in this extended somatic sphere. She must make (or else neglect) decisions as a citizen and worker, and of course, as an individual; and the modern world offers her ever greater leeway in choosing, planning, or renouncing her somatic tasks more knowingly and responsibly.

The sphere of *citizenship* I call Polis because I want to emphasize that it reaches as far as the borderlines of what one has recognized as one's "city," and it is clear that modern communication makes such a communality ever larger if not global. In this sphere women can be shown to share with men a close sameness of intellectual orientation and capacity for work and leadership. "Political" equality, however, can live up to this fact only by encompassing for women a position in the political sphere which goes beyond an occasional voice (whispered or shouted) and a periodic vote for male politicians and for issues exclusively determined by men. It even goes beyond the active participation in politics and government. In this sphere, too, the influence of women will not be fully actualized until it reflects without apology the facts of the "inner space" and the potentialities and needs of the feminine psyche. It is as yet unpredictable what the tasks and roles and opportunities and job specifications will be once women are not merely adapted to male jobs but when they learn to adapt jobs to themselves. Such a revolutionary reappraisal may even lead to the insight that jobs now called masculine force men, too, to inhuman adjustments.

In the sphere of Psyche, psychoanalysis has come to understand an organizing principle called ego.° Ego-organization mediates between somatic and personal experience and political actuality in the widest sense. To do so it uses psychological mechanisms common to both sexes—a fact which makes intelligent communication, mutual understanding, and social organization possible. It is in the ego that the equivalence of all truly individualized experience has its organizing center, for the ego is the guardian of the *indivisibility of the person.* No doubt militant individualism has inflated this core of individuality to the point where it seemed altogether free of somatic and social considerations. However, psychoanalysis is making it clear that the active strength of the ego (and especially the identity within the individuality) is inseparable from the power of somatic development and of social organization. Here, then, the fact that a woman, whatever else she may also be, never is not-a-woman, creates unique relations between her individuality, her bodily intimacy, and her productive potentials, and demands that feminine ego-strength be studied and defined in its own right.

° The term ego—in all but narrow professional circles—is fighting a losing battle against its popular and philosophical namesakes, the inflated and the self-centered and self-conscious "egos." Nevertheless, the term must be used as long as the concept represents an important trend in psychoanalytic theory.

It should be clear, then, that I am using my definitions concerning the central importance of woman's procreative task not in a renewed attempt to "doom" every woman to perpetual motherhood and to deny her the equivalence of individuality and the equality of citizenship. But since a woman is never not-a-woman, she can see her long-range goals only in those modes of activity which include and integrate her natural dispositions. An emancipated woman thus does not necessarily accept comparisons with more "active" male proclivities as a measure of her equivalence, even if and after it has become quite clear that she can match man's performance and competence in most spheres of achievement. True equality can only mean the right to be uniquely creative.

We may well hope, therefore, that there is something in woman's specific creativity which has waited only for a clarification of her relationship to masculinity (including her own) in order to assume her share of leadership in those fateful human affairs which so far have been left entirely in the hands of gifted and driven men, and often of men whose genius of leadership eventually has yielded to ruthless self-aggrandizement. Mankind now obviously depends on new kinds of social inventions and on institutions which guard and cultivate that which nurses and nourishes, cares and tolerates, includes and preserves.

Before he left Harvard, Paul Tillich in a conversation expressed uneasiness over the clinical preoccupation with an "adaptive ego" which, he felt, might support (these are my words) further attempts at manufacturing a mankind feeling so "adapted" that it would be unable to face "ultimate concerns." I agreed that psychoanalysis was in danger of becoming part of such vain streamlining of existence; but that in its origin and essence, it intends to *free* man for "ultimate concerns." For such concerns can begin to be ultimate only in those rare moments and places where neurotic resentments end and where mere adaptation is transcended. I think he agreed. One may add that man's Ultimate has too often been visualized as an infinity which begins where the male conquest of outer spaces ends. As a young woman poet has put it, when man finally "reaches infinity," he wants "to punch a hole in it." Thus he can truly respect as superior only a domain where an even more omnipotent and omniscient Being must be submissively acknowledged. The Ultimate and the Infinite thus is easily overlooked in the Immediate, which has so largely been the domain of woman and of the inward mind. Such considerations would lead us to the *temporal* aspects (here neglected throughout) of the space-time experience of the two sexes.

ROBERT JAY LIFTON

Woman As Knower: Some Psychohistorical Perspectives

Is IT NOT TIME for us to turn from the question (and expression of weary male chauvinism)—"What does a woman want?"—to the more pertinent inquiry: "What does a woman know?" My assumption, of course, is that women do know something *as women,* not entirely different from what men know but in a different way. In speaking of woman as knower, I refer to her potential for possessing insight or wisdom. My emphasis is upon experiential patterns of cognition and feeling, particularly in relationship to changing social forces.

I shall shift back and forth between specific observations and highly speculative suggestions which emerge from a generally psychoanalytic orientation but move in directions quite outside prevailing psychoanalytic theory. I follow the perspective outlined in earlier work, within which every psychological pattern is seen as part of a trinity, including universal psychobiological tendencies (in this article, those notably strong in women, but by no means entirely absent in men), currents given special stress within a particular cultural tradition, and modern (especially contemporary) historical influences. By referring frequently to Japanese (and occasionally to Chinese) women, as well as to American women, I shall try to explore patterns common to all women. This requires consideration of enduring tendencies as well as of those in flux, since only in this interplay can we glean what is most true of our subject and most pertinent for us to understand.

1.

There is some usefulness in distinguishing three general aspects of womanhood, and in doing so in a culture that has institutionalized their discreteness. For in Japan women have long been divided, at least to a very considerable extent, into those who primarily nurture, those who provide sensual pleasure, and those who convey social wisdom.

The nurturers, of course, have been the culture's wives and mothers, the great majority of its women. And there has been no society anywhere in which the nurturing function has received greater emphasis. Indeed, there is evidence that, over the centuries, Japan has evolved a mother-child pattern unique in its stress upon symbolic oneness—upon a shared image of inseparability that continues to dominate much of Japanese psychological life and to serve as a model for relationships quite beyond those between parent and child. We may thus, in relationship to Japan, speak of a *cult of nurturence* based upon a kind of utopian imagery held by both nurturer and nurtured: through their earliest exchange of gestures and other emotional messages, they come to agree upon a standard of more or less absolute care and dependency which has no clear point of termination. A woman's life-tasks come to center on nurturing, particularly in relationship to her children, but also to her husband, and, in fact, to almost every task she performs. Japanese culture has thus made a way of life out of this aspect of essentially feminine potential.

In Japan, as throughout East Asia and much of the non-Western world, marriage is essentially a vehicle for the procreation and nurturing of children, rather than in itself a "holy bond" as in the Christian West. Marriage has been one thing, and sexual pleasure—either of love or simple lust—quite another. This separation necessitated the existence of woman as temptress in a form quite distinct from woman as nurturer. The woman dedicated to sensuality has had her special social identity within a large category of amusement professions—prostitutes, geisha, entertainers, servants at inns and restaurants, and recently bargirls—or what has become known as the *mizu shōbai* or "water world," so named because of the amorphous ebb and flow of life within it. We shall not concern ourselves here with the elaborate rules governing the sexual availability of women in the "water world": these relate to the specific profession and position within it, as well as to the status and wealth of patrons and to elements of mutual attraction and taste—but it is probably safe to say that few if any women in the water world are entirely unavailable, given a sufficiently favorable commercial or personal situation. For the seductive pleasures of atmosphere, artistic performance, conversation, or personal service, as well as sexuality per se, have been the raison d'être of the woman living and working in the water world, and of the water world itself. While such women have undoubtedly varied in their own capacity for sexual pleasure, it has been they, rather than conventional wives and mothers, who have been the traditional female participants in romantic love and lustful encounter; and it is significant that, at least according to literary legend, a frequent combination for a geisha was to become the long-term mistress of a man of wealth and high social standing for the sake of her personal security and prestige within her profession, and at the same time engage in briefer, clandestine affairs with actors, reputed to be skilled in the arts of love, for the sake of personal romance and sensual pleasure.

Literary legend thus suggests that the water world, to which actors of course belong, alone possessed the key to erotic mysteries. Given this general cultural imagery, and the absence of ideologies which denigrate the experience of pleasure in the sexual act or of pleasure in general (Japanese ideologies tend rather to place restrictions on appropriateness of time, place, and partner, and upon the proper balance of sensual activity with the more obligatory aspects of life), it is probably fair to say that the temptress in Japanese society has preempted much of the sexual pleasure available to women in that society.[1] Such institutionalizing of woman as temptress, not only in Japan but in traditional cultures throughout the world, may be seen as the social formulation of a universal psychological pattern: namely, the unspoken assumption that a psychic emanation from woman's being sets in motion the sexual act, that the woman, in sexuality, is acted upon, literally entered into—which makes her by no means necessarily "passive," but rather, in a fundamental psychobiological sense, the source and the ground of heterosexual encounter.

Woman as knower has been best exemplified in Japan by creative women, particularly women writers, beginning with Murasaki Shikibu, author of the *Tale of Genji*, not only one of the first novels ever written (early eleventh century) but one of the greatest as well. Nor was Lady Murasaki the only prominent female knower of her era. As Ivan Morris points out, "During the period of about 100 years that spans the world of the *Tale of Genji*, almost every noteworthy author who wrote in Japanese was a woman."[2] Morris goes on to note the uniqueness of such female literary dominance in any culture at any time, as well as the paradox "that it should

29

occur in a part of the world where women have traditionally been condemned to a position of irremediable inferiority." But Heian women, particularly court ladies like Lady Murasaki, had considerably more freedom than did women in subsequent periods of Japanese History;[3] moreover, as we shall soon see, the "irremediable inferiority" of Japanese women, even under conditions of their greatest social suppression, has by no means been what it has appeared to be.

In this literary emergence of women during the Heian period, there is one factor of particular psychological significance. Men who had literary aspirations persisted in the use of the Chinese language, then considered elegant, dignified, and prestigious—"the language of scholars, priests, and officials, occupying a role analogous to that of Latin in the West." But women, unburdened by psychological pressures of the socio-political hierarchy, "were free to make the fullest possible use of the *kana* phonetic script, which allowed them to record the native Japanese language, the language that was actually spoken, in a direct, simple fashion that was impossible either in pure Chinese or in the hybrid Sino-Japanese known as *kambun*." So sharp was this differentiation that the term used for the native syllabary (*onnade*) literally means "woman's hand," while that used for Chinese ideographs (*otokomoji*) means "men's letters." It is true that men were much more likely to have the educational opportunities to learn the Chinese language, but it is also probable that women turned naturally to the vernacular in order to describe the kinds of things they were most interested in. For women writers presented

a one-sided picture, concentrated almost exclusively on the social and cultural aspects of life. From reading works like the *Tale of Genji, Gossamer Diary*, and the *Pillow Book* (all classics by women of that era) we should hardly guess that the men described were often leading figures in the government of the day and that they spent at least as much of their time in political intrigues as in those of an erotic nature. Still less should we imagine that many of them, especially members of the northern branch of the Fujiwara family, were hard-working officials, seriously devoted to their public duties. . . .

Similarly Arthur Waley, referring to the same era, speaks of the "extraordinary vagueness of women concerning purely male activities." Women writers, in other words, in direct contrast to their male counterparts, dealt with immediate, personal, mostly sensual experience; with feelings, longings, aesthetic responses, and personal encounters. They concerned themselves with what might be termed *informal knowledge* rather than with the more structured, theoretical, and formal knowledge of men. And in this and other respects, woman as knower in Heian Japan was not a unique entity, but merely more advanced than her counterparts in other cultures.

These three categories—nurturer, temptress, and knower—are clearly aspects of a psychic unity. Every woman, tenth-century Japanese or twentieth-century American, is in some measure all three. But what, we must then ask, is their unifying aspect? Are they merely, as some might claim, expressions of male fantasy—in the way that Freud described the need of many men to envision women as either asexual mothers or debased—and debasing—seductresses,[4] that is, as "madonna" or "whore"? There can be no doubt that elements of male fantasy—and, for that matter, female fantasy as well—enter into the formation of cultural institutions delineating the three types of women, but it would be misleading to attribute the categories to such fantasy alone. Rather we are confronted with three aspects of woman's psychic potential to which the institutions of every society have given expression during the course of cultural evolution. And the unifying element in all three categories—the focus from which woman's psychological life emanates—is *close identification with organic life and its perpetuation.*

This identification with organic life is most obvious in woman as nurturer, since this function stems directly from her role in procreation and is psychologically inseparable from it. But the identification holds in the other two categories as well. Woman as temptress, in a fundamental sense, creates conditions which favor procreation. And even where she contributes to the cultivation of sexual pleasure per se rather than to a procreative outcome, such cultivation may be part of a psychosocial balance between pleasure and procreation that enhances both. Moreover, in Japanese culture we are particularly struck by the way in which a nurturing aura dominates even seductive behavior. The present-day temptress, whether geisha or bargirl (and presumably prostitute, though prostitutes are now officially outlawed), approaches the male in a manner that is at the same time sexually provocative and maternal, seeming to combine encouragement of his manhood with an assumption of his childlike helplessness. It is, in fact, specifically this combination of attitudes that constitutes the much appreciated Japanese style of feminine service. Woman as knower similarly allies herself to organic life by drawing upon her functions as nurturer and temptress, which become not only starting points for her knowledge but the source of specific qualities in her style of knowing. This prominent psychological tone of nurturence throughout all female function is made unusually explicit in Japanese culture and demonstrates that the most complex attainments of women are likely to be colored and enriched by it.

2.

During periods of rapid historical change, the social structuring of these three feminine identities becomes unstable and confused, and women most sensitive to such change experience considerable psychological discomfort. Again the tendency is dramatically visible in Japan. The patterns found there have been bound up with social, economic, and sexual exploitation of women; and modern, mainly Western, ideologies of self-realization for men and women (beginning in the late nineteenth century and achieving particular force during the recent postwar era) have brought them under sharp attack. The resulting institutional breakdowns or, more frequently, partial breakdowns, have created a special form of conflict. We usually think of modernization, or of patterns of postmodern development, as requiring a high degree of specialization; but in the case of contemporary trends of individuation in women, the reverse is true. Each woman tends to become a "generalist"—to become, in a new way, nurturer *and* temptress *and* knower.

In work with young Japanese women, most of them in their early twenties, from middleclass backgrounds, and at the time of our interviews in a transitional state between completing their university work and moving out into "the world," I discovered how difficult this contemporary task can be. For many in this group, conflicts are made vividly manifest by the opportunity and threat of marriage, and in relationship to the already classic, modern Japanese ambivalence in the choice between the "arranged marriage" (*miai kekkon*) and the "love marriage" (*ren'ai kekkon*), and the often ingenious compromises which the culture has evolved—as four very brief examples suggest.

One girl spent much of our interview time, over a period of many months, castigating the institution of the arranged marriage, articulately exploring its derivation from feudalistic patterns of feminine inferiority, and affirming the importance of the love marriage as an expression of the individuality of the two people concerned. But just before her graduation she suddenly agreed to a marital arrangement initiated by the two families, in which there was only a single more or less formal meeting, in a group situation, with her prospective husband. She expressed the vague hope that she would be able to salvage some of her original personal and intellectual ideals by becoming a working wife.

Another girl wavered in her actions concerning marriage, backing out of one parentally-engineered arrangement at the last moment through a show of tears, after having seemed, in her ambivalent silence, to have acquiesced to it. Meanwhile she continued an affectionate but rather theoretical relationship with a reticent male fellow student whose ambivalence and search matched her own. In the process, her scholarly interests in contemporary literature waned. She complained of feeling purposeless, as if "floating," but she persisted, though with limited enthusiasm, in her efforts to find a teaching position that would give expression to this intellectual interest.

A third student became involved in an affair with a married writer whose unstable emotional pattern included feelings of guilty obligation toward his wife and concern for his infant child. When the student herself became pregnant, she suddenly shifted her full commitment toward *her* (unborn) child and refused to have an abortion performed (a legal medical procedure in Japan) despite urgent advice from many sides that she do so. After several conferences among the various parties involved over a considerable period of time, during which the student herself experienced feelings of unreality and depression and had occasional thoughts of suicide, a solution seemed to be in the offing: the wife kept her child (something of a concession in Japan where, until recently, children of broken marriages were generally given to the husband or his family); and the student, encouraged by her lover's hesitant steps toward committing himself to her in eventual marriage, began to make plans not only for having her baby but for returning to her university and continuing studies that would prepare her for professional work with children.

A fourth girl identified closely with the writings and the life-pattern of Simone de Beauvoir and rebelled vigorously against her comfortably conventional middleclass background. She succeeded in gaining admission to a leading national university (something of an accomplishment for a girl, but often looked upon as an equivocal one, since those who did so were labeled "unfeminine"), where she went through relatively familiar patterns of enthusiastic embrace of, then disillusionment with, Marxist ideology and action programs; she also embarked upon a love affair with a brilliant fellow student who shared many of her intellectual and literary interests, and to whom she eventually became engaged. But with the approach of her graduation and wedding date, she felt increasingly moody and pessimistic, seemed at times depressed and complained

33

of feeling unreal. Although she still considered herself to be in love with her fiancé, she had strong doubts about her capacity to tolerate life in the provincial area to which he had been temporarily assigned, and about their longer-range ability to achieve happiness and fulfillment with one another.

I have of course omitted the complex individual-psychological factors which contributed to these outcomes, or temporary outcomes. My only purpose here is to suggest the difficulties faced by young women at the forefront of their culture's historical development in coming to terms with changing combinations of imagery and self-imagery concerning what a woman might or should be. As they perceive ever enlarging and confusing possibilities (not only from reading Simone de Beauvoir, but from the various communication media, and from the examples of prominent women within Japanese culture), such young women quickly form partial identifications with these new patterns, and evolve new criteria of judgment according to which they find themselves wanting. They are likely to internalize ideal visions which require that they themselves not only become feminine "generalists," but that they do so in "expert" fashion. They expect themselves to become not only a mother but a "modern mother" conversant with the latest approaches to child-rearing; not merely a sexual partner, but one capable of giving and receiving pleasure according to the latest ideas of how such pleasure is defined; not only an intellectual but a holder of ideas of depth and relevance equal to those held by men. No wonder, then, that these young women frequently falter, make sudden retreats into earlier cultural patterns they have seemingly abandoned but which actually still hold great emotional force, make blind forays of a self-destructive nature, achieve "victories" in which the accomplishment is so fraught with ambivalence and guilt as to be almost incapacitating. No wonder, also, that, whether retreating, advancing, or making intricate compromises, such women experience feelings of transience and unreality which epitomize their sense of historical dislocation, their inability either to live by the old imagery or master the new. Much of their discomfort may be thought of as the adult psychohistorical counterpart of the phenomenon of "separation anxiety"; for the imagery of helplessness and abandonment experienced by the very young child when separated from its mother can be unconsciously revived with every subsequent act of individuation.

Contributing to this separation anxiety is acute sensitivity to stringent criteria for what constitutes femininity. The dreaded accusation of being "unfeminine" becomes an all-too-easy epithet which may reflect both male anxiety concerning woman's increasing explorations and female anxiety lest these explorations result in disqualification from participation as women in the various male-female rhythms which each culture establishes and defines, as well as universal anxiety that woman's quest for knowledge might impair her sensual and nurturing capacities. A vicious circle then develops: these very anxieties, together with persisting rigidities of definition (for instance, Japanese feminine requirements of reserve, acquiescence, and a semblance of ignorance), make it almost inevitable that women who break out of these limitations do so by way of identification with their fathers and brothers, competition with men, and the acquisition of "masculine" traits—which in turn stimulate the anxieties, and so on. Only gradually, after many generations, are such definitions enlarged and women given more leeway for imagery concerning their own femininity. But the dilemma persists in all cultures, ever fed by new anxieties of both men and women.

3.

Conflicts, however, beget possibilities. I have suggested that much of woman's psychic potential stems from her close identification with organic life and its perpetuation; from this potential she derives a special capacity to mediate between biology and history. Such mediation becomes particularly necessary under present conditions of unprecedented historical velocity. For with so much of psychic imagery confused and in flux, biologically rooted modes of knowing could have a uniquely steadying influence. Mediating between biology and history, of course, is by no means solely a female function; and exploring it in women may well shed light upon man's related, though not identical, psychic possibilities.

Woman's organically rooted traditional function as informal knower can be distinguished from man's traditional explorations of ideas and symbols on abstract planes far removed from organic function.[5] Yet her knowledge has been "informal" only in the sense that it has been relegated to a kind of social underground, as if such knowledge were not quite proper or acceptable, unworthy of having its forms recognized. But recent developments in many fields of thought have created radical shifts in standards of intellectual acceptability, and have, in fact, placed special value on those very modes of knowing which had been previously part of the feminine informal underground. Michael Polanyi, for instance, traces the evolution of—and sees as crucial to man's future—a form of "personal knowledge" characterized by "the personal participation of the knower in the knowledge he believes himself to possess," and which "transcends the disjunction between subjective and objective."[6] The concept which Polanyi evokes here might also be termed *organic knowledge;* it requires rigorous cognitive standards but at the same time takes account of the self-process of the knower. It parallels the recent emphasis of depth psychology, social science, biology, and even physics, upon the significance of the contribution of the "observer" or knower to the outcome and formulation of his scientific work. The prevailing male domination of these sciences (with the possible exception of depth psychology) makes clear that women have no monopoly on "personal" or organic knowing; and it is difficult to gauge the extent to which women may have indirectly played a part in bringing about the present emphasis upon this form of knowing. What we can say is that given women's special aptitude in this direction—along with the instability of cultural contexts and criteria for knowledge in general—we may well expect a series of extraordinary developments in modes of knowing in which feminine influence becomes increasingly significant, though in ways we can as yet only dimly perceive.

Also operating here is what I would call a general shift in the psychology of knowing, affecting men and women alike: a change in the way ideas are held, which depends in turn upon a new form of self-process. In more than a decade of work with Chinese and Japanese young adults, I have found them, and many of their elders as well, to be capable of surprisingly rapid shifts in ideas, imagery, and ideology, even when these have been related to the most central issues of individual and group existence, and often without undergoing the painful sequence of resistance, internal conflict, and dramatic "conversion" which we traditionally tend to associate with such shifts. East Asian cultural patterns play a part here: rather than the Western focus upon the fateful encounter between self and idea, they have stressed group hegemony at the expense of either self or idea. But this cultural principle does not, in itself, suffice as a causative explanation. For one can observe a similar tendency in young people, and in some older ones too, in America and elsewhere. There would appear to be a convergence between pre-modern, non-Western patterns and post-modern tendencies, a much more frequent convergence than is generally realized. In any case, this *mutability of ideation and imagery* is a function of a contemporary style of self-process that has emerged from the breakdown of stable sources of identification (which in the past made shifts in ideation a more serious internal matter), and from the unprecedented flux in new objects of identification, ideational and technological, to which everyone is exposed.

We may thus speak of a *Protean style of self-process* characterized by an interminable series of experiments and explorations in identity which may come to resemble what Erik Erikson has called "identity diffusion" or "identity confusion." But rather than necessarily leading to impaired or pathological functioning, the Protean style may simply become, or perhaps already is, one of the functional patterns in our day. Proteus, of course, was able to change his shape without difficulty—from wild boar to lion to dragon to fire to flood. What he did find difficult, and would not do unless seized and chained, was to commit himself to a single form, his own, and carry out his prophetic function. The present day Proteus—and who is not one to some extent?—faces similar dilemmas and possibilities, and here feminine knowing may once more make a contribution.

For lurking beneath the Protean style of self-process—perhaps primarily reactions to it—are a pair of related myths, essentially male in their theoretical absoluteness: the myth of the magnificently independent and wholly unfettered self; and the polar myth of the totally obliterated self, whether obliterated in the service of an all-embracing social movement or of an equally imprisoning "spontaneity".[7] Elements of both myths are everywhere operative, in music and painting as well as in philosophy and politics. Both can tend toward that combination of psychic and ideational excess, or ideological totalism, which we have come to associate with severe historical dislocation; but both are also capable of serving as evocative, if unattainable, ideals for creative Protean exploration. And it is just possible that woman's way of knowing can help guard against the former danger and enhance the latter possibility; that her form of organic knowledge may humanize these harshly abstract polarities sufficiently to permit the contemporary Proteus to exercise his prophetic function without recourse to the Protean chains. As to the prophetic function itself, might that not be the creation of a form of self-process which is equal to our present historical dilemmas? A gifted young American novelist suggests, through one of his female characters, the kind of feminine knowing I have in mind; he has her speak as the wife of an artist, but in a way that applies for women in general:

We women are only human . . . and . . . no matter how we feel we can touch . . . on their masculine power, we still remain rooted in life, at a much more primitive, invariable, more logical level . . . and we are never capable of a total sacrifice of ourselves to their ends. . . . We must go along, *but we must not leave the ground.* (italics his)[8]

Important here is the refusal of self-surrender and the reassertion of the organic foundation of feminine knowing. Identification and empathy are distinguished from total merging, to create the psychic basis of what Camus has called "thought which recognizes limits."

To suggest an even more speculative possibility, woman's innate dependence upon biological rhythms—particularly the several rhythms central to her nurturing capacities—may provide her with psychobiological sensitivities useful for grasping the more irregular historical rhythms which confront us. This potential insight into the rhythmic is of course difficult to assess; and I in no way wish to suggest that magic combinations of numbers derived from physiology can be applied to social process. But neither should we assume that woman's accustomed psychobiological rhythmicity has no relevance or potential value for comprehending events in the cultural sphere.

Whether or not we are justified in such speculation, it is possible to identify more specific features of woman's relationship to historical change. Here one often encounters the assumption that "women are more conservative than men," that during periods of change women tend to cling to old forms of custom and belief that men are more willing to relinquish. There is some truth in this assumption; the organic aspect of feminine knowing can lead women to distrust and resist technological and ideological innovation that seems to threaten the structure of longstanding, biologically based social patterns. But woman's attachment to the old and familiar has been both exaggerated and oversimplified. For there are significant ways in which her organic conservatism, epitomized in her nurturing, and specifically maternal, function, becomes a crucial vehicle of social change. The set of feelings and images she transmits to the infant constitute an individual basis for cultural continuity and a psychic imprint of the perpetuation of life itself, surely a genuinely conservative function. But during periods of great historical pressure toward change, precisely this imagery makes possible the individual participation in change by providing a source of constancy—what I have elsewhere called an "emotional-symbolic substrate"—with which subsequent imagery of change can interact without threatening the basic integration of the self. And even when this substrate becomes a psychic basis for nostalgic, or restorationist, longings for the individual or cultural "golden age" of harmony and unity, the dynamic interplay of past- and future-oriented imagery becomes a propulsive force toward change.[9]

I encountered specific examples of this change-enhancing potential when examining the parental relationships of Japanese students. Militant leaders of the Japanese student movement, the Zengakuren, often turned out to have particularly intense relationships with their mothers, who had not only applied to their sons' upbringings the cult of nurturence I have already mentioned but also played a special role in their later rebellious ideological activities. In contrast to the boys' fathers, who opposed such activities on both personal and political grounds but found themselves able to do little but withdraw ineffectually from the whole problem, the mothers tended warmly to support their sons. While usually claiming little knowledge of the ideological issues involved, they simply expressed the conviction that their sons' goals and motives, and those of their fellow students, must be "pure" and worthy, and raised objections mainly because of fears that their sons might meet with physical harm in clashes with the police which sometimes occurred. This emotional support tended to confirm the students' own sense of the nobility of their group's vision. Here the emotional-symbolic substrate transmitted in the mother-son relationship served not only as a source of constancy for these students, but also provided, in its original stress upon "purity," an ethical model for the son in his ideological aspirations and for the mother in her support for these aspirations. Her support in turn tended to reinforce his innovative identity and "confirm" him in his change-promoting activity. In these ways the mothers' nurturing function provided something very close to a psychic mandate for change.

But there were also pitfalls. There was an emotional price paid for this maternal support in the form of lifelong patterns of marked dependency—not only that traditionally transmitted in mother-son relationships, but magnified by the special nurturing these mothers had been called upon to provide under changing social conditions. This dependency was evident in the students' exaggerated group needs in relationship to the Zengakuren itself, and to the decision many of them subsequently made to put their radical pasts behind them in favor of a career in one of Japan's large, paternalistic industrial organizations. Thus in a sense the mother-son alliance played a part in subverting the very autonomy sought in the change-promoting involvements that it supported. Maternal support also did much to ease the "moral backsliding" (or what the Japanese call *tenko*) inherent in this switch to the "enemy camp," and to minimize, though by no means eliminate, feelings of self-betrayal and permit these young men to function successfully in their new occupational (and in a different way still change-promoting) identities. These psychological pitfalls therefore do not negate the woman's influence in promoting social change; they merely suggest its complexity.

4.

Hidden feminine influences operate in historical change in America no less than in East Asia. Depth-psychological work with American students, notably that of Kenneth Keniston,[10] suggests the importance of the mother-son relationship for creating and sustaining innovative potential among young Americans; Keniston's group was both intellectually outstanding and psychohistorically alienated, and probably reflects generalized American patterns writ large.

But there are also important differences in the way in which women affect social change in America and in East Asia, differences growing out of very divergent histories. Important here is the fact that America has not only lacked a feudal social structure but has grown out of a series of specific breakdowns of feudal structures in other cultures, or else out of the piecemeal sequestering of deviant individuals and groups from every variety of larger social unit. The resulting strain upon Americans' sense of the past—our polar tendencies to deny on the one hand that any past has existed or is needed, and on the other hand to expand in idealized, sometimes desperate, terms the past we possess—can hardly be argued. Nonetheless, compared to the radical upheavals that have taken place in modern Asia, America has emerged out of relatively mild social and psychological dislocations. We have, moreover, at least until recently, evolved a cultural style for the channeling, even taming, of ever-present social change. Since the rapid development of movements for feminine self-expression, including ideologies of feminism, may be looked upon at least in part as phenomena of release accompanying social breakdown and historical change, we are not surprised that American versions of these, however lurid they may have appeared to many, have also been relatively mild. And the American struggle for women's rights has been tempered by a frontier tradition—and later, in a different way, a tradition for acculturating immigrants—which either contained imagery of equality consistent with the expression of such rights or at least did not serve as a nucleus for absolute opposition to them.

The "release phenomenon" of which I speak—the sudden emergence in often exaggerated form of psychological tendencies previously suppressed by social custom—has been much more dramatic in China and Japan. One can, for example, contrast the classical stance of the Chinese woman, her bound feet literally restricting her motion and symbolically restricting her "life space," with the recent displays of assertion and unwavering ideological aggressiveness by female cadres in Communist China. This does not mean that the women of China have been suddenly transformed from weakness to strength. Rather, it suggests that an important group of them have undergone a shift in the areas within which they can operate as knowers, from family to society, along with a similar redirection of intellectual and emotional expression. Such release and redirection often tends toward excess, as was made clear to me not only in the behavior of female cadres, but in the examples I encountered of extraordinarily domineering and shrewish behavior in Chinese women who were still operating primarily within their families at a time when the society surrounding these families was literally falling apart. Indeed, it may well be that "the shrew," whenever she appears in significant numbers, whether in China or Elizabethan England, is a specific product of social breakdown and of such a release phenomenon.

By these standards, American shifts in the life space permissible to women have been minor ones, taking place within a more established ideological tradition of feminine self-realization. Educated East Asian women are well aware that their historical experience with such ideologies is brief indeed, and that their serious confrontation with them is still in its infancy. Leaving aside the psychological complexities and mixed benefits of this confrontation, my point here is that American women, and in different ways European and Russian women, are in a real historical sense a vanguard group. Indeed, although American and East Asian women tend to have complicated feelings about one another—or about themselves in relationship to each other—they seem to agree upon the observation that East Asian women have only begun to experiment with matters that their Western counterparts have been struggling with for centuries. (No doubt the time will come when East Asian women will feel the need to rediscover some of their own cultural values here as in other areas, but that is another matter.)

As a vanguard group, American women are capable of institutional inventions that are bound to be of interest to the rest of the world. One of these inventions, made, of course, in collaboration with men, is the new marriage pattern described by Edna Rostow,[11] in which mutuality of care and individual realization, as well as intellectual and emotional sharing, have been achieved, or at least sought after, to an unprecedented degree. But it inevitably follows that American women must also be in the vanguard of despair—despair related to the gap between the nobility of this kind of vision, whether in marriage or other aspects of life, and the more ambiguous, disappointing, often painful actualities. Yet large groups of women throughout the world seem determined to have an opportunity to experience this vanguard despair.

One sometimes has the impression that such feminine despair increases directly in proportion to the development of feminine capacities. There are additional reasons for this, one of which is suggested by the simple, somewhat accusatory claim, made about thirty years ago by a prominent American journalist, that "modern women are . . . unhappy and . . . unconsciously hate men . . . because they have gotten better and men have gotten worse."[12] Rather than simply dismissing this statement by Dorothy Thompson as that of an aggressively competitive woman, or as merely an expression of "penis envy," we do better (whatever her psychological makeup) to see in it the possible suggestion of a general principle: Both men and women experience considerable psychological conflict in relation to rapid historical change, but the conflict in women is more likely to carry at least the seed of personal liberation, while in men the greater commitment to the ideological superstructure which is undergoing deterioration is likely to imbue the conflict with profound psychological threat. This principle is, of course, bound to have a great number of exceptions, depending upon the nature of the change and the context in which it takes place. But I have found it to apply in a variety of situations under differing conditions, and I believe it to be generally consistent with the psychohistorical factors we have so far discussed. If the principle is true, and there will be additional evidence for it in what follows, historical change creates a disparity in psychological balance between the sexes in which feminine achievement becomes something of a pyrrhic victory, accompanied as it is by impaired capacity of both men and women to relate to one another. Yet precisely this combination of disappointment in male partners and expanding criteria for self-realization gives women particular capacity for new kinds of accomplishment, for the development of new forms of knowing. Men may then feel themselves doubly threatened: not only dislocated and possibly emasculated, but also "seen through" in their weaknesses more clearly than ever before by women whom they can no longer dominate and to whom they feel distinctly inferior. At this juncture, their latent psychic tendency to view all women as dangerous devourers is likely to be activated, whether or not these devourers are felt to be allied with an imprisoning society, as Diana Trilling suggests is the case in contemporary American masculine literary fantasy.[13] This particular aspect of historical dislocation, however uncomfortable, seems to be the source of a great variety of literary and depth-psychological discoveries by both men and women.

We would seem now, willy-nilly, to have entered into the arena of the "battle of the sexes," an arena which the historically minded psychiatrist should neither flee from nor accept on its own terms. Substituting the metaphor of the dance for that of the arena, we may say that in all cultures there is a complex rhythmic patterning of emotions between men and women, in the continuous effort at definition and reassertion of what is to be considered properly "masculine" and "feminine." Within the dance one inevitably encounters a discrepancy between public and private gestures, between outer appearance and inner actuality. For the Japanese woman, for instance, the definition of femininity has traditionally contained requirements of charm and service; definitions of femininity have been less precise for the American woman, but, at least when compared to the Japanese, she has been permitted much greater public assertion. I have, in fact, repeatedly noted the fascination and horror with which Japanese men and women alike have observed the American woman's public self-assertions, and particularly her readiness to contest male authority. But when we

43

look at the more hidden aspects of the dance within the two cultures, a very different image presents itself. It turns out that the Japanese woman has an actual authority in human relationships within the family, often over her husband as well as her children, in many ways far greater than that of her American counterpart. Within this realm her service to others—her nurturing function—is her means of rule; her influence is all-pervasive as she doles out both financial (she tends to be in control of the purse strings and to receive her husband's paycheck in toto, from which she grants him his allowance) and emotional succor to those around her. And when Americans have become sufficiently intimate with Japanese life to observe these patterns, it has been their turn to look on with horror and fascination at the Japanese woman's way of treating her husband in public as uncontested lord and master, and in private as another child in need of maternal care.

But what of the *direction* of the movements of the dance within the two cultures? In Japan, there is a saying that during the postwar period "women and nylon stockings have grown stronger." The first part of the claim is untestable. But whatever the fits and starts and mutual ambivalence (and we have seen that women can be very ambivalent about becoming "stronger"), there has been a clear if grudging tendency toward the loosening of existing definitions of femininity. This tendency shows itself in beginning opportunities for women to work in areas previously confined to men, and to participate in various intellectual activities without totally destroying their capacity to be considered, and to consider themselves, feminine. We have already witnessed the difficulties of achieving even this much; and there have inevitably been enormous strains, residual forms of discrimination (not only financial, but more subtle patterns which include relegating women employees to serving tea and in various ways waiting on men), and even "restorationist" demands that all of society return to an idyllic past that never was, in which women were totally subservient to men and all lived in perfect harmony. But these resistances do not alter the basic direction of the dance.

For the American woman, the direction, as might be expected, is considerably less specific. For she lacks both the exaggerated restrictions of traditional definitions of femininity (although restrictions have of course been present) or actual models to follow (such as her Japanese counterpart has in identifying with American or generally Western patterns). Still subject to psychological and financial discrimination in her efforts to broaden her knowing, her social gains offset by her culture's traditional stress upon something resembling a male-female "alliance for progress" (that is, for visible, often technological, accomplishment) rather than upon celebration of the genuinely sensual and spiritual possibilities of male-female interplay, it is no wonder that she often seems brittle beneath her attainments, uncertain of her femininity, and equally uncertain of what would improve her situation. Yet out of this very ambiguity of direction, new generations of American women are engaging in a variety of experiments, sexual and otherwise, which would seem to offer as much promise for creative innovation as they do cause for concern.

The strains that accompany changing definitions of femininity can cause women to retreat into highly damaging distortions of their nurturing function. What we Americans so possessively refer to as "Momism" is by no means confined to American culture, but is rather a compensatory plunge, taken by dislocated women of any culture, into a more or less *totalistic nurturing ethos:* into a despair-ing effort to achieve self-esteem and power through a mother-child relationship which goes even beyond that of a cult of nurturence in the direction of total maternal control over the child, achieved by the alternate promise of total sustenance and threat of abandon-ment, neither of which is carried out.

Such totalistic nurturing imagery can, moreover, lead to malig-nant consequences, whether or not these take the form of mental illness per se.[14] Children so brought up may not only go through life unconsciously seeking new combinations of total dependency and total submission, but, equally important, inevitably experience a sense of profound disillusionment at the failure to achieve what they seek, the disillusionment itself a repetition of the original mother-child pattern. They may come to distrust all relationships as falling short of what is craved, and develop a sense of what Japanese intellectuals have termed (referring to themselves and their fel-low countrymen) "victim-consciousness"—which, in psychological terms, really means a gnawing sense of resentment over unfulfilled, and unfulfillable, dependency. Those so affected can become sus-picious to the point of paranoia, and particularly *suspicious of counterfeit nurturence:* that is, exaggeratedly on guard lest the help or sustenance they seek be predicated upon their being con-sidered weak and inferior—precisely the way they feel about them-selves. Such patterns of suspicion of counterfeit nurturence can operate within any group of people who feel themselves unusually dependent and helpless in relationship to stronger groups—whether arising from actual victimization of any kind, such as racial prejudice, or even from the circumstances of international politics, particularly those involving programs of economic or other aid. I do not wish to suggest that totalistic nurturing imagery (or "Momism") in itself causes these momentous problems, but rather that it becomes part of an active constellation of psychological and historical elements for which there is no clear starting point; it is both a product of, and a further stimulus to, the essential historical dislocation.

I have confined myself to Japanese examples because I have had specific opportunity to observe them, but my impression is that people in non-Western cultures are more generally prone to patterns of totalistic nurturing imagery and suspicion of counterfeit nurturence than are Americans. There are several reasons for this: Non-Western cultures have traditionally emphasized the unity of the mother-child relationship to a greater extent than in the West, to a point sometimes approaching totalism; these same cultures have undergone much greater modern and contemporary historical upheavals; and, equally important, the nations formed from non-Western cultures find themselves in the position of requiring various forms of help or sustenance from Western countries.[15] Yet American culture may, in a special way, have a particular sensitivity to "Momism" precisely because it has long emphasized an opposite myth of absolute "individualism"—that of the child's eventual capacity to achieve total independence from its parents (and from everyone else)—and this sensitivity makes us the first to seek out "Momism" in our midst.

The alternative to these dislocations and explosions of mistrust lies in various kinds of social inventiveness. New psychological discoveries concerning the interplay of the sexes and the special potential of each sex are as necessary as are political and economic advances. All three may, in fact, be inseparable; women might, for instance, be able to make use of their characteristic focus upon immediate human relationships to evolve modes of knowing that could "soften" prevailing political and economic approaches, and bring enriching elements of sensuality and nurturence back into knowledge itself. But a conspiratorial theory which sees the difficulty as the imposition of feminine standards by women's magazines or psychoanalysts is not adequate for grasping the dilemma.[16] The actual problem is a more difficult one: How can women make their way in a technologically dominated, in this sense "man-made," world and claim their full share of the contemporary historical adventure while remaining true to their psychological nature as women?

5.

There is an additional expression of feminine knowing that could have enormous significance in our present historical situation, pertaining to ways of symbolizing death and immortality in relationship to the needs of life. It stems from the general human need for a sense of connection, for meaningful ties to people, ideas, and symbols, derived from the past and projecting into the future. This sense of connection is initiated through innate patterns of the human infant toward what John Bowlby has called "attachment behavior."[17] Bowlby has identified five "component instinctual responses" (sucking, clinging, following, crying, and smiling), inborn impulses in the infant which both promote, and are further stimulated by, maternal care, and which therefore have "survival value" to the child and "underlie the child's tie to his mother," his earliest and most fundamental human bond.

I would make the further claim that the sense of connection so initiated extends not only into adult life but beyond it. That is, for a sense of connection to be experienced during adult life, one requires a form of imagery, conscious or unconscious, which is felt to perpetuate that connection after one's death. This inner imagery constitutes what I have referred to as a *sense of immortality*,[18] and may be expressed in the biological, theological, and interpersonal or creative spheres, or through identification with nature itself. This sense of immortality, in turn, reflects what I have spoken of as "a symbolic need to transcend individual biological life; rather than consisting of mere denial of death, it represents a compelling universal urge to maintain an inner sense of continuous symbolic relationship, over time and space, to the various elements of life."

I have also suggested that the existence of nuclear weapons has, in itself and independently of any use of these weapons, posed a significant, though usually unrecognized, psychological threat in the form of interference with this symbolic need. For in the post-nuclear world (and probably no one's imagination, from the age of seven or eight, is entirely free from internalized images of nuclear destruction) we can imagine no biological or biosocial posterity,

47

little or nothing surviving of our works or influences. Theological symbolism of an afterlife becomes threatened or blurred, leaving only nature itself as a potentially important but ambiguous means of perpetuating a sense of individual connection and maintaining a sense of immortality.

I believe that this fundamental threat to human connection must inevitably affect attachment behavior in a more general sense. Our imagery of connection does not necessarily distinguish between present and future attachments, and if one is threatened so is the other. It may not be too much to say that the combination of unprecedented historical velocity (which in itself presents a severe threat to connection and attachment) and the existence of nuclear weapons create a revolutionary degree of potential suspiciousness of all human connection. There results not only the sensitivity to counterfeit nurturence I have already mentioned, but also a variety of psychosocial patterns both destructive and potentially creative: these include such things as severe youth rebellions, widespread lassitude and rote behavior, engagement in various forms of pseudo-attachment characterized by the appearance of a meaningful bond without its emotional content, every form of plunge into social movements that promise new solidarity, followed by rapid disillusionment with these movements and with the possibility of achieving solidarity or connection. These reactions to impaired connection represent another form of separation anxiety, which, according to Bowlby, is a "primary anxiety . . . not reducible to other terms." Therefore, to say that we are faced by psychohistorical threats to our sense of connection of a revolutionary intensity is also to say that we are faced with unprecedented eruptions of anxiety of the most elemental nature.

These are root problems of the human situation, and can hardly be solved by any individual or group, or by members of either sex alone. But it would seem that women have a special relationship to them that we may do well to explore, and to a degree quite beyond the fragmentary suggestions presented here, a relationship based upon her nurturing function and upon her particular capacity to bridge biology and history. If, as I am suggesting, an impaired sense of immortality, severed symbolic connection, and intensified separation anxiety are all of a psychohistorical piece, they create a self-reinforcing cycle which threatens not only general psychic balance but the continuity of the human species. Insofar as women can contribute to counter-tendencies which interrupt this cycle in favor of constructive and even extraordinary possibilities equally open to the human future, her capacity as knower meets its ultimate test. We might of course say that she makes just this kind of contribution through each child she helps to instill, during its earliest years, with a reasonable balance of connection and autonomy, in the face of pressures that make even this modest contribution ever more difficult. But I am suggesting something more: that, given the precarious nature of our psychic and physical existence, we have no choice but to return to organic principles even as we extend our cognitive and emotional discoveries; and that woman as knower, closest to these principles, can—like the goddess Demeter, who taught mankind to raise itself "above the life of beasts" and became the "giver of immortality"[19]—bring her wisdom to bear where it is most needed.

REFERENCES

1. I assume here that the psychology of the divergent group of women who entered—or, in most cases, were sold into—the Japanese "water world" cannot be directly equated with that of contemporary Western prostitutes; and that psychological studies which have demonstrated various kinds of sexual aberration in the latter do not necessarily apply to the former.

2. Ivan Morris, *The World of the Shining Prince: Court Life in Ancient Japan* (New York: Alfred A. Knopf, Inc., 1964). Subsequent quotations concerning women writers in the Heian period, in this and the next two paragraphs (including the quotation from Arthur Waley), are from Morris's book.

3. Morris, *op. cit.*, points out that "it is not only since the Second World War that the position of Japanese women has become better than that of their ancestors a thousand years ago." And indeed, these feminine "ancestors" of the Heian period—or at least those elevated few who were part of Court life—were notable not only for their literary interests but for their erotic ones as well. Their tendency to combine feminine functions at so advanced a level anticipates the modern condition, as I shall attempt to demonstrate. Women of their literary attainment and individuated life patterns do not seem to have again made their appearance in Japanese life until well after the Meiji Restoration of 1868. For this long period of feminine decline, in China as well as in Japan, many historians blame the suppressive influence of Neo-Confucian doctrine in both countries.

4. Sigmund Freud, "On the Universal Tendency to Debasement in the Sphere of Love (Contributions to the Psychology of Love II)," *Standard Edition*, Vol. XI (London: The Hogarth Press and The Institute of Psycho-analysis, 1957), pp. 177–190.

5. See Erik H. Erikson, "Inner and Outer Space: Reflections on Womanhood," this volume, for a discussion of these psychobiological distinctions —particularly that between feminine "inner space" and masculine "outer space"—and their appearance early in life.

6. Michael Polanyi, *Personal Knowledge* (Chicago: The University of Chicago Press, 1958), pp. 300–303.

7. I have discussed some of these issues at length in my book, *Thought Reform and the Psychology of Totalism* (New York: W. W. Norton, 1961), and other related matters in my paper, "Youth and History: Individual Change in Postwar Japan," *Dædalus* (Winter 1962), reprinted in Erik H. Erikson, ed., *Youth: Change and Challenge* (New York: Basic Books, 1963).

8. Charles Haldeman, *The Sun's Attendant* (New York: Simon and Schuster, 1964), p. 256.

9. See my "Individual Patterns in Historical Change: Imagery of Japanese Youth," in *Comparative Studies in Society and History*, Vol. 6 (1964), pp. 369–383; also in *Disorders in Communication*, Vol. 42, *Proceedings of the Assn. for Research in Nervous and Mental Disease*, David McK. Rioch, ed. (Baltimore: Waverly Press, 1964), for a discussion of these ways of psychologically symbolizing time; and "Youth and History . . .," *op. cit.*, deals with some of the observations on Japanese students that follow.

10. Kenneth Keniston, "Inburn, an American Ishmael," in Robert W. White, ed., *The Study of Lives* (New York: Atherton, 1963), and a book by the same author now in preparation. See also, Ellen and Kenneth Keniston, "An American Anachronism: The Image of Women and Work," *American Scholar*, Vol. 33 (1964), pp. 355–375.

11. Edna Rostow, "Conflict and Accommodation," this volume.

12. Vincent Sheean, *Dorothy and Red* (Boston: Houghton Mifflin Company, 1963), p. 340.

13. Diana Trilling, "The Image of Women in Contemporary Literature," this volume.

14. Such totalistic nurturing imagery also bears considerable relationship to the kind of mother-child relationship which is thought to contribute to the development of schizophrenia. Recent work on schizophrenia emphasizes the entire family constellation rather than the mother-child relationship alone; but if an actual increase in the incidence of schizophrenia has been occurring during the past few decades in America and elsewhere, a debated issue, it is quite possible that the patterns of historical dislocation and attendant disturbances in mother-child relationships we have been discussing might be a factor in this increase.

15. The great exception in American life is, of course, Negro culture, in which suspicion of counterfeit nurturence as well as patterns of maternal domination are strong. Especially crucial here is the long victimization of the American Negro in American life and his continuing position of inferiority

and dependency, though the other features I mentioned in relationship to non-Western cultures also play a part.

16. A recent, forceful presentation of what comes close to this conspiratorial point of view is that of Betty Friedan, in *The Feminine Mystique* (New York: W. W. Norton, 1963). While I am sympathetic to Mrs. Friedan's concern with enlarging prevailing imagery about what constitutes femininity, and would agree that women's magazines and psychoanalysts have at times promulgated overly narrow definitions of femininity, I would insist upon the importance of broader psychohistorical currents rather than the groups she singles out for attack.

17. For this and subsequent references to Bowlby, see his "The Nature of the Child's Tie to his Mother," *International Journal of Psycho-analysis,* Vol. 39 (1958), pp. 350–373; and "Separation Anxiety," *International Journal of Psycho-analysis,* Vol. 41 (1960), pp. 1–25.

18. Robert J. Lifton, "On Death and Death Symbolism: The Hiroshima Disaster," *Psychiatry,* Vol. 27 (1964), pp. 191–210.

19. W. K. C. Guthrie, *The Greeks and Their Gods* (Boston: Beacon Press Paperback Series, 1955), pp. 284, 286.

DIANA TRILLING

The Image of Women in Contemporary Literature

IN UNDERTAKING to speak to you this evening on the influence of
our contemporary literary culture on the gifted young college
woman, I realize, of course, that I have moved rather far afield from
the precise area this Conference has set itself to explore. You have
come together for these few days to deal with honors programs
and with the educational problems of superior women students—
and I have chosen to talk to you about literature. I hope, however,
that I am not being unduly confident in giving you my assurance
that my subject is considerably more relevant to the theme of
your meetings than it may appear to be on the surface. In earlier
sessions of this Conference there has been discussion of some of
the social-psychological realities affecting the life of women in
present-day American life—the impulse, for instance, of young
women, in a situation which doesn't permit them the special considerations of their sex, to give up the careers for which they were
trained rather than give up their role as mothers. This discussion
was largely derived from the observations of sociology as they coincide with our practical experience of the world in which we live.
But art, too, has something to tell us about the contemporary experience, and something not the less cogent because it is intuitive
rather than scientific and because it may at many points contradict
our own social perceptions or those of the professions devoted to
formal social study. In *The Two Cultures* C. P. Snow describes the
large separation which he believes now exists between science and
the humanities. I also have it in mind this evening to speak of two
cultures, but in a very different sense than Sir Charles's. The oppo-

A speech delivered to a conference on the superior woman student
held by the Inter-University Committee on the Superior Student, Columbia University, May 23, 1964.

sition with which I shall be dealing here is not the division between science and the humanities but the extraordinary antithesis between the view of life to which we subscribe as teachers, university administrators, counselors of students, even as citizens or parents—participants, that is, in the ongoing enterprise of society—and the view of life now being proposed in our literary culture.

Although usually, in the past, when the literary critic spoke of literary culture, he meant a quite limited phenomenon—the activity of the most conscious segment of society as it deals with books—a premise of my remarks tonight is that this strict definition no longer applies. Parallel to the social and economic mobilities of which sociology has taken account, there is another movement in American life which has not been sufficiently studied, the cultural mobility which accompanies the breakdown of the old barriers of class. While note has been taken of the diffusion of standards of domestic taste through large sections of the American population, this development has been chiefly examined in its relation to the impact of advertising and merchandising on people who suddenly have enough money to acquire the questionable benefits of a consumer culture. What has not been properly commented upon is the diffusion of tastes, ideas and attitudes whose ultimate source is not Madison Avenue but art, and art at its top reaches of seriousness, where Madison Avenue is the declared enemy.

Up to a short time ago, it was perfectly accurate to speak of American literary culture in terms of a highbrow and a lowbrow culture, a literature for the elite and a literature for mass consumption; I think, however, that that time is now past. I am not implying that we have achieved the total democratization of literature, and that there is no longer any distinction to be made among many levels of literary performance and audience. But the unbridgeable gaps which once divided the various sectors of American literary production and response are closing. In another context, I referred recently to the information given me a few years ago by the editor of a semi-popular periodical—that there had been a moment, in the '50s, when the smooth-paper magazines of this country were faced with a major decision, either to lower their denominators and aim for a truly popular readership, or, as she put it, raid *Partisan Review*. The magazines that lowered their standards suffered a fall in circulation. The magazines that stormed the bastions of high culture rose in circulation.

We are all of us familiar with the result. It is not only

that magazines as different in their intention and diversified in their content as, say, *Esquire, Show, Holiday, Mademoiselle, Redbook, Good Housekeeping,* even *Nugget* or *Playboy,* now make their way by offering the general public the work of some of our most "advanced" writers. Nor is it only that our serious authors can now, if they wish, reach very wide audiences, or that our popular or semi-popular magazines are staffed by men and women for whom it is a qualification for their jobs that they have a ready familiarity with the best writing being produced here and abroad. After all, it could be pointed out that even several decades ago F. Scott Fitzgerald published in the *Saturday Evening Post* and Ernest Hemingway in *Cosmopolitan.* The more important fact is that it is by employing writers of the greatest adventurousness of mind that our large-circulation periodicals now make their general appeal for readers. And more important still is the fact that even where our advanced writers may not themselves appear in magazines of large circulation, their attitudes and their forms of sensibility have penetrated to such an extent that we no longer even notice it as an intrusion.

But this is only one route by which the dissemination of contemporary literary values is proceeding. In addition to the magazines, there are the theater, movies, television, in all of which, no matter how wide and various the audience they hope to reach, we see the mark of literary modernity as it is now being formulated on our most advanced cultural fronts. That the intention of the serious artist has often been grievously diluted or distorted in the process of popularization goes, of course, without saying. The line of descent is nevertheless unmistakable.

It follows, then, that the college student of today does not have to be especially "literary" to be influenced by contemporary literary thought. Nor does the sex of the student either increase or decrease this susceptibility, so far as I can make out. Male or female, gifted or only average in endowment, any student who is part of the present-day world is also part of the world that is being reflected in, and created by, contemporary literary art. I know, of course, that it is one of the assumptions of education that a well-trained mind is better capable of resisting influence than an untrained mind. It is my own opinion that this assumption is largely a piety. By my observation, the influences from the side of rebelliousness, whether in art or politics, are as compelling among the well-educated classes as those of conservatism are in other sections of the community. Perhaps what marks the person of superior intellectual training in our society is not so much his actual capacity to think for himself as his happy belief that he thinks for himself. Surely none of us is proof against the pressures of fashionable ideas. It is therefore to some purpose, I think, that if we are to deal with the special problems of the superior young woman in our colleges, we also try to understand her in her *un*specialness—through an understanding of what it is she is now being told about herself and her relation to society in the novels she reads, the plays and movies and television programs she sees, even perhaps by the pictures in the fashion magazines she leafs through at the beauty parlor. For this is the other education to which she is being exposed along with her schooling, and it may be equally or even more persuasive.

Confronting such a huge area of investigation, one must necessarily narrow the range. I can suppose it would be possible to treat this evening's subject by limiting myself, say, just to the image of contemporary young womanhood in a magazine like *Mademoiselle;* in fact, by limiting myself to the fashion models who display the clothes and cosmetics in magazines for young women—those extraordinary creatures whose harsh, hard outlines are presented to us as, presumably, the very distillation of female charm; whose angularity of figure and posture are, purportedly, the sign of their womanly grace; whose fierce air of wonder and question is, paradoxically enough, the key to their knowingness. Surely none but an affluent society could afford to represent its well-being in girls as underweight as these; it is very expensive to stay this thin and yet sufficiently strong to achieve the bizarre poses which celebrate the freedom and despair of the contemporary young. It also takes much knowledge of the racial unconscious to project, in the handling of one's body, Dostoyevsky's remarkable insight that there is no such thing as an ugly woman. But although there is undoubtedly much to be said of the relationship between today's fashion model and the view of life that is current in our elite literary quarterlies, I'll resist the urge to explore it further, and, instead, take my point of departure in television, by recounting a story I chanced upon one evening not long ago in a series called *The Nurses.* The series was designed, I gather, to challenge the hegemony of the male doctors, but, expectably enough, I suppose, the male characters, at least in this particular program, soon took the center of the stage.

The episode, on the evening I tuned in, concerned a young intern recently married to a nurse in the hospital. The young man is accused of having cheated on his examinations in his last year of medical school; he is brought up on charges before the hospital board of inquiry. Although he swears, publicly, that he is innocent, the young doctor admits to his wife that he is lying; he did cheat on his examinations but for what he considers a sound reason; he was a good student but he was not top of his class and he had to lead his class if he wanted an appointment to this hospital, where he could work with one of the foremost endocrinologists of the country. His wife is horrified and confounded; she, too, is to be called up before the board; shall she also perjure herself to protect her husband? The young man has no doubt but that this is where her duty lies, and not only her duty but common sense—after all, is it not motive that counts, rather than honor in the abstract? And in this view he has the support of the great endocrinologist himself, who argues that the young intern's superior talent for medicine is really all that matters; what difference does it make that he got his hospital post dishonestly since he has turned out to be so worthy of the appointment? In fact, the only people in the story who share the moral scruples of the young wife are the hospital administrators; and of these we were told in an earlier episode of the serial that they are not only squares but hypocrites: they are interested, not in the patients in the hospital, but in the rich donors; and they don't pay their kitchen staff a living wage. Well, the wife fails to persuade her husband to confess the truth or even to feel guilty about his lie, so she leaves him. But her inviolate morality turns out to be the loneliest of virtues; gift, originality, charm, humor, flexibility, even conscience itself would seem, all of them, to be lined up on the side of the intern. As the door closes on her departure at the end of the film, we have the firm impression that a talented young doctor is well rid of a wife so lacking in realism. Our hero will no doubt find himself a life partner who understands that it is sometimes necessary to discard the traditional moralities for the sake of one's ultimate goal.

Now a story of this kind was obviously created for what we think of as a popular audience. It is apparent, however, that it has its cultural antecedents far from the advertising office in which it was designed, perhaps with some degree of conscious cynicism. First of all, there is its implicit political reference. Ever since the McCarthy period, when writers for movies and television lost their jobs for political reasons, it has been one of the tokens of conscience and seriousness in Hollywood or on Madison Avenue to introduce into popular films this or that bit of social propaganda: one's duty to resist an investigating committee is one of the familiar messages from this quarter of political enlightenment. Then there is the relation the narrative establishes between gift and moral independence: were the young man in the story less talented as a doctor, we can suppose he'd not have earned the right to make his own moral laws. A similar assumption, of course, underlies some of our best writing of the last seventy-five years, in which the hero of literature has regularly been conceived as someone whose special endowment of sensitivity or imagination or spirit puts him beyond the reach of ordinary moral imperatives. It is a point of view which reaches its present-day climax in Mailer's Hipster, Genêt's criminal, even in James Baldwin's Negro. And one of its corollaries is the special virtue which is now assigned to sexual deviation, as if a deviant sexuality is itself a sign of superiority, like a talent for painting or poetry: the homosexual in current literature is exempt, not merely from the sexual rules of our society, but from its prescriptions for moral behavior. Or another offshoot of the same premise is our assumption that the artist or intellectual has the inherent right to civil disobedience; this is surely not a right we readily grant to the reactionary politician, or even to the businessman.

But the connection between our TV story and present-day literary culture in its more advanced sectors doesn't stop here. We recall that in the literature of forty years ago, the conflict in the life of a young doctor named Martin Arrowsmith concerned his choice between pure and impure science: that is, between research and the practice of medicine. Basic to the choice with which Sinclair Lewis confronted the hero of his novel about the medical profession was the problem of financial security. In our story, idealism and financial security are no longer in opposition to each other. Apparently the Foundations—or if not the Foundations, then a burgeoning economy—have taken care of *that* drama. Indeed, money is not mentioned at all in our film; and this is not an accidental or minor omission. It indicates far more than merely our current economic upsurge.

Certainly, of the many conditions by which society asserts its reality, none is more forceful than the making and spending of money. Therefore to make money real is to make society real. But this reality is exactly what contemporary literature would now put under question. According to advanced literary opinion, modern society is not lacking in power; it has the giant implacable power to destroy the individual. It has weight, dread and inchoate. What it does not have is such concreteness, structure, particularization of good and bad purpose as once gave the individual his best means of self-definition and the novelist his richest material. The reason money has disappeared from fiction is that society has disappeared from fiction.

As a matter of fact, I think it would be fair to say that if we had to name one test by which we can now distinguish between seriously ambitious writing and writing which has no proper claim to art, it would be the amount of reality given to the social organization. The more art in any literary work, the less social reality—the less allusion, that is, to money, class, manners, property, profession. There are even some few television programs—*Route 66* is an outstanding recent example—which, aping their betters in this as in other ways, do make a claim to art, basing this pretension precisely on their abstractness. For the most part, however, television and the movies still do not dare the abstractness which is already so much the fictional vogue. For instance, in the story I have recounted, although the problem of money is avoided, we still find a deference to the old popular preference for social representation: the narrative provides its main characters with a local habitation and with professions. But the professions, being nothing if not social particularizations, have virtually disappeared from a fiction which means to deal acutely and consciously with the modern condition, especially that branch of fiction which is most highly subjective in inspiration, the developmental novel concerned with the coming of age of a young man.

In the past the hero of the developmental novel was always either a writer, like his author, or some surrogate for the writer—a painter, perhaps, or a lawyer, an architect, a scientist. Today, these professional surrogates for the writer are more and more being substituted for by totally amorphous projections of the author, persons without roots, social delineation or educational advantage—a baseball player as in Bernard Malamud's *The Natural*, an ex-basketball player as in John Updike's *Rabbit, Run*, a man of—what?—some unspecified universal genius such as Salinger's Zooey Glass. And it is interesting that where, as in Malamud's more recent book, *A New Life*, or Updike's more recent *The Centaur*, the protagonists *are* given professions consonant with the experience of their authors, the jobs they do are robbed of their traditional coherence. For instance, in *A New Life*, although the hero is technically a college instructor in English, he is presented to us not merely as an unusually depressed figure but as a displaced person, a born Easterner dropped without passport in the wastes of the far West; also as an ex-alcoholic, which further authenticates him as a man without context. In Updike's *The Centaur*, the situation is even more heavily charged against professional reality; although the leading character is a teacher in a high school, he spends every other chapter in the novel as a centaur, Chiron, teacher to Achilles, the point being, one gathers, that the profession of teacher in our society is half mythological. Which, of course, it may very well be.

In serious contemporary fiction, the interest which once attached to the social scene now has a different object: it is directed to the self. The hero's exploration of an external and objective world has yielded to the effort of self-exploration and self-explanation. And here, again, our television story reveals its high antecedents, for only that is right for our young intern which makes him feel right, feel "good" (as the current phrase has it) within himself. The idea of personal or social morality as a more or less fixed code which guides the conduct of people living together in the community of a nation cedes to the idea of morality as an entirely *ad hoc* affair, something we devise for ourselves according to our subjective needs of the moment.

And yet the subjective moral test is not as anarchic as it may sound when we examine it outside its usual narrative frame. We remember that in our television story the young intern who cheated and lied was not planning to be a gangster; he was going to be one of the great doctors of the future. That which was good for him was also good for *us*, for the future of mankind: we must be willing to grant our need for gifted endocrinologists. And this is the familiar basis of moral judgment in most of our serious contemporary writing. The hero, with or without profession, is the voice of the author-artist. *His* need, *his* choices, are actually our needs and our proper choices, too, had we but the wits to recognize them.

The difference between anarchy and virtue turns out, that is, to be the ability to name the problem whose solution requires an act of moral improvisation. Whoever is aware that modern society is not designed for the best uses of man has, so to speak, a built-in guaranty that his own moral decisions are the best ones, however wrong they may seem by traditional standards. Consciousness is ultimate conscience. Indeed, I cannot overemphasize the degree to which, in the modern literary view, a proper awareness of self is equated with social morality. The view has perhaps its most arresting statement in the recent work of James Baldwin. For Baldwin— I put it crudely—his own sensibility, with all that this implies of one individual's distinctive gift and personality, is extended to represent the sensibility of the whole Negro population. A race which has been brought to its present plight by a vast complex of economic, social and psychological forces is shorn of these *real* conditions of its dilemma and becomes the object of one individual Negro artist's passionate quest for self-definition and self-justification.

As an artist, Baldwin is not a Negro, any more than a young Jewish writer like Philip Roth, say, is a Jew. If there are no significant distinctions of class in our contemporary literature, neither are there valid distinctions of race or creed: the multiplicities of cultures within the American group, once so absorbing to the novelist, are now no more than a tease of the memory. What divides the black and the white characters in Baldwin's *Another Country* is not their differing human characteristics but only Baldwin's undemonstrated assertion that there *is* a human and characteristic difference. It is all but impossible to recognize the girl's family in Philip Roth's *Goodbye, Columbus*, as Jews.

It is to *self*-knowledge, *self*-awareness, *self*-validation that the consciousness of the modern writer and hero is directed. The selfhood of others exists but without exciting any feelings of connection; passion we reserve for ourselves, to others we bring that modern substitute for passion, understanding. This is of course one of the techniques for living that we have been taught in our nursery schools for some years now. We must learn, not to *feel* for each other, but to understand each other. It is also the method of conducting our foreign relations which, over the last decades, has been suggested to us in substitute for a clear, principled foreign policy: if we understand other nations—understand, that is, that the citizens of other countries are no less human than ourselves—presumably this will eradicate our antagonistic goals. In television, understanding is what keeps the dramatic wheels moving. The more we are told about both sides of any issue, the higher the quality of the program: *The Defenders* is of course the obvious example. Conflict may or may not be resolved in these dramas; usually it is not. But at least everyone has been given a big therapeutic dose of tolerance of other peoples' points of view and of insight into their motives.

The Image of Women in Contemporary Literature

But the big question which is seldom asked, let alone answered, is bound to occur to us: where, in the midst of all this insight with which we are being supplied, is feeling? We return to our television story: at the close of the episode, when the wife tells her husband she has decided to leave him, the husband says, "But I love you." Touched, but not to be deterred in her decision to separate from him, the wife departs. We hear the telephone ring; we see the young doctor move firmly to answer it, a smile—wan, to be sure—of anticipation on his face, and yes, it *is* the great endocrinologist calling him. Our hero may be debited one wife but to his credit he has the continuing support of his chief—what better bargain could he ask for? So much for feeling, and it makes the rather quiet scene of Nora's departure from the Doll's House sound like a full orchestration of expressed emotion.

Indeed, we grope back over the ages to a novel, *Farewell to Arms*, in which the loss of a wife spelled the defeat of all of life and hope for Hemingway's hero, and we wonder how many light-years now divide us from our world of thirty-five years ago, in which people who loved each other gave hostage to more than fortune, to one another. Today, if we are to believe our fiction, the individual is not only isolated from society, he is isolated from everyone he knows, even his own love partner. The connection between people, which we once so much relied upon, breaks, or, at best, is diverted from its former channels, and man lives alone in marriage, in friendship, in non-business, in business, in every area with which the contemporary imagination concerns itself. Only where our literary arts are themselves frankly retrograde—as, say, in conventional war stories; for what could be more retrograde than old-fashioned war?—do we find any celebration of comradeship, mutuality, self-sacrifice for the sake of another, or, for that matter, any acknowledgment of a reciprocal relationship between love or anger on the one hand, and that which we love or hate, on the other. While typically the hero of current fiction talks a great deal about his feelings—the English language, in fact, is put under some strain to cope with the volcanic surge of contemporary emotion—it is only with difficulty that one discovers the specific human object of this much urgency, except it be the author himself.

And it is especially in the relationship between lovers that emotional isolation is the order of our literary day. If we think of Hemingway as the last writer to give us love stories, we realize that he was also the last significant novelist to engage in anything like an equal dialogue with society; we begin to realize, that is, that where there is no dialogue between society and the individual, there can be very little dialogue between individuals—which is of course exactly what the writer since Hemingway has been trying to tell us. Instead of the dialogue between man and society of Hemingway's best work, we now have the interior monologue of fiction, man talking to himself, without certainty that he is even being listened to. In *A Farewell to Arms*, Lieutenant Henry was on a quest for personal identity; he sought it and found it, though only temporarily, in his love for Catherine Barkley. In *For Whom the Bell Tolls*, Jordan's dedication to the cause of the Spanish Loyalists had its paradigm in his intensity of feeling for the girl, Maria. But both such efforts have now met the defeat foretold for them by the unhappy endings of these two novels.

To measure the distance between the fiction of World Wars I and II we need only examine even the first, and quite traditional, novel of Norman Mailer, whose name has since become synonymous with the moral revolution of our time. For in Mailer's war novel, *The Naked and the Dead*, published in 1948, the Army is not simply one unit in the social entity. It is society itself, in all its giant malign indifference to the human destiny, within which there is room for neither loyalty nor affection nor yet ordinary concern for one's fellow creatures. The emotions of Hemingway's war are more than inappropriate in Mailer's war; they are downright dangerous, they can get you killed. As for love between man and woman, in *The Naked and the Dead* women exist only as offstage noises, the distant rumble of remembered sexual excitement.

Between the publication of *The Naked and the Dead* and the appearance of an important story of Mailer's called "Time of Her Time," some twelve years elapsed. The character of the later story was nevertheless implicit in Mailer's war novel, for concrete as it is in its physical detail, "Time of Her Time" is a story totally mythological in its force and import. It is a story about the sexual relations of a young bullfighter—I don't think that qualifies as a profession—in Greenwich Village and a young woman from New York University. The young woman is determined not to allow her partner the pleasure of giving her sexual satisfaction. The young man, challenged, inflicts this beneficence upon the girl despite her resistance, by resorting to methods of lovemaking which, because they violate social sanction, dispel her self-protections. But the girl, far from being pleased or softened by her experience, solidifies in hostility; the story ends with its heroine bitterly accusing its hero of being a homosexual. Manifestly, this is not a love story, nor even the story of an "affair" in the sense of suggesting, as an affair once did, some degree of continuity, mutuality, romance. It is a story of personal war. Just as in *The Naked and the Dead* the Army symbolizes the destructiveness of modern society, so in "Time of Her Time" woman, the female, represents the fearful social power against which man must defend himself: woman and society have become synonymous. The castrating woman is not new in literature any more than the male phantasy of the castrating woman is new in life; but what Mailer's story demonstrates better than any piece of contemporary fiction I can bring to mind is the new impulse of the writer to identify the destructive female force with the destructive social force: woman *is* society in all its dark, unspecifiable lust and horror. The sexual battle between the male and female characters in "Time of Her Time" is more than the projection of a common male castration phantasy, although it is certainly that too. Looked at more broadly, in the context of the modern writer's disgust with civilization—and we remember that it is Mailer's announced pro - gram, as, in a different way, it was D. H. Lawrence's before him, to work a renovation in our consciousness in order to bring us closer to our life of instinct—"Time of Her Time" represents the doomed, last-ditch struggle of man to preserve his selfhood and his decent manly pride under the assaults of a predatory society.

The woman in advanced present-day fiction, in short, is no longer recognizably related to the "ball and chain" of American folklore, a goddess knocked off the pedestal of romantic courtship to become that most dismal of folk figures, a wife, who saddles her poor husband with a home whose mortgage he cannot meet, with children who squabble and brawl, with a furnace to stoke and a lawn to mow. Feminism and technology have transformed the harassed shrew of a few decades ago to someone who is man's equal, even his superior, in the ability to meet the requirements of daily living, and woman becomes something far more insidious than a mere scold; she becomes that force in life which not only has its own unconquerable and even indefinable power but also operates to rob man of his last shred of purpose and dignity. Sexually, she is all hunger and depredation. In terms other than those of sexual desire she is an empty shell, as empty and meaningless as the society in which we find her and with which she has come to be so disastrously identified.

And how is man to cope with society, so-to-speak right in his own bed, except by isolating himself from it—her—and ridding himself of his root emotional tie to her? Except by treating her like an abstraction, just as he treats society as an abstraction? We observed the vital separation of the young intern and his wife in our television story. But this is only a shadow version of the barrier dividing men and women in the seriously ambitious fiction of our day. In Philip Roth's *Goodbye, Columbus,* for instance, the young lovers have their most brilliant meeting at the bottom of a swimming pool, where the contact can be sustained only the length of one deep intake of breath and is dissolved and made unreal by the dark moving water in which it takes place. In Updike's *Rabbit, Run,* the hero's skill as a high school athlete is recapitulated, in manhood, in the swiftness with which he makes his escapes from the women with whom he has will-lessly involved himself, flights which require no causal explanation other than resides in a man's natural right to resist death. In Malamud's *A New Life,* the hero is explicitly incapable of controlling his own sexual fate: of the three sexual encounters in which he is involved, in the first the connection is irremediably broken by a farcical incident; in the second, a snowstorm, a recalcitrant car and an overeager young lady conspire to thwart the promise of romance; in the third, the very availability of the much-desired woman is sufficient to translate the dream of love into a reality of dreariness and despair. Or we consult Golding's great best seller, *Lord of the Flies,* as appealing to young people today as Salinger's *Catcher in the Rye* was to a previous generation of adolescents, where finally there are no women at all to impose the dictates of civilization, and where we find man alone, in the infancy of the race and in all his grim submission to natural instinct. Surely it was no mere personal whimsy that impelled Nabokov, in *Lolita,* to write the love story of a grown man and a child. Only in perversity and the violation of social law is passion between the sexes now possible to the literary imagination.

What we have, then, is a literary culture, if it is only a literary culture, in which man lives in isolation from his society and in which his society reannounces itself in woman; in which, that is, woman is in essence either a predator or a husk, an uninhabited body supplied with the mechanical appurtenances for the satisfaction of the sexual appetites and the continuation of the unhappy human kind. At any rate, such is the situation as it exists for the male writer. And what about the woman writer? Does she subscribe to a similar view of society and herself?

This question is not easy to answer, largely because there is more cultural contradiction and paradox in female than in male fiction. Being neither the pathfinders of culture nor its creative historians, women always tend to represent the principle of conservatism as opposed to the greater adventurousness of the male: it was the observation Freud made about our differing sexual dispositions even at the beginning of civilization. Much female writing, indeed, constitutes the overt, highly conscious and articulate effort of women to deal with the attack which men are now making upon culture, an attack which women properly understand as an attack upon themselves as women and upon their own legitimate demands for a new life which will not be the new non-life being offered to them by Malamud and his colleagues. The work, for instance, of Doris Lessing has this as its substance; and to call Miss Lessing's novel, *The Golden Notebook,* or her stories an enterprise of conservation is distinctly not to pass pejorative judgment on them; it is simply to describe them in their essential motive.

Margaret Mead, in *Male and Female,* remarks upon the salient fact that in all known societies the work which occupies men is the superior work. If men hunt and fight, then hunting and fighting are the superior occupations of that society; if men weave and care for the babies, then weaving and baby-care have the superior prestige. The principle inherent in this observation operates unmistakably in our literary society: the way men write is apparently the superior and more prestigeful way to write, and the woman who would win a high literary status is constrained to conspire in man's view of the world; and this is especially the case at the top levels of literary seriousness. Thus, in *The Benefactor,* the recent first novel of a young woman writer of notable gift, Susan Sontag, there is nothing in either its matter or manner to suggest the sex of its author. Not only is the central character a man but a man who is the very personification of depersonalization, if we can put it so. In the story Miss Sontag tells, a man lives his dreams; it is all the life he can have. Certainly there couldn't be a more contemporary conception.

But this is a very conscious, even consciously fashionable, exercise Miss Sontag is engaged in; as I say, her novel cannot be read as special to her sex. For the most part, the present-day serious female writer echoes the male voice in ways far more unconscious than this and even—which is the significant point—in the very midst of following her own more conservative, or conserving, line. A striking, and surprising, instance is Mary McCarthy. Although as a critic Miss McCarthy stands in the forefront of the modern movement in literary thought—she has been a most ardent celebrant, for instance, of Burroughs' nihilistic *Naked Lunch*—as the author of *The Group* she has frankly undertaken to revive the novel of social specificity. It is of more than casual interest, however, that *The Group* could not be set in the contemporary world; it is a historical novel of the 1930s, when society was admitted to literary awareness in a way that it no longer is. Still, modernity intrudes itself even into Miss McCarthy's reconstruction of a period whose sensibility was so different from ours: certainly the distance between the men and women in *The Group* is a strong premonition of the isolation we know now in the '50s and '60s. It is as if Miss McCarthy cannot ascribe even to an earlier decade than ours emotions which are not now permitted to a writer in tune with her times. As a matter of fact, the intense loyalties that are supposed to bind Miss McCarthy's Vassar classmates have a sharp ring of falsification, at least to one reader; I find the close relationships of these seven girls forced, overcreated, factitious, to the point where I begin to wonder whether Miss McCarthy's seven heroines are really seven differentiated individuals or merely seven aspects of herself—seven facets, that is, of an author unwillingly and unwittingly snared in the contemporary commitment to self.

A case could be made, I think, for the thesis that the commitment to the self was, in fact, contributed to contemporary fiction by the woman writer and that it is an evidence of the demasculinization of modern man—an evidence he fails to recognize—that in his role of author he has borrowed a peculiarly female way of taking his stand against the savage impersonality of modern life. Perhaps women were quicker than men to perceive the cruel direction of the modern world, if slower to canonize the belief that society has scored its final triumph over the individual. In our own century, certainly, from the time of Dorothy Richardson right down to our present-day women writers for *The New Yorker*, the female self has been the locus of all the sensibility presumed to have been left us by modern life. Katherine Mansfield, who put herself to school to Chekhov, could learn from him only a style of objective narration; her stories were actually dedicated to the celebration of her own precise and delicate spirit. And it was Virginia Woolf who formalized the stream-of-consciousness technique as the most suitable method for re-enacting the miracle of being oneself in an environment bent on one's destruction. This self-mythologizing impulse has far from played itself out in the work of women: Katherine Anne Porter's *Ship of Fools,* also a historical novel, is a useful statement about life as it is, or even as it was, only insofar as we are willing to generalize from one woman's exercise in self-definition. And manifestly this is not very far, although it is hard to see why, except for reasons of man's dominance in culture, there should be more validity in generalizing about the Negro population from James Baldwin than about the white population from Miss Porter.

What I mean to say here, in short, is that if men have appeared to take the lead in making our contemporary spiritual formulations, they have had, and continue to have, considerable cooperation from the opposite sex which, in so many of its expressions, would seem to exercise a restraining or even a retrograde force in the cultural movement of the times. Or perhaps the nub of the situation is that art tells the truth, whatever the sex of the artist or the conflicts peculiar to only one sex, and that the real world *is* deserting us, society *is* destroying us, leaving us nothing but the immediate and existential self with which to try to counter the dark external power.

At any rate, a culture in which men tell women that they are neither loving nor lovable is no more likely to produce love stories written by women than a culture in which women tell men that they are incapable of appreciating the special female sensitivities is likely to produce, from men, a fiction of solid and shared feeling. The gap between classes closes in the modern world; the gap in the emotional connection between men and women widens—desperately widens, if we are to judge by literature and by the peripheral literary arts. We return, in fact, to the fashion models of whom I was speaking earlier with a new perception of what it is that makes for the bizarre postures in which we meet them and for those familiar expressions of outraged bewilderment. It is now a tired insight that women's clothes are designed for them by homosexuals who, because of their hostility to women, distort their appearance. What we must recognize as well is that these clothes are being exhibited by a race of female creatures who no longer know how to look their female best, where they stand or how to stand, what to think or whether they should think at all. Such being the extreme dilemma of the contemporary young woman, small wonder that she undertakes to deny her isolation and to confirm her womanliness in the quickest possible public assertion of her connectedness, in marriage and in rapid and repeated childbearing. The suburbanization of our well-educated young women, which has been much talked about in this Conference, her retreat from a professional career, is not, I'm afraid, a retreat only from unfavorable working conditions.

Sometimes, to confront boldly the image of contemporary young womanhood as it is presented by our literary culture is indeed to confront such an extravagant evidence of emotional waywardness and disconnection that it is difficult to align this picture with our everyday experience of decent, hardworking girls going to college, studying, making friends, engaging in athletics, graduating from college, worrying about jobs, worrying about beaux, worrying about the managing of their homes, worrying about the baby's sinuses and schooling, coping, progressing. For the image that has been suggested by art is virtually that of a mutation in the species. I daresay there has *not* been a mutation of the species, actually. Yet I can in all gravity raise the question whether we have not already been faced, in the contemporary practice of psychiatry, with a premonition of such a mutation, psychological to begin with but with imaginable physiological consequences. I intrude here into the province of the psychiatric professions; it may be that they have the data with which to dispute my surmise that what we observe in the literary culture already has its clinical counterpart: in the disappearance, say, of the old hysterical neurosis and its replacement by what I believe is called the characterological neurosis, where the complaint which brings the patient into treatment is so frequently *just* the inability to feel, and where the illness exists on some dim borderline between neurosis and psychosis. Certainly the striking currency of words like "isolation" and "affectlessness" in present-day psychiatric studies suggests a new prevalence of the symptoms these words describe, just as the practice of the new ego psychology—the concentration upon the mechanisms by which the ego defends itself—suggests a clinical analogue to the increasing emphasis on the self in literature. I am not of course saying that our literature is making us ill. On the other hand, I would not rule out the likelihood that modern art abets, quite as much as it mirrors, the "sickness" of our world. What I mean to stress, however, is a point which we tend to overlook in our investigations into culture, that in the reiteration of a given pattern of sensibility in the art of a period we may even have a clue to corresponding physical and psychic changes in the species, nonetheless actual for being of a most subtle kind.

And it is with this grim, even melodramatic, proposition that I come back to the situation of the woman of superior talent in our colleges. I am afraid that if my portrait of the modern human condition, of the modern female condition, as I find it in contemporary writing is accurate, it cannot be much of a female student we are teaching in our schools, but only some poor lost creature, unloved, unloving, unconnected with either her fellows or the ongoing enterprise of society, considerably paranoiac in relation to the social authority, perhaps a borderline psychotic, her best and most creative energies devoted to a self-definition whose sole goal is the knowledge of how little of possibility she is permitted by contemporary life. Well, this is the trouble with allowing oneself to be captive to a diagnostic plausibility—for we all know that for every generalization I have made tonight, there could be offered a countergeneralization just as well based in our everyday experience of modern young people. That such contradiction exists, I of course do not deny. Only a few weeks ago I had, indeed, a most striking exemplification of the contradictoriness through which we must beat our way in any effort to formulate accurate statements about the "tendencies" of the contemporary young. I had been asked to be a judge in a literary competition in a woman's college. Not many manuscripts had been sent to me, they had been weeded through by preliminary readers, but in those I did receive there was more evidence than anyone needs of a culture profoundly at odds with itself. Certainly there was proof extraordinary of the tendencies I have dwelt on this evening, stories which might have been written to specification by the movement of modernity. There were also stories which so opposed themselves to the view of life which I have been describing as the dominant view in our literary culture that they stood like a caution against the conclusions which I have permitted myself.

The story that particularly impressed me, perhaps because I had already begun to think about this speech, was about a young man, bored and lonely on a New York summer evening, who, in trying to reach a friend on the phone, reaches instead an unknown girl named Myrtle, with whom he arranges a meeting at a bar. Except that her name, he discovers, is not Myrtle; in fact, she has no fixed name, she is anything one chooses to call her. It turns out that this vagueness of identity is joined to a vagueness in her apprehension of reality so acute that communication between the young man and herself, once they meet at the bar, is restricted to such charged remarks as "What about another beer?" or "Shall we go now?"—to both of which the answer is yes. The young man takes her to his apartment where she readily, and still without verbal communication, undresses and lies naked on the bed. But when the young man thinks to make love to his beautiful visitor, he looks into her eyes to lose himself in their fathomlessness; even the next morning he cannot approach her except by closing his eyes and forcing himself upon all this vacuity. The girl leaves and the young man finds himself desperate for her return. But he cannot find her; his new acquaintance is utterly without habitation or connection. Then, as suddenly and inexplicably as she had first appeared to him, the girl reappears—and again the young man takes his fierce isolate pleasure from her. Finally, the girl disappears for good, and with her departure from the young man's life, we gather that a huge nameless significance has departed as well. Emptiness has entered emptiness and begotten emptiness.

Now, it happened that I recounted this story to a literary young man with whom I was speaking a few days later. His response was "Say, that sounds good." I don't know why I was surprised. He asked me if I had given Myrtle my vote for the prize, and when I replied "No," he commented on a note of disapproval he said he heard in my voice. Why, he asked, did I disapprove of such a story. The question was difficult to answer briefly; by way of a quick explanation I told him of the stories for which I *had* cast my votes. These were a story about a family taking an aged grandmother to a nursing home, a story about a young architect who becomes involved with some neighbors whose personal history fascinates and baffles him, a story about two young country girls who feel themselves to be the spiritual custodians of the graveyard of their forebears, a truthful and touching story about two young boys, high school friends, who are reunited after a year in which one of them has been away at college. Were the stories I had favored better stories, more talented than the story of Myrtle, my literary friend inquired. This, too, was a difficult question to answer, except by saying that I was not prepared to specify what I meant by literary talent in writers as young and untried as these. For the fact was that I had voted not so much *for* talent, as *against* chic, against the easy availability of current style and attitude: if there is to be a moral revolution in my lifetime, I prefer that it involve a certain moral strenuousness to guaranty it to me; I do not conceive it to be my role to push what is already going down such a well-greased slide.

I am not sure that my answer was useful to the young man. It would be my guess that he felt that I had betrayed my responsibility as a judge of literature by basing my decision on what he would call social or moral, rather than literary, values. Certainly it would be hard to persuade anyone committed to the modern spirit in art that its existence as anything except a force for devastation depends upon the continuing presence of an opposition based in a more traditional morality.

It is not so much the part played by education in providing this traditional framework as the part played by the movement of the new that I have had it in mind to emphasize this evening. Perhaps it is just in the degree that the picture of life which I have drawn from contemporary literature will seem to be remote from the life of your own dedication as teachers and student counselors that it is important for you to recognize this other term of a dialectical process in which we are all of us engaged.

DAVID RIESMAN

Two Generations

IN THE arguments about whether women's roles have really changed, I have tried to take account of scholarly discussion, as I would if I were a stranger in the land; but in addition I am stubbornly and perhaps mistakenly influenced by my own personal history. I know that the world in which my mother grew up is very different indeed from the world in which my children are growing up, and the shift here is not due primarily to a shift in class position, region, or schooling. But in the pages that follow I do not argue the case, let alone review the social histories that might support it. Instead, I have been selectively autobiographical, essayistic, and discursive. I shall try to contrast the life I saw around me as a boy during and just after the First World War, as illustrated by a vignette of my quite idiosyncratic mother, with the life of the young people in the elite colleges whom I see now as a parent and teacher. It goes without saying that nostalgia and selective perception can bias me in both directions, and that the generations tend to be opaque to one another. Moreover, it remains true that both generations of women, whether they choose to struggle or not to struggle against prevailing definitions of femininity, cannot help being what Simone de Beauvoir calls "the second sex." In both epochs, men have tended to define the major aims of life for Americans, reluctantly leaving it open to a few women to pursue the same aims as feminists or to pursue complementary ones as what I have termed "femininists." Seeking self-definition in a fluid society, most women have tended to fall back on the cultural interpretations of their biological distinctiveness—a femininism that could be acquiescent and passive or (as Sonya Rudikoff has pointed out in her article, "Feminism Reconsidered") as mystically assertive as the French West African concept of *négritude*. Indeed, as Alice Rossi notices in her paper in this volume, many women deprived of function outside the home respond by forcing their menfolk into an ancillary position within the home, the sort of antagonistic co-operation that one also finds in many other relationships tainted by irrational authority on the one side and submissiveness on the other.

And even if I am correct that competitiveness and invidiousness are not as overwhelming motifs in American society today as at earlier times, they are still surely powerful enough so that any differences, including those between the sexes, will tend to be interpreted in terms of better and worse; and in a society where one's antecedents are seldom known, visible differences—whether of color or sex or size or imposingness—will be used to mark the boundaries of privilege and possibility. As Gunnar Myrdal and many observers have pointed out, the so-called Negro problem is for the most part a white problem; and the many symposia and conferences on "the woman problem" tend to displace the accent from where it largely belongs, on the pace-setting and boundary-creating men.

My Mother's Generation

My mother and her younger sister both assumed that they would attend college, although of course at that time, unlike today, women were not expected as a matter of course to attend college, no matter what their intelligence or social position. My mother graduated from Bryn Mawr College in the class of 1903. She led her class in scholarship, was befriended by some of her teachers in English literature, and was given the European Fellowship, handed each year to the outstanding senior for study abroad. There were some women in my mother's day and many more in my own generation who hoped to pursue both marriage and a career (as against the more common pattern today of taking on marriage first of all and then a job rather than a career). My mother was confronted with the dilemma that the post-feminist generation also encountered, for it had not occurred to her to seek a career, academic or otherwise; she was under no compulsion to marry immediately, but she was expected to wait for callers from the small covey of eligible men, one of whom, a Philadelphia physician already thirty-seven years old, had made a shy but persistent presence felt. She declined the fellowship, while treasuring the honor and resenting her lot. She and her friends had discovered the excitement of ideas and books in college; and a very few of these women did go on to pursue careers, for example in settlement house work, never marrying, while more of those I later had a chance to meet ended up as gracious housewives. My mother's family was too traditional, fearing the fellowship would lead to spinsterhood, and she herself was too timid to embark on such an independent course.

She postponed marriage to the doctor for five years, while she read novels; in her last years she was proud of the many first editions she possessed of writers who were later famous and whose worth she recognized on their first appearance: Proust, Joyce, D. H. Lawrence, Faulkner, Virginia Woolf and Gertrude Stein. She also absorbed high culture in other spheres. She knew painting and painters (and the terrible-tempered Albert C. Barnes), music and musicians (Beethoven's late quartets were her favorites but she also loved Wagner); in general, she held the romantic view of art as the only worthwhile human activity, for which all else is infrastructure or, as she would have put it, "merely second-rate." Physicians, like her husband and younger son; lawyers, like her brother and older son; bankers and brokers, manufacturers and investors, like her father and other relatives; even founding the Graphic Sketch Club like one cousin or being a foreign correspondent in the Far East like another —all these callings which help make the world go round were by definition dull and uncreative; only the arts had a place in the sun, with perhaps a lunar place for great metaphorical scientific gifts such as those of Freud or Einstein.

This romantic cult of creativity and uniqueness my mother shares with some of the young, highly educated housewives of today, although her verdicts were probably harsher and more narrow as to the orbits within which creativity might be found while at the same time being more sentimental. But very little else in my mother's life as a housewife would be acceptable to people of similar privilege today. My mother was not alone in her outlook; many of her bluestocking friends had a similar insatiable hunger for culture; it is possible that, lacking any function in society that made full use of their talents, the voracity for culture served as a kind of substitute. Anglophile and Francophile, my mother learned Italian in her forties so as to be able to read *The Divine Comedy* in the original (not at all so as to converse with Italians on visits to artistic monuments in Italy). Still later, she herself, her sister and another friend decided that they did not understand modern physics and took a course in it at the University of Pennsylvania, proudly pulling down the top grades and besting even those majoring in the subject.

My mother felt no social pressures or personal responsibility to put her learning and (rather limited) energies to any kind of use, even while she suffered as I have suggested from watching the underemployed engine of her talents keep turning over in the same place. True, she served on various Bryn Mawr boards and fund drives, and helped found a progressive secondary school near Philadelphia; during the First World War she sewed bandages, knitted stockings, and sold War Bonds. She helped my father both with medical and less specialized papers, organized his office, and familiarized herself with many diagnostic problems. But good works seemed worthless and unsatifying to her, save perhaps in the cause of education.

Correspondingly, as I have said, most menfolk were, for my mother, beneath contempt because they simply did the work of the world; if they were happy doing it, they must be stupid. The men she knew, including her spouse, did work very hard, and most of them left culture to their wives. These other women admired and envied my mother because at least her husband could talk about ideas and would not fall asleep at the opera—although he would often disappoint her by not being able to go (so he said and believed) on account of a patient. The idea that men could share cultural matters on a basis of equality did not occur to many women of my mother's generation and style, any more than it occurred to Carol Kennicott in Sinclair Lewis's *Main Street*.

According to an analogous logic, the idea that a woman of means or quality should do housework or cooking would have seemed absurd to my mother's generation. My mother prided herself on knowing foods, but only as a consumer; she could direct the cook, but she would no more think of preparing dinner than she would think of driving a car or taking direct care of her children. On a camping trip in Maine or in the Adirondacks there would always be a guide along to cook meals; and the annual summer hegira to Maine was always an elaborate Pullman convoy, complete with iceboxes enroute, and a chauffeur sent ahead with the Phaeton. My mother collected antiques somewhat ahead of the fashion, but in other material things, except for painting, she was of her time and place; she was *avant garde* principally in her imagination—and since she was not an artist, she doubted if she had much imagination, and this made her feel a failure. Once when my father was having a stag dinner party, our Scottish maid came to my mother and suggested that she put on an apron and help wait on table since the talk was so interesting. Much of her life my mother waited vicariously on the men's table, feeling frustrated because of inability to deploy talents she was not actually sure she possessed. She very much enjoyed talking to my own friends, especially the more literary ones, who were in turn surprised to find that she had read the books they were reading and that she seemed to have stripped from life the illusions under which they believed their own mothers still dwelt.

Although my mother lived until 1945, the world in which she matured was a stable Edwardian one against which her rebellions of the mind could occur without upsetting accustomed routines. She devoured Freud and D. H. Lawrence, yet when my young German governess was late returning with her boyfriend, my mother, acting *in loco parentis*, would be terribly upset; she was somewhat more responsive to servants than her own mother had been, but expected from them the same kinds of innocence outside the house and exigent performance within it. Very likely her hunger for art sprang partly from a sheltered and isolated existence whose limitations she was intelligent enough to sense without being courageous or ingenious enough to overcome. All in all, this provided a substitute window on a world that was still fairly small, in which, for example, Russian Jews were regarded by Spanish or German Jews as intruders, pushy people (unless they were artists), and in which Negroes, although regarded with Abolitionist sympathy, could not be viewed with empathy. My mother believed that she saw through possessions and people, but she never escaped their prison.

My mother did not regard herself as rich, but rather as in comfortable circumstances; she saved string. By differentiating herself from the very rich and by regarding plentiful money with disdain, she was able to escape a large part of the social guilt that some people even in her younger days were beginning to feel vis-à-vis the oppressed. Moreover, although she read *The New Republic* and admired Woodrow Wilson and his New Freedom, these political considerations were again secondary to cultural ones; even the greatest political leaders or political writers such as Walter Lippmann or Walter Weyl were at best stage managers for the high drama of art itself, the performing acolytes of which (such as Leopold Stokowski or the flautist William Kincaid or the oboist Marcel Tabuteau) gained a kind of subsidiary glory. My mother did serve on a commission of Governor Gifford Pinchot on Mother's Assistance and was involved in volunteer social work, but this, like raising money for

Bryn Mawr College, was felt as a civic obligation, not as an outlet for hemmed-in talents.

But before I leave my mother's generation, I should make clear that even in her circle there were women who were precursors of a later outlook. There was my cousin, Mrs. Alice Liveright, who became Commissioner of Welfare of Pennsylvania and later worked under Harry Hopkins in the New Deal. She enjoyed gourmet cooking and informal entertaining, and did not have a maid who lived in. Another cousin in middle life went back to school and became a successful architect. Still other women in my mother's small orbit did not merely hunger for culture but helped contribute to it, writing novels or reviewing books or painting.

My Daughters' Generation

Whereas I used my mother as an exemplar, though of course a very peripheral one, of her own generation, I speak of my daughters here only analogically, and what I have to say will be drawn more from what I have seen of college students and young married couples today than from any specific individuals. However, what I have to say is subject to the same limitations of scope and the same dangers of impressionism.

With rare exceptions, in our daughters' generation, servants are thought of as a liability, an obstacle, and a remnant of social injustice.[1] It is generally contended, and with some reason, that servants have virtually disappeared; the census figures show as much. Unquestionably it is difficult to get any servants and nearly impossible to get competent ones, for the democratization of our society and the reduction of immigration from Europe have meant that people no longer want to endure either the hours and limits or the felt humiliation of serving in a household, though they are perfectly willing to be "servants" more generically in a hotel or restaurant or in the glamorized position of airline stewardesses. Thus today one does not think about servants very much: except for amateur babysitters and part-time cleaning ladies, they are not part of the visible social landscape. Hence only among the very rich, where one has to make a decision not to have servants, does conscious asceticism enter as a factor in the failure of the young to pursue the servants who might be available. Even so, there is a streak of asceticism or at any rate of a feeling that one would rather not have servants, even where they might be available and where money is available to employ them. To be sure, if one is not in the Peace Corps and is living in an Indian village or even in Tokyo with a busy husband and small children, one may succumb to the rigors of a strange land and its relatively low wages even by having a servant who lives in, although of course one would still drive one's own car and would not allow a nurse to interfere between mother and child. Here at home, it is said by most young couples, even when they have money and when the wife has career ambitions, that it is "impossible" to get help.

A number of issues, both practical and ideological, have to be unraveled here. Young people do get married today before the husband is well launched on his career, and the economic base for marriage depends to some extent on the parents or on fellowships. The young people live in apartments too cramped to have room for a servant who lives in and too filled with conveniences to give a servant a full day's work to do. Moreover, these young people cannot treat the help as non-persons; hence, even if quarters were less cramped, they would feel their privacy interfered with. The young people I am speaking of have an understandable and even attractive difficulty in acting as masters and mistresses; for free and liberal women to delegate chores they are physically themselves capable of performing to members of the "suppressed race" seems to add insult to injury. Quite a few, if they must have someone living in the home, compromise by having a college student or, if they can afford it, by bringing into the home not a country cousin but a European (or Japanese) girl who wants to work and perhaps marry in America. Moreover, although it is possible to get Negro or Puerto Rican domestic labor in the great cities (indeed, such women have an easier time getting jobs than their menfolk and sometimes than white women), this is much more difficult for the young people who live in the suburbs far from public transport.

At the same time, there are a number of mothers who too quickly use the alleged impossibility of getting and deploying competent servants to rationalize the sacrifice of career and other ambitions in their absence, contrary to the pattern of an earlier day when women used rationalizations to justify luxuries their husbands could not afford. Some of today's young mothers in the educated strata are frightened at the thought that they might not love their infants enough or might be tired by them and want a surrogate to help care for them. For such mothers, a babysitter is perfectly all right for special occasions, and even one's own mother or relatives can be trusted with a small child, for there is not such a fear of spoiling the child as there was in my mother's day. Egalitarianism has also had a hand here, so that Freud and Marx have combined to make nurses and governesses seem wrong or obsolete. There are exceptions to this canon among perhaps a growing group of mothers who have gained sufficient confidence in their love for their children to be willing to search for ingenious arrangements to give themselves periodic sabbaticals from them: they may build up babysitter pools, teach older siblings to look after younger ones, or arrange to share a cleaning lady who will also look after children, and so on.

Whatever the attitude towards "help," all these young mothers have gained the right to enjoy their own children. They nurse them when they can and enjoy nursing (indeed a few seek natural childbirth, and they fight for the right to have their infants with them in the lying-in hospital). The mothers also, with intermittent help from other family members, are prepared to cope and enjoy coping with their rambunctious two-year-olds (an age to weary all but the most athletic mothers) until the nursery school takes over for part of the time as the legitimate, collective nurse. (In the preschool years young mothers may take turns watching over each others' children, although hardly in such organized fashion as in a kibbutz, but again they would not pay someone of humble origin to do this for them full time.) Moreover, the young husband has become, as much by his own volition as by pressure on him, part of the maternal task force, helping his wife with the children on all occasions and not only on such ceremonial ones as a trip to the circus or being a spectator (as in the movie *Executive Suite*) at a Little League baseball game. To visitors from other cultures it often appears that American men have been feminized by this assignment and by a certain blurring of sex roles in the home. But the visitors fail to see that the wives still have the main responsibility for the home, the husband playing the part of a volunteer aide, and that the women have made a tacit bargain with their husbands not to compete with them professionally or in career terms; thus, if the men have moved (largely to their own liberation) in the direction of accepting some of the more maternal sides of themselves, the women have also moved away from feminist (that is, masculinist) ambitions.

Alterations in the culinary realm are also striking. Recognition of the sensuous pleasures of infant care is matched by alertness to nuances of taste and to the aesthetics of preparing food. While it is legitimate to have a cleaning woman come in once or twice a week to do the heavy housework, to have someone else do the cooking would be thought of as an interference with an intimate function. Students at a college such as Bryn Mawr today are avid devotees of cookbook lore, and here too their boyfriends may join them, not simply in the steak-in-the-backyard pattern of the middle strata, but in the exploration of casseroles, wild rice, and gourmet soups. In young married dwellings where there is the strictest simplicity in furniture, where the foot-high bed may be unmade and the bathroom shared with children a total mess, dinnertime may be an occasion of ritual, with candles and Mexican pottery and the right kind of wine. Perhaps only in the playing of chamber music or the singing of madrigals and motets is a similar formality possible, for in other aspects of family life informality rules with an iron hand, and any other style would be thought insincere and lacking in proper casualness.[2]

Often, dinner is served very late, at 8 or 9 or later still, in the expectation that the children by then will be put to bed and that the young mother can devote herself to her guests in a welcomed change of pace from the child's world. Of course, the children don't always stay put. But in other homes such staging is not undertaken, and the children, at once free-wheeling and exhausted, may make even the most carefully prepared meal a social shambles. As in the home of a poor peasant which is shared with goats, chickens, and other livestock, guests here may face the hazard of children who are treated as pets and who are not put away with a babysitter when company comes. The children in their innocence may poke forks at the guest or throw food or scream; but the parents, to their great credit, are seldom embarrassed or flustered; the guests, indeed, if they are young enough, may bring their own children, unworried about the damage they may do to the hosts' furniture or to themselves. While, as I have said, some of the young mothers are extremely anxious lest they discover that they don't love their children every moment, they are, in comparison with my mother's generation, most unanxious with respect to physical hazards such as germs, sharp objects, or critical-minded and terrible-tempered adults. There is certainly not the feeling that children should be in bed at a Watsonian hour that made my mother's generation rigid and my own only slightly less so; Dr. Spock has brought the gospel of relaxation to all these more mechanical aspects of child-rearing. It is even possible that the more secure young mothers, who feel confident of their love and competent in their handling of their children, can afford the slightly greater formality which I mentioned above, and can be firmer with disruptive children. Having thrown off older restraints, it has taken time and tact to discover the limits of permissiveness, and some have done so.

Many observers of the American scene, notably Margaret Mead, have commented on the ways in which the reduction of adult supervision and the general vogue of permissiveness have freed children from traditional restraints but have put them more at each other's mercy. Today's young married couples may have begun dating in junior high school, and the marriage may either benefit from the wisdom gained in earlier experience or represent a mutual defense pact against the competitive turmoil of the rating-dating pattern in high schools and colleges. In the high school years boys may suffer because the girls who are their own age are more mature (although there are always a few boys who are or appear to be ahead of their fellows in social and sexual maturity). But boys can always take refuge in the boys' culture of sports, mechanics or ham radio—a culture that has no feminine protective counterpart, since girls' hobbies, apart from studying, are only boys and each other (a few unusual girls may take ballet or piano lessons). Many of the boys' activities, notably sports, anchor team members in a group; as James Coleman points out in *The Adolescent Society,* a basketball or football player is a member of a communal enterprise for which his own individual excellence provides group solidarity rather than rivalry. Girls, however, have no comparable sorts of solidarity. Often the principal way for a girl to become known outside her small clique is as a baton twirler or cheerleader, in both of which posts it is her sex appeal which is emphasized (along with a modicum of dexterity); from such positions, one may be elected to the isolated post of prom queen. Then and later the girls are potential rivals for all that matters, namely, boys.*

Going steady would appear to be the "solution" to which my daughters' generation has arrived in coping with the problems of rivalry and mutual exploitation among the sexes. Of course, it is no new practice but has been common in rural and lower middle class

* Margaret Mead has also pointed out that the more popular a girl is with boys, the less she has to "give" in order to hold them—an exploitative pattern hardly conducive to intense attachments. On the other hand, if she "gives" too freely, there may be enough of the double standard left so that she will lose her popularity; the solidarity of the boys with each other often means that girls are damned if they do and damned if they don't.

groups for many decades. What is relatively new is the extension of the practice to the more educated and upper social strata where, in many circles, young men in an earlier day played the field (perhaps including the red light district) while girls "came out" and in that way also played the field. Going steady implies that once a boy and girl in high school or college have put their brands on each other, their friends keep hands off. And it obviously means that there is no oligopolistic or haremlike monopolization of girls by the most attractive boys, or vice versa—though, to be sure, the practice does nothing to help the always sizable fraction of students in college as well as in high school who hardly ever date and who languish in the shadows even when it appears that "everybody" is doing it. Going steady creates many dilemmas for the partners as to the appropriate or tolerable degrees of intimacy, while also offering greater opportunity for sincerity and directness and minimizing the extent to which the boy and girl become trophies for the same-sex friends of each of the couple, rather than human beings in their own right. (There are, of course, exceptions, as when the basketball star dates the prom queen in an almost ascribed relationship.)

The emphasis on real or inner personal qualities that going steady allows, even while the practice limits the range of exposure to wider orbits among the opposite sex, exemplifies one of the paradoxes which may be a consequence of the emphasis on sex in contemporary culture. By making sex at once the central goal of existence and the central definition of oneself as a human being, much that was thwarted and inhibited in an earlier day has been banished to the far fundamentalist corners of society. A divorce from one's own body has seemed to me characteristic of the British public-school boy, whose very accent and posture are, as it were, laid on as signs of educated alienation; these characteristics are extremely rare in American young people, whose armoring is much less, even in private sex-segregated schools, whether parochial or elite imitations of the British pattern. In athletics, in food, in sex, in comfort, American young people are bodies first of all—even if at their worst they are simply bodies, from their gum-chewing jaws, to their slovenly shuffling feet. There is here a fundamental equality at least for the vast majority who, in their own view of themselves and the view of others, fall within the increasingly tolerant boundaries of their own sex group. However, the equalization provided by the emphasis on the physical oneness of mankind—or its sex-typed halves—does tend to cut off alternative paths of life that might be chosen by a minority oriented primarily to other things than sex roles.

In my mother's generation, the nun who chose a vocation or the school teacher or librarian who, whether by choice or not, remained a spinster, was not made to feel that there was something monstrous and unnatural about her life; such women were often extremely spirited and lacking in any feeling of deprivation. Today even a bachelor, let alone a spinster, is made to feel that there is something wrong with him, and it is a rare person who does not internalize this feeling and who does not become defensive about it. Partly, this reflects the sheer demographic fact that 94 per cent of all women will be married before age 40—an incomparably higher proportion than ever before; a very different situation from earlier America or from a country like Ireland, where even today marriage is still often late and not a near-unanimous choice. Being single, furthermore, is neither a defense nor a prohibition against having some sexual relations in one's life. While it would seem to be true that the path of sexuality cannot live up to its billing, so that many young people are disappointed that they cannot experience the ecstasies extolled in the movies and novels and by the very look of sexiness that people parade today, those who do not choose the path cannot use its disappointments as a defense of their own course—especially since the disappointments are thought to be the result of poor technique or poor choice of partners or other remediable imperfections (rather than the kind of disappointment in sex itself of which Freud wrote in *Civilization and Its Discontents*). Consequently, since the spinsters whom young women meet are less and less possible models for them, still more emphasis must be put on the emotional gold standard of men and marriage as the only "careers" for women who are, or fear they might not be, truly human.

So far as one can tell, there are very few girls who retreat from this pressure into Lesbianism. I do not know whether close friendship among women is declining as the neighborhood is exclusively tipped toward persons of the opposite sex. I do know that my mother maintained to the end of her life friendships with some of her Bryn Mawr classmates, that my wife too had deep friendships in college, some of which persist. Whether sorority friendships are deep as well as close I do not know. A Radcliffe senior, Mary Haywood, in her undergraduate thesis, "Were There But World Enough and Time . . . ," studied a group of Radcliffe freshmen living together in a dormitory and found that for them boys and studies were worthwhile work, but friendships among themselves were, if not a waste of time, as many thought, then at least something for which there wasn't enough time alongside the high pressure for scholastic achievement and for locating oneself as a woman in relation to men. This double bind leads many girls, precisely as a counterweight to high academic performance, to feel that they must sleep with men in order to prove to themselves as well as to anyone else that they are really women. Viewing other girls as rivals, both in their academic and nonacademic roles, they may save real intimacy, if not for the boy with whom they are going out at the moment, then for a hoped-for improvement. At other times, since their behavior is often bolder than their values and often less bold, they may talk compulsively with each other in a mutual exchange of anxieties that may pass as friendship. But it has for a long time been perfectly acceptable for a girl to say that she doesn't like members of her own sex and prefers men.[3]

To be sure, at least after emerging from the protective solidarity of teams and gangs, boys are subject to somewhat comparable although less divisive pressures. In the lower classes, pressure on them to prove their manhood through sex has always been strong— a milder American version of the Latin cult of *machismo*. However, in my mother's generation, upper and upper middle class young people were to some extent exempt from such demands and were both forced and allowed to postpone full sexuality—indeed were defined as persons of promise rather than attainment by such postponement. Many factors have operated to reduce this exemption. The spread of affluence downward in the society and the greater confidence in one's long-run future that many college-educated people now possess, thanks to full employment for them, large organizations which seek them out, and a more meritocratic way of life, permits the middle class to depart from its earlier orientation toward saving, thrift, and postponement of gratification. Installment buying is no longer confined to the impulsive lower class, and hedonism penetrates where pinched gentility once prevailed. Furthermore, affluence has meant not only the ability to enjoy now and yet get ahead, but a declining age of puberty as better nutrition has moved it steadily downward. And affluence also compels a far greater exposure to the lures of commercial vendors of sexuality, in which smoking a cigarette, putting on perfume, driving a car, and many other forms of consumer behavior have become sex-linked.

At the same time, some of the occupational and cultural bound-

aries have broken down which help men rest assured that they are
men. While girls are more universally preoccupied with personal
relations, men increasingly pursue careers which explicitly, as in
clinical psychology or counseling or many business callings, make a
profession of such relations. Likewise, many cultural areas are no
longer so closed off from the young men as was true when I was an
undergraduate, although in the South and Southwest the older patterns may still hang on (as might be tested if Southern writers dis-
proportionately continue to be homosexuals,* as if there were no
role within their own sex for their kind of calling and orientation).**
Whatever line they may use, boys feel under pressure to put pressure
on girls to prove to them that they *are* boys while also establishing
that the girls are truly female and able to "give."

And it should be clear that the disappearance or virtual disappearance of the double standard has meant that it is those girls who
once would have been considered "nice" girls who are under this
pressure. Among educated young people today, prostitutes are as
much anathema as servants. One can still find college students and
prep school boys who look for town girls outside their social class
for their first or later sexual experience. But amateur competition
has made such quests largely unnecessary, even while the rise of
egalitarian sentiment has made them seem undesirable. Going steady
is not necessarily an "occasion of sin" as many priests contend;
what it does do is alter the occasion as far as the girl is concerned

---

* I have heard college girls say in open discussion that boys have asked
them to sleep with them in order to save them from the fate of homosexuality
(hardly a "line" that would have been employed before the war).

** Overall, of course, the gap between the "two cultures" of the two sexes
remains great. For example, hardly any girls read science fiction or take an
interest in hot rodding (when they do, it is usually because they are trying to
keep up with a particular boy). In school and college the boys tend to cluster
in science or mathematics or shop, while the girls concentrate in literature,
including Romance languages, and (in certain colleges where they think these
fields may be "human") in sociology or psychology or anthropology (where
these areas are treated like natural sciences, the girls tend to be driven out,
one aim, no doubt, of their instructors). One should add that there are many
exceptions. Thus, upper-class boys have the freedom and also the limitation to
pursue nonscientific careers in literature, museum work, and so on, while
equally intelligent boys of lower social origin may be going into engineering
or other applied sciences. One can find bluestocking college girls pursuing
biology or in rare cases physics with fierce energy, as if to prove that the going
definitions of proper feminine incompetence in these areas are a canard. Moreover, mathematics, at least for purposes of teaching it, is not an uncommon
choice.

by making her a full partner rather than, as in the traditional South, a white woman on a pedestal who is miserably if complacently exempt because the boys (in Kinsey's depressing phrase) have other "outlets."

Hence marriage is now the unquestioned goal of *both* sexes. The older Maggie and Jiggs type of joke about the ball and chain, like the older type of pre-wedding bachelor's party, is pretty much a thing of the past. The married GI's in our universities after the Second World War set a new norm of adulthood; and fraternity and sorority single-sex mystiques have been under uneven pressure ever since. Because there is such a demand for places in all our good colleges, even the isolated women's colleges today are able to attract students. But at the same time, an increasing number of girls seek to attend the coed institutions (which in the selective institutions are much harder for them to enter than for the young men) because the girls want both a good education and to be near available men.*

Since in my mother's generation an upper-class girl had to make a decision to go to college when coming out was regarded as more important and worthwhile, those who did go (somewhat like Roman Catholic girls more recently) were often in effect deciding that they did not put marriage before all else.** Today a marriage-oriented

* In the East, Roman Catholic institutions of higher education remain largely sex-segregated. In the *Time*-sponsored study *They Went to College* (Ernest Havermann and Patricia Salter West, Harcourt, Brace [1947]), it appears that only 50% of the graduates of Catholic women's colleges had found husbands as against 80% or 90% of the Protestant and Jewish women college graduates, suggesting the possibility that at that time Catholic men were still too patriarchal to want college-educated wives. I have the impression that today, however, Catholic men are no longer so resistant to higher education for their wives (or daughters) even though some of the smaller Catholic women's colleges continue to advertise induction into gracious living and produce or continue a particular Catholic sort of docility which is often a despair of the Sisters on the teaching faculty. Yet even at such institutions I believe that a single-sex mystique finds little place. Cf. on women graduates of Catholic colleges pursuing advanced degrees, Andrew M. Greeley, *Religion and Career: a Study of College Graduates* (New York: Sheed and Ward, 1963). On the outlook of women in some of the Catholic women's colleges, see the data in James W. Trent, "The Etiology of Catholic Intellectualism," Ph.D. dissertation (Center for the Study of Higher Education, University of California, Berkeley, 1963).

** Lower down in the social structure, money even now can often be spared for a son's education but not for a daughter's. And, as Mirra Komarovsky has pointed out, when girls are sent to college they are not sent as far from girl who graduates from a reasonably good high school has to make the opposite decision, namely, *not* to go to college; our colleges harbor a great many girls with little academic interest who often drop out in the course of their studies in order to get married (or perhaps to get a job in a milieu which doesn't rule marriage out). One result of these changes in the composition of the college-going population is that there is often panic among college seniors who remain unpledged and unmarried; educated young women of age 23 or 24 may feel that they are old maids already, as only a lower-class girl would have felt in my mother's generation or even a generation ago.

Marriage, moreover, almost invariably involves the expectation of children. The optimal family of the present college generation seems to have dropped slightly from around four to three; and except among Roman Catholics there is no wish for five or more children. But the two-child family—an older boy and a slightly younger girl—which is still featured in so many advertisements and stories is no longer the norm. (There is some demographic evidence that if a family has three or four girls they will keep trying for a boy for at least one or two more times. There is less tendency, if one has all boys, to keep trying for a girl; this may be a measure of the extent to which we are still patriarchal or to which mothers feel deprived of their menfolk and seek substitutes in a son.) There is thus very seldom a marriage in which both partners pursue professional ambitions and decide that they will not have children because this would tie the wife's hands. If one cannot beget children oneself there is a considerable freedom in America to adopt them, for we lack the feeling of blood connection that is much more characteristic of Europe and Latin America; our attitude here also owes something to egalitarianism.* Furthermore, the children are not only a necessary part of marriage eventually, but they are necessary almost at the outset; one wants children while one is

---

home as sons are. See Komarovsky, *Women in the Modern World: Their Education and Their Dilemmas* (Boston: Little, Brown, 1954). As indicated later, Negroes are an exception here since many more Negro women attend college than men, for a whole complex of reasons relating to the lack of opportunity, especially in the South, for educated Negro males, and the greater drive and docility of the women in a matriarchal sub-culture.

* Eric Larrabee rightly points out, commenting on the foregoing, that the freedom to adopt an outsider into the family business, common in Japan and not infrequent in Germany, is alien to the American male's patronymic sense; the only people who can be adopted are infants too young to refuse.

young.* And once there is a single child, few want the near-orphanage of an only, lonely child; he must be surrounded by siblings, and the family must have a certain festive range of noise and hubbub to feel like a family.

This early philoprogenitiveness is a complex matter. The young couple want to be human not only in their relations to each other but in their relations to small children, toward whom they have a Salinger-like feeling. It is as if the young people were saying, "Who are we to put our personal development and rapacious ambition ahead of the equal rights of the yet unborn? Our future children are as alive and as interesting as we are; we would rather add them to our own and to the world's stock than to add material possessions or even to contribute ideas or the service of extra-familial causes."[4] Most well-educated and even well-to-do young women have been babysitters during their high school and college years. They are not afraid of childbirth and child care but rather look forward to them as one of the tests of womanhood; and they can count on the co-operation of their husbands. The career plans of the husband may be greatly influenced by his family situation or rather by the same values that have led him to place such an emphasis on the family: he may give up the idea of medical school, because this takes too long, and become a biochemist instead (an increasingly prestigeful if less remunerative career in any case); or even if he does attend medical school he will come home early to help with the children and the dishes, and, to the dismay of his professors, spend evenings at home rather than at the hospital (although here there are many exceptions, and interns and residents seem to work or be worked about as hard as ever). Or he may prolong getting his Ph.D. because he has to teach part time to support his family. Many sensitive young men, in fact, reject careerism, deprecate what they call the rat race, and oppose the ambitions their parents often project on them. A certain blurring of sex boundaries has liberated them from old constrictions of male ambition.

My focus, however, in this paper is primarily on the college-edu-

*Having watched so many young couples where the husband is a graduate student and the wife still in college begin having children when it is most inconvenient, I have come to suspect among non-Catholics a certain casualness about birth control, perhaps reflecting the cult of spontaneity or a kind of Russian roulette where the stakes are not very great! Of course, attitudes toward birth control are changing among Catholics, and as the demographers have shown, family norms, and especially family size, are declining.

cated woman and the ways in which the attitudes of the still-domi-
nant men influence her choices. In a world perspective, she is certainly among the freest of women. Japanese girls, for example, want
to marry American men in the hope they will gain a greater scope
(while conversely, some American men seek the seeming submissiveness and unthreatening demeanor of Japanese women). This comparative freedom of the American girl is not new. Alexis de Tocque-
ville was struck by the American girls he saw traveling alone without
fear for their virtue or safety; somewhat like Henry James later, he
saw these girls as persons of independent minds, upright and
virtuous character, and eagerness for culture. He noted, however,
that once the girl was married her freedom, unlike that of a French
woman, came to an end; she was the mistress of the house, perhaps
the founder of the temperance society, but not the mistress of a man
or of her own time. Many, wearied by child-bearing and toil, died
prematurely, leaving their husbands to marry again and perhaps
even a third time (as one can discover in old graveyards). My
mother's grandmothers had each had ten children, but she herself
was one of but three and she in turn had three children. The
relative ease cf life of women of her class meant that they often
began to outlive their hard-working menfolk—and to complain of
the fact. At the same time, in her feminist generation, women who
embarked on careers tended to pursue the approved goals of the
more powerful and established sex.

The women of our daughters' generation are somewhat less in
the position of a new nation, torn between pursuing the goals valued
by the former colonialists or retreating into a refusal of integration
and an insistence on a separate but superior world of women. The
relaxation of the older feminist intransigence has freed many women
to make a more personal choice of occupational goals. Yet I should
make clear that it ill becomes a man to say to a woman: "Why
must you be as foolish as we are? Why do you want your name on
the door and all that nonsense?" Women must have the chance to
discover all this for themselves and to inherit all the foolishness
that men have made to seem important.[5]

And it is at this point that we realize that the new forms of
women's freedom have brought subtle constrictions in their wake.
My mother studied English at Bryn Mawr without a thought that
this would help her either in a career or a job. My wife also studied
English, both for its own sake and with the hope that it might help
her in a career as a writer—although not well-to-do, and with what

now looks like a very unrealistic lack of concern as to how one could make a living as a writer. College was a sanctuary; the issue of career could be postponed; men's judgments concerning the ways young women were developing their intellects could be postponed also or left outside the college gates.

College, or at least a good college, is less of a sanctuary today for anybody. Young men as well as young women can neither be so frivolous in abstention from studies nor so wholly non-vocational and "liberal" as in the period before the Second World War. This reflects partly the greater intensity of instruction, partly the increasing number who go on to graduate and professional school, and partly what seems to be the secular growth of precocity among young people. Thus in a woman's college today, the students are conscious simultaneously of the future and of the boys they hope to marry, even if the boys are not physically present, and of what sorts of intellectuality these boys may welcome or resent. As a teacher in coeducational settings, I have watched some of the ways in which women students presently try to cope with the dilemma of being at once women and students. For some, to have men around is a liberation and provides an impetus to a more dialectical and less docile approach to learn than might be the case if they attended college only with their own sex. But perhaps the greater number, trained to be socially conscious since childhood, are intensely aware of how their class performance is viewed both by boys and by their own sex: facing a double audience, they are inhibited from expressing themselves as rambunctiously or spiritedly as they might do in a single-sex setting.[6] The girls are responsive to what others in the class say, including the teacher; they are better listeners than the boys, preparing in this way for a life-long role of listening to menfolk and responding to others in a responsive and responsible way. But there are always a few women, at least in the better colleges, who, as it were, go through the sound barrier and throw traditional canons of femininity out; to do this they must have more brass than the average boy, or at least they appear to, and they create a stereotype of the aggressive woman who is characteristically American as against the more gentle assertiveness of the European career woman, who appears able to retain her feminine responsiveness without loss of the power of assertion or even of command. Both groups of women, the small minority who, as it were, flee forward in the face of the enemy, and the large majority who are passive, diligent, and shy, suffer from the constrictions which the insecurities both of men and of women place upon them and upon what they can accomplish. At the same time, responsive as little girls to their mothers and school teachers, they continue in college to want to do well. In the better institutions they scorn dilettantism while yet understandably regarding deep intellectual involvement as a potential threat; looking perhaps at some of the unmarried women on the faculty, they may fear that such involvement would cut them off from the life of a normal, average woman, and they are persuaded that it is more important to be a woman than to become some kind of specialist: as the phrase goes, they seek to be rather than to do.[*] Paradoxically, many women students enlist themselves industriously and even pedantically in proto-graduate undergraduate specialties, as if they were still underprivileged battlers for the main chance— it sometimes seems that the co-eds would regard it as high hat to love learning for its own sake and pretend instead that they must earn a grubby keep through the discipline that they pursue as their major.

At the same time, many young women in colleges such as Radcliffe, Swarthmore, or Oberlin have a hard time thinking of themselves as pursuing a career (rather than a job) after their children are grown, and of using their premarital years to prepare for that period in a fully professional sense. Instead they pursue the liberal arts with the thought—and they do think about it—that on graduation they will get the sort of job open to any reasonably intelligent and attractive A.B. The girls who have taken over so many previously masculine preserves, in sports (notably horseback riding), clothing, and outlook feel diffident about identifying themselves with a specialized occupational achievement that would stamp them as perhaps not "feminine": thus, the helping professions are open to them where they can serve familylike constituencies as teachers, social workers, and in rare cases as pediatricians or psychiatrists; the arts are open to some degree; but the old feminist drive to enter engineering and architecture, law and business, economics and archeology is much attenuated. Instead, even very gifted

[*] Nevitt Sanford and others at Vassar have studied the way in which this outlook cuts the present generation of students in an academically oriented women's college off from their women teachers; and these latter in turn often feel let down because their exceedingly bright and gifted students decline to extend themselves to their fullest lest they fall in love with a career that might restrict their choices in marriage. See the chapters by Sanford and Mervin B. Freedman and articles cited therein in Nevitt Sanford (ed.), *The American College* (New York: John Wiley, 1961).

and creative young women are satisfied to assume that on graduation they will get underpaid ancillary positions, whether as a *Time-
Life* researcher or United Nations guide or publisher's assistant or
reader, where they are seldom likely to advance to real opportunity,
whether in terms of status or freedom of choice in their work. A
certain throttling down occurs, therefore, both in college and later
on, which then, in the usual vicious circle, allows men so minded to
deprecate women as incapable of the highest achievements.

Such deprecation is often a subtle affair. Young men in the better colleges today believe in equality; they certainly believe that
women have as much right as men to be educated and to graduate
from college. But these young men's ideals are to some extent
sabotaged by their insecurities. They are insecure in their occupational role, feeling themselves inadequate to meet the competition
of other men. In many colleges they are, beneath apparent good fellowship, related to other men as gamesmen or antagonistic coopera-
tors. They are convinced that they inhabit a rivalrous world. And
as many observers have pointed out, they are insecure also in their
roles as males, in part because, as one of the liberations of our time,
men must help women enjoy sex and enjoy their company (only in
the pages of *Playboy* and in the advertisements do the girls say, in
effect, "Whatever you do, darling, is great by me"). All this makes
young men ambivalent—not in all cases, of course, but in many—
about serious career ambitions on the part of prospective wives;
they do not want to be faced with competition from the feminine
side.*

Several years ago I attended a discussion at Radcliffe College
where a group of unusually able students were discussing the sorts
of career they would consider ideal. Several were going into medicine and others were pursuing Ph.D.'s, but none was doing so
without ambivalence. In the arts, less traditionally closed to women,
they faced not only the issues of careers vs. marriage, but an insistence akin to my mother's that only first-rate work is worth doing
at all. To mess around with paint, for example, was no longer satisfying when even as an undergraduate one was exposed to world-
wide standards of excellence and one would have to have unusual
arrogance to feel qualified to enter a global competition. One girl

* Many observers have pointed out the threat to men implicit in the greater
equality of women in sexual relations which allows them to take the initiative
and to insist on the right to sexual pleasure; they have become critical consumers of male performance.

going into medicine said that her ideal would be a marriage to a physician serving in Africa who needed her to help take care of his medical clinic; they could serve together, both of them needed, and each needing the other. (My mother, I can well imagine, would have regarded this, much too proudly, as being an auxiliary to a "serving man," not an outlet for the great esthetic talents which were the only ones which counted in her eyes.) The group of girls seemed to agree that this would be idyllic: the situation of danger and service, not competitive as between the two spouses nor between them as a couple and the surrounding community. Here the wife could extend herself to the fullest without raising problems for her identification as a woman or as a professionally useful individual. The uniqueness of the marriage and of the couple's mission could substitute for the marginal surrender of uniqueness of the hypothetical wife.

Whereas my mother deprecated both most men and most careers, it is clear from this example and many others that gifted, college-trained young women today do not look down on men as drones performing the world's dull work—the men, in fact, as already indicated, are less apt to be such drones. The men are less philistine, and the women, having persuaded themselves, understandably enough, that marriage is the one ingredient that makes life worthwhile, do not undervalue what they so eagerly cherish by running men down. (They may indeed complain of a certain passivity among men, whose introspectiveness and therefore greater attractiveness for educated women, can have this quality; similarly, they may find their menfolk too dependent.) And just as girls six feet tall complain of the still taller men who marry girls who are five feet two, since there are not enough really tall men to go around, so girls who are six feet tall in intellect and drive realize that many men of comparable power will marry very low-pressure, eye-fluttery girls, and that there will not be enough secure, non-dependent men left (given the imperfections and irrationalities of the marriage market) for the women who could grow and develop in marriage to such men. Hence girls who feel that if they do not marry early (when the men around are perhaps even less secure and differentiated) they may not marry at all are prepared unconsciously if not consciously to surrender chances for personal distinction in order to be fairly sure of pleasing a larger range of men.

In a more aristocratic society, women (provided that they belong to the upper class) may have a freedom to excel because their special class position counts for even more than their general position as women. Moreover, while marriages may no longer be formally arranged among families of the aristocracy or the haute bourgeoisie, marriages may remain in such a society less committed to romance and more to convenience. (The class position, to be sure, has its own constraints, as registered for example in Simone de Beauvoir's *Memoirs of a Dutiful Daughter.*)

In our society, exceptional women are protected neither by class nor of course by arranged marriages. Such women perhaps face fewer obstacles in a Jewish family than, for example, in an Italian or fundamentalist Protestant one—here, as so often in America, ethnicity seems more important than social class; among urban Negroes, where men have a more difficult time securing or maintaining employment, mothers are often more successful in passing on their ambitions to their daughters than to sons growing up in a matriarchal home or what passes for a home. If, as many Negro women have sufficient reason to believe, men are a necessary evil, then the men's prejudices concerning women may be a practical problem for a woman but not an inner drag. But outside such ethnic enclaves and to a large degree also within them, a ceiling is placed over the ambitions of young women by anticipations of what men are likely to tolerate. And since women, as with many minority groups, bitterly resent and envy those among them who break out of confinement, as an implicit verdict on their own failure to do so, these anticipations concerning men are reinforced by mothers and same-sex peers.°

° Attending conferences with educated middle-class women over a number of years, I have again and again observed the vehemence of the attack by those who call themselves "only housewives" against those who are active outside the home, accusing the latter of neglecting their children and being accused in turn of neglecting their responsibilities to themselves and to the society. The intelligent, fairly affluent "housewife" who knows perfectly well that her home is not quite a full time job can often be shrewish and vindictive toward the active women who remind her of this fact. On the other side, the more career-minded women, ambivalent toward their occupational successes as well as their occupational failures, and wondering if after all they have not sacrificed family life, may have the impetus to despise the "mere" housewife. There are always a few exceptionally energetic women, fortunate in their spouses and family situations, who appear to be omnicompetent and who as often arouse envy as admiration among other women. In the absence of a spirit of live and let live among these embattled groups, personal temperament and situation are not a sufficient reason for one's way of life and thin ideologies take the place of self-assurance.

> Sigh no more, ladies.
> Time is male
> and in his cups drinks to the fair.
> Bemused by gallantry, we hear
> our mediocrities over-praised,
> indolence read as abnegation,
> slattern thought styled intuition,
> every lapse forgiven, our crime
> only to cast too bold a shadow
> or smash the mould straight off.[7]

In the response readers have made to the cross-generational comparisons of *The Lonely Crowd*, I have found a very great tendency for readers to deprecate our own age and to look back to nineteenth-century values and attitudes with nostalgia and admiration. This should have prepared me for the fact that readers of an earlier draft of this essay for *Dædalus* responded in many cases by saying that my mother's generation of women was better off than my daughters' generation. I was not then thinking in terms of such evaluation. There are, of course, a few people around who find even today that there is too little permissiveness and too much of the Puritan ethic. The greater majority, perhaps especially among the young, who regard the present age as a decline should perhaps be sentenced by some Alice in Wonderland procedure to reliving the Edwardian and Georgian years. As a young man I could read such Victorian commentaries as Samuel Butler's *The Way of All Flesh* and Edmund Gosse's *Father and Son* with at least a distant sense of recognition, while Holden Caulfield in *Catcher in the Rye* complains of far subtler oppression from his family's insincerity and

---

The ceilings over the ambitions of women who want to combine a career with a family do not operate in those areas the culture has defined as feminine, such as homemaking, tutoring of one's children, and whatever civic and philanthropic activities have not yet been engrossed by the professionals. Moreover, although girls in school and college are more or less subtly discouraged from pursuing certain fields of intellectual work, they are encouraged to cultivate their uniqueness as persons outside these areas. Women, no less than men, want to be individuals, non-conformist, autonomous. And while in college this may take the form of a search for personal identity and uniqueness, after 10 or 15 years of marriage women often decide that they want to do something of significance as well as to be somebody; at this point, as Esther Raushenbush and Robert Blood have pointed out to me, continuing education comes into its own: women who have already made a "career" of marriage and starting a family now turn with greater realism and more self-confidence back to the occupational world, at least in those few locales where they can find appropriate guidance and training or retraining.

phoniness. Any change brings losses as well as gains, but among the educated we have become almost too disenchanted today with progress, and enamored in contrast with original sin, tragedy, and a neo-orthodox pessimism which is becoming the opiate of the classes. The circle of privilege in my mother's generation was narrow and, for those within it, confining though comfortable and complacent. The widening of the circle of privilege is a good thing, even if its first consequences are often a widening of shallowness. Though they have faced psychic rather than physical hardships, the most alive young women today have an exceptional resilience, more so than all but a tiny handful in my mother's day, and they number much more than a tiny handful.

Moreover, I must emphasize that much is still open to the women of my daughters' generation. It is true that a number have married, perhaps prematurely, in order to "solve" the persisting residues of the debate of marriage versus career. But other career-minded women have married men who have graduated, followed them to where they are doing graduate work, and continued their college careers in the new locale. Some of these women, having put their professional interests to simmer on the back of the stove during the early family-building years, will have the energy and resourcefulness later on to refurbish their professional concerns, returning to study and/or to work and thus re-emerging from the familism of an earlier stage of the life cycle. The response to the few programs we have for the continuing education of women would seem to indicate that the still young married woman of early middle life wants to delegate some of the responsibilities for the home and the no longer so helpless children and to re-enter the labor market. Our society (as we wrote in *The Lonely Crowd*) remains inflexible when it comes to employing women in superior positions on a part-time basis, with allowances made for their dual roles as housewives and career women. This is so in spite of the fact that many men, as things are now, also work "part time," and spend the rest of the time in office sociability or makework; they are nevertheless identified with their work full time and of course, as Mrs. Hanna Papanek has pointed out to me, they have an opportunity not open to the working wife to choose the part of the time that they will work. Alice Rossi's paper in this volume suggests some of the devices and arrangements that would be desirable to give women greater freedom of choice by pooling resources on the side of domesticity and child care. But while she also suggests the extent to which cultural attitudes toward appropriate sex roles limit the horizons of women from the earliest years onward, I would still say that there is much less resignation and inhibition in these young women than my mother suffered. Instead there is an effort to lead a full, multidimensional life without storming the barricades at home or abroad.

REFERENCES

1. See to similar effect the witty comments by Russell Lynes in *Harpers*, July, 1963 (now published in *The Domesticated Americans* [New York: Harper and Row, 1963]).

2. For comparable attitudes toward informal sociability, see David Riesman, Robert Potter, and Jeanne Watson, "Sociability, Permissiveness, and Equality," in *Psychiatry*, Vol. 23, No. 4 (November, 1960); and "The Vanishing Host" in *Human Organization*, Vol. 19, No. 1 (Spring, 1960).

3. Concerning the subtle ways in which girls are very early taught by both their mothers and fathers to respond coquettishly, see Evelyn Goodenough Pitcher, of the Gesell Institute, "Male and Female," *Atlantic Monthly*, 211 (March, 1963), 87–91.

4. Compare the discussion in Riesman, "The Found Generation," in *The American Scholar* (reprinted in *Abundance for What? and Other Essays* [New York: Doubleday, 1964]), and also "Permissiveness and Sex Roles," *Marriage and Family Living*, Vol. 21, No. 3 (August, 1959), pp. 211–217.

5. Cf. Bruno Bettelheim, *Symbolic Wounds; Puberty Initiation Rites and the Envious Male* (Free Press, 1954), for a suggestive and preliminary discussion of ways in which men, jealous of women's biological creativity, create all sorts of rituals to sustain their own sense of their fitness in the scheme of things. Diana Trilling, writing in *The Reporter* some years ago, said in defense of Radcliffe College that women had to get an education as bad as a man's in order to believe they were getting as good a one!

6. For a fuller discussion, see my essay, "Continuities and Discontinuities in the Education of Women," Bennington College, 1956.

7. "Snapshots of a Daughter-in-law," from Adrienne Rich, *Poems, 1954–1962* (New York: Harper & Row, 1963), p. 26.

ALICE S. ROSSI

Equality Between the Sexes: An Immodest Proposal

. . . the principle which regulates the existing relations between the
two sexes . . . is wrong in itself and [is] now the chief hindrance to human
improvement; and . . . it ought to be replaced by a principle of perfect
equality, admitting no power or privilege on the one side, nor disability
on the other.

John Stuart Mill, 1869

Introduction

WHEN John Stuart Mill wrote his essay on "The Subjection of
Women" in 1869, the two major things he argued for with elegance
and persuasion were to extend the franchise to women, and to end
the legal subordination of married women to their husbands. The
movement for sex equality had already gathered considerable momentum in England and the United States by 1869, reaching its
peak fifty years later, when the franchise was won by American
women in 1920. In the decades since 1920, this momentum has
gradually slackened, until by the 1960's American society has been
losing rather than gaining ground in the growth toward sex equality.
American women are not trying to extend their claim to equality
from the political to the occupational and social arenas and often do
not even seem interested in exercising the rights so bitterly won in
the early decades of the twentieth century in politics and higher
education. The constitutional amendment on equal rights for men
and women has failed to pass Congress for seventeen consecutive

I wish to express my gratitude to Peter H. Rossi for his critical assessment
of several drafts of this essay; to the Social Science Research Committee at the
University of Chicago for a research grant that supported part of the research
on which this essay is based; and to Stephen R. Graubard for his generosity of
time and editorial skill.

years, and today a smaller proportion of college graduates are women than was true thirty years ago.

There is no overt antifeminism in our society in 1964, not because sex equality has been achieved, but because there is practically no feminist spark left among American women. When I ask the brightest of my women college students about their future study and work plans, they either have none because they are getting married in a few months, or they show clearly that they have lowered their aspirations from professional and research fields that excited them as freshmen, to concentrate as juniors on more practical fields far below their abilities. Young women seem increasingly uncommitted to anything beyond early marriage, motherhood and a suburban house. There are few Noras in contemporary American society because women have deluded themselves that the doll's house is large enough to find complete personal fulfillment within it.

It will be the major thesis of this essay that we need to reassert the claim to sex equality and to search for the means by which it can be achieved. By sex equality I mean a socially androgynous conception of the roles of men and women, in which they are equal and similar in such spheres as intellectual, artistic, political and occupational interests and participation, complementary only in those spheres dictated by physiological differences between the sexes. This assumes the traditional conceptions of masculine and feminine are inappropriate to the kind of world we can live in in the second half of the twentieth century. An androgynous conception of sex role means that each sex will cultivate some of the characteristics usually associated with the other in traditional sex role definitions. This means that tenderness and expressiveness should be cultivated in boys and socially approved in men, so that a male of any age in our society would be psychologically and socially free to express these qualities in his social relationships. It means that achievement need, workmanship and constructive aggression should be cultivated in girls and approved in women so that a female of any age would be similarly free to express these qualities in her social relationships. This is one of the points of contrast with the feminist goal of an earlier day: rather than a one-sided plea for women to adapt a masculine stance in the world, this definition of sex equality stresses the enlargement of the common ground on which men and women base their lives together by changing the social definitions of approved characteristics and behavior for both sexes.

It will be an assumption of this essay that by far the majority of the differences between the sexes which have been noted in social research are socially rather than physiologically determined. What proportion of these sex differences are physiologically based and what proportion are socially based is a question the social and physiological sciences cannot really answer at the present time. It is sufficient for my present purposes to note that the opportunities for social change toward a closer approximation of equality between the sexes are large enough within the area of sex differences now considered to be socially determined to constitute a challenging arena for thought and social action. This is my starting point. I shall leave to speculative discourse and future physiological research the question of what constitutes irreducible differences between the sexes.

There are three main questions I shall raise in this essay. Why was the momentum of the earlier feminist movement lost? Why should American society attempt to reach a state of sex equality as I have defined it above? What are the means by which equality between the sexes can be achieved?

Why Feminism Declined

I shall discuss three factors which have been major contributors to the waning of feminism. The chief goals of the early leaders of the feminist movement were to secure the vote for women and to change the laws affecting marriage so that women would have equal rights to property and to their own children. As in any social reform movement or social revolution, the focus in the first stage is on change in the legal code, whether this is to declare independence from a mother country, establish a constitution for a new nation, free the slaves, or secure the right of women to be equal citizens with men. But the social changes required to translate such law into the social fabric of a society are of a quite different order. Law by itself cannot achieve this goal. It is one thing to declare slaves free or to espouse a belief in racial equality; quite another matter to accept racial integration in all spheres of life, as many northern communities have learned in recent years. In a similar way, many people accept the legal changes which have reduced the inequality between men and women and espouse belief in sex equality, but resist its manifestation in their personal life. If a social movement rests content with legal changes without making as strong an effort to change the social institutions through which they are expressed, it will remain a hollow victory.

This is one of the things which occurred in the case of the feminist movement. Important as the franchise is, or the recent change in Civil Service regulations which prevents the personnel specification of "male only," the new law or regulation can be successful only to the extent that women exercise the franchise, or are trained to be qualified for and to aspire for the jobs they are now permitted to hold. There is no sex equality until women participate on an equal basis with men in politics, occupations and the family. Law and administrative regulations must permit such participation, but women must want to participate and be able to participate. In politics and the occupational world, to be able to participate depends primarily on whether home responsibilities can be managed simultaneously with work or political commitments. Since women have had, and probably will continue to have, primary responsibility for child-rearing, their participation in politics, professions or the arts cannot be equal to that of men unless ways are devised to ease the combination of home and work responsibilities. This is precisely what has not occurred; at the same time, since fewer women today choose a career over marriage, the result has been a reduction in women's representation in the more challenging and demanding occupations.

By itself, the stress on legal change to the neglect of institutional change in the accommodations between family and work does not go very far in explaining why the feminist movement has lost momentum. There is an important second factor which must be viewed in conjunction with this first one. The feminist movement has always been strongest when it was allied with other social reform movements. In the nineteenth century its linkage was with the antislavery movement, and in the early twentieth century it was allied to the social welfare movement. There is an interesting and a simple explanation of this: unlike any other type of social inequality, whether of race, class, religion or nationality, sex is the only instance in which representatives of the unequal groups live in more intimate association with each other than with members of their own group. A woman is more intimately associated with a man than she is with any woman.* This was not the case for lord-serf, master-slave, Prot-

* This is one among many points of crucial and still relevant significance to be found in John Stuart Mill's essay "The Subjection of Women" (London, 1869)

ALICE S. ROSSI

estant-Roman Catholic, white-Negro relationships unless or until
the social groups involved reach a full equality. By linking the
feminist cause to the antislavery or social welfare movement, women
were able to work together with men of similar sympathies and in
the process they enlisted the support of these men for the feminist
cause. To a greater extent than any other underprivileged group,
women need not only vigorous spokesmen and pacesetters of their
own sex, but the support of men, to effect any major change in the
status of women, whether in the personal sphere of individual relationships or on the level of social organization.* The decline of
political radicalism and the general state of affluence and social
conservatism in American society since World War II have contributed in subtle ways to the decline of feminism, for women are
not joined with men in any movement affecting an underprivileged
group in American society. At the present time, marriage remains
the only major path of social mobility for women in our society.

The general conservatism of the total society has also penetrated
the academic disciplines, with side effects on the motivation and
ability of women to exercise the rights already theirs or to press for
an extension of them. Feminism has been undermined by the conservatism of psychology and sociology in the postwar period. Sociologists studying the family have borrowed heavily from selective
findings in social anthropology and from psychoanalytic theory and
have pronounced sex to be a universally necessary basis for role
differentiation in the family. By extension, in the larger society
women are seen as predominantly fulfilling nurturant, expressive
functions and men the instrumental, active functions. When this
viewpoint is applied to American society, intellectually aggressive
women or tender expressive men are seen as deviants showing signs
of "role conflict," "role confusion," or neurotic disturbance. They

* In recent years of acute manpower shortages in scientific, professional
and technical fields, there has been a growing awareness of the fact that women
constitute the only sizable remaining reservoir of such talent. Many men whose
administrative or policy responsibilities alert them to this fact have been eagerly
exploring the ways by which female brainpower could be added to the national
pool of skilled manpower. The contemporary period is therefore ripe with opportunities for talented women, and women can anticipate a welcome from male
colleagues and employers. I shall not discuss any further the current societal
need for women in the labor force, because I would argue for an extension of
female participation in the higher levels of occupations even in an era with *no*
pressing manpower shortages, on the grounds of the more general principles to
be developed in this essay.

102

are not seen as a promising indication of a desirable departure from traditional sex role definitions.* In a similar way, the female sphere, the family, is viewed by social theorists as a passive, pawnlike institution, adapting to the requirements of the occupational, political or cultural segments of the social structure, seldom playing an active role either in affecting the nature of other social institutions or determining the nature of social change.** The implicit assumption in problem after problem in sociology is that radical social innovations are risky and may have so many unintended consequences as to make it unwise to propose or support them. Although the sociologist describes and analyzes social change, it is change already accomplished, seldom anticipated purposive social change.† When the changes are in process, they are defined as social problems, seldom as social opportunities.

Closely linked to this trend in sociology and social anthropology, and in fact partly attributable to it, is the pervasive permeation of psychoanalytic thinking throughout American society. Individual

* Often the conclusion that sex differentiation is a basic and universal phenomenon is buttressed by pointing to a large number of societies, all of which manifest such sex differentiation. Since Americans are easily impressed by large numbers, this does indeed sound like conclusive evidence against the likelihood of any society's achieving full sex equality. Closer examination of such samples, however, reveals two things: very little representation of numerous African societies in which the instrumental-expressive distinction is simply *not* linked to sex in the predicted direction, and second, they are largely primitive societies, a half dozen of which might equal the size of a very small American city. Such cultural comparisons assume every possible kind of societal arrangement is represented, but this is not the case: Sweden, China, Yugoslavia, the Soviet Union, Israel are not represented on such a continuum. I believe we may learn more that is of relevance to a future America by studying family patterns in these societies than from a study of all the primitive societies in the world. Unfortunately, most of contemporary sociology and social anthropology is far less concerned with the future than the present as molded by the past.

** A rare exception is the recent work by William J. Goode, who has focussed precisely on the active role of the family in determining the course of social change in the non-family segments of social structure. See his *World Revolution and Family Patterns* (Glencoe: The Free Press, 1963).

† When the sociologist finds, for example, that the incidence of divorce is higher for those who marry outside their religion than for those who do not, he concludes that intermarriage is "bad" or "risky"; he does not say such marital failures may reflect the relative newness of the social pattern of intermarriage, much less suggest that such failures may decline once this pattern is more prevalent. In fact, the only aspect of intermarriage which is studied is the incidence of its failure. Sociologists have not studied *successful* intermarriages.

psychoanalysts vary widely among themselves, but when their theories are popularized by social scientists, marriage and family counselors, writers, social critics, pediatricians and mental health specialists, there emerges a common and conservative image of the woman's role. It is the traditional image of woman which is popularized: the woman who finds complete self-fulfillment in her exclusive devotion to marriage and parenthood. Women who thirty years ago might have chosen a career over a marriage, or restricted their family size to facilitate the combination of family and work roles, have been persuaded to believe that such choices reflect their inadequacy as women. It is this sense of failure as a woman that lies behind the defensive and apologetic note of many older unmarried professional women, the guilt which troubles the working mother (which I suspect goes up in direct proportion to the degree to which she is familiar with psychoanalytic ideas), the restriction of the level of aspiration of college women, the early plunge into marriage, the closed door of the doll's house.

Our society has been so inundated with psychoanalytic thinking that any dissatisfaction or conflict in personal and family life is considered to require solution on an individual basis. This goes well with the general American value stress on individualism, and American women have increasingly resorted to psychotherapy, the most highly individualized solution of all, for the answers to the problems they have as women. In the process the idea has been lost that many problems, even in the personal family sphere, cannot be solved on an individual basis, but require solution on a societal level by changing the institutional contexts within which we live.

The consequences of this acceptance of psychoanalytic ideas and conservatism in the social sciences have been twofold: first, the social sciences in the United States have contributed very little since the 1930's to any lively intellectual dialogue on sex equality as a goal or the ways of implementing that goal. Second, they have provided a quasi-scientific underpinning to educators, marriage counselors, mass media and advertising researchers, who together have partly created, and certainly reinforced, the withdrawal of millions of young American women from the mainstream of thought and work in our society.*

* A full picture of this post-World War II development is traced in Betty Friedan's *The Feminine Mystique* (New York: W. W. Norton, 1963). See particularly Chapters 6 and 7 on the "Functional Freeze" and the "Sex-Directed Educators."

Why Seek Equality Between the Sexes

This brings us to the second question: why should American society attempt to reach a state of sex equality? If women seem satisfied with a more narrowly restricted life pattern than men would be, why should we seek to disturb this pattern? To begin with, I do not think this question is really relevant to the issue. There have been underprivileged groups throughout history which contained sizable proportions of contented, uncomplaining members, whether slaves, serfs or a low status caste. But the most enlightened members of both the privileged and underprivileged groups in such societies came to see that inequality not only depressed the human potential of the subject groups but corrupted those in the superordinate groups. The lives of southern whites are as crippled by racial inequality as the lives of southern Negroes are impoverished. In the same way, many men spend their daytime hours away from home as vital cognitive animals and their nights and weekends in mental passivity and vegetation. Social and personal life is impoverished for some part of many men's lives because so many of their wives live in a perpetual state of intellectual and social impoverishment.

A second reason why American society should attempt to reach a state of full sex equality is that at the level our industrial society has now reached, it is no longer necessary for women to confine their life expectations to marriage and parenthood. Certain of the reasons for this have been increasingly stressed in recent years: with increased longevity, and smaller sized families, the traditional mother role simply does not occupy a sufficient portion of a woman's life span to constitute any longer the exclusive adult role for which a young woman should be prepared.* American girls spend more time as apprentice mothers with their dolls than they will as adult women with their own babies, and there is half a lifetime still ahead by the time the youngest child enters high school. Although studies have shown that women today are working in the home roughly the same number of hours a week as their mothers did,[1] this is not because they have to do so: technological innovations in the produc-

* Demographic changes in the family life cycle between 1890 and 1950 are shown in great detail in Paul Glick's *American Families* (New York: John Wiley, 1957). It should also be noted that even in contemporary families with four or five children, child-bearing occupies a far shorter portion of a woman's life span than it did to achieve this size family fifty years ago, because infant mortality has been so drastically reduced.

tion and distribution of food, clothing and other household equipment have been such that homemaking no longer requires the specialized skills and time-consuming tasks it did until early in our century. Contemporary women often turn what should be labor-saving devices into labor-making devices. In the light of the many time-consuming tasks the American mother fifty years ago had to perform, and the much longer work day for those in the labor force then, the woman in 1964 who holds down a full-time job will probably have as much or more time with her children as her grandmother had. Furthermore, most of the skills needed for adulthood are no longer taught within the family: child socialization is increasingly a shared enterprise between the parent and teachers, doctors, nurses, club leaders and instructors in an assortment of special skills.

These are perhaps all familiar points. What has not been seen is the more general point that *for the first time in the history of any known society, motherhood has become a full-time occupation for adult women.* In the past, whether a woman lived on a farm, a Dutch city in the seventeenth century, or a colonial town in the eighteenth century, women in all strata of society except the very top were never able to be full-time mothers as the twentieth-century middle class American woman has become. These women were productive members of farm and craft teams along with their farmer, baker or printer husbands and other adult kin. Children either shared in the work of the household or were left to amuse themselves; their mothers did not have the time to organize their play, worry about their development, discuss their problems. These women were not lonely because the world came into their homes in the form of customers, clients or patients in villages and towns, or farm-hands and relatives on the farm; such women had no reason to complain of the boredom and solitude of spending ten-hour days alone with babies and young children because their days were peopled with adults. There were no child specialists to tell the colonial merchant's wife or pioneer farmer's wife that her absorption in spinning, planting, churning and preserving left her children on their own too much, that how she fed her baby would shape his adult personality, or that leaving children with a variety of other adults while she worked would make them insecure.

There are two important questions this analysis raises: why has full-time motherhood been accepted by the overwhelming majority of American women, and how successful has been the new pattern of full-time motherhood of the past forty years or so? I believe the major answer to the first question is that the American woman has been encouraged by the experts to whom she has turned for guidance in child-rearing to believe that her children need her continuous presence, supervision and care and that she should find complete fulfillment in this role. If, for example, a woman reads an article by Dr. Spock on working mothers, she is informed that any woman who finds full-time motherhood produces nervousness is showing a "residue of difficult relationships in her own childhood"; if irritability and nervousness are not assuaged by a brief trip or two, she is probably in an emotional state which can be "relieved through regular counseling in a family social agency, or, if severe, through psychiatric treatment"; and finally, "any mother of a preschool child who is considering a job should discuss the issues with a social worker before making her decision."[2] Since the social worker shares the same analytic framework that Dr. Spock does, there is little doubt what the advice will be; the woman is left with a judgment that wanting more than motherhood is not natural but a reflection of her individual emotional disturbance.

The fundamental tenet of the theory underlying such advice is that the physically and emotionally healthy development of the infant requires the loving involvement of the mother with the child. If an infant does not receive stable continuous mothering there is almost invariably severe physical and emotional disturbance. There is apparently ample clinical evidence to support these points. Studies have suggested that prolonged separation from parents, and particularly from the mother, has serious effects upon infants and young children.[3] However, practitioners make unwarranted extrapolations from these findings when they advise that *any* separation of mother and child is risky and hazardous for the healthy development of the child.* Despite the fact that the empirical evidence stems from instances of prolonged, traumatic separation caused by such things as the death or serious illness of the mother, or the institutionalization

---

* A few authors have seen this claim that all separation of the child from the biological mother or mother surrogate, even for a few days, is inevitably damaging to the child, as a new and subtle form of anti-feminism, by which men, under the guise of exacting the importance of maternity, are tying women more tightly to their children than any real clinical or cultural evidence indicates is necessary. See Hilde Bruch, *Don't Be Afraid of Your Child* (New York: Farrar, Straus & Young, 1952); and Margaret Mead, "Some Theoretical Considerations on the Problem of Mother-Child Separation," *American Journal of Orthopsychiatry* (1954), 24: 471–483.

of the child, this viewpoint is applied to the situation of an employed mother absent from the home on a regular basis. No one predicts that any dire consequences will flow from a woman's absence from home several afternoons a week to engage in a shopping spree, keep medical appointments or play bridge; nor is a father considered to produce severe disturbance in his young children even if his work schedule reduces contact with them to the daylight hours of a weekend. But women who have consulted pediatricians and family counselors about their resuming work are firmly told that they should remain at home, for the sake of their children's emotional health.*

What effect *does* maternal employment have upon children? Many sociologists of the family have raised this question during the past fifteen years, expecting to find negative effects as psychoanalytic theory predicted. In fact, the focus of most maternal employment studies has been on the effect of mothers' working upon the personalities of their children, somewhat less often on the tensions and strains between the mother role and the occupational role,** seldom on the question of how maternal employment affects the woman's satisfactions with herself, her home and marriage. To date, *there is no evidence of any negative effects traceable to maternal employment;* children of working mothers are no more likely than children of non-working mothers to become delinquent, to show neurotic

* It is interesting in this connection that studies concerning the separation of the mother and child are frequently cited as cases of *maternal deprivation,* but those concerning the separation of the father and child are cited more neutrally as cases of *father absence,* never as *paternal deprivation.*

** Social scientists raise the question of whether there are not such diametrically opposed requirements of an occupational role from the mother role as to involve great strain between the two. It is argued that because of this contrast between the two spheres, one or the other role must "suffer," there will be "role conflict." The researchers were not prepared to find either that women could slip back and forth between these two spheres just as men have done for decades without any of the same difficulty predicted for women, or that the mother role may be subtly changed in the direction of more rationality, greater stress on independence and autonomy in children than is found in the child-rearing values of non-working mothers (See Faye VonMering, "Professional and Non-Professional Women as Mothers," *Journal of Social Psychology* [August, 1955], 42: 21–34). Rather, the researcher expected to find maternal neglect, negative effect on children's personality, or inadequacy in occupational roles, such as absenteeism, overly personal view of work relationships, etc. As in many areas in which role conflict has been predicted, human beings have a greater tolerance for sharp contrasts in role demands than social scientists credit them with.

symptoms, to feel deprived of maternal affection, to perform poorly in school, to lead narrower social lives, etc.[4] Many of the researchers in the 1950's frankly admitted surprise at their negative findings. In a study reported in 1962,[5] the only significant difference found between working and non-working mothers was the mother's confidence about her role as mother: 42 per cent of the working mothers but only 24 per cent of the non-working mothers expressed concern about their maternal role, "often by explicit questioning and worry as to whether working is interfering with their relationships and the rearing of their children." Yet these working women did not actually differ from the at-home mothers in the very things that concerned them: there were no differences between these women in the emotional relationships with their children, household allocation of responsibilities, principles of child-rearing, etc. The working mothers appeared to share the prevailing view that their children would suffer as a result of their employment, though in fact their children fare as well as those of non-working mothers.[6]

It would appear, therefore, that the employment of women when their children are eight years of age or older has no negative effect on the children. What about the earlier years, from infancy until school age? In the American literature, there is little to refer to as yet which bears directly upon the effect of maternal employment on the infant or toddler, partly because employment of mothers with preschool children is so negligible in the United States, partly because the measurement of "effects" on young children is difficult and cannot be done with the research tools which have been used in most studies of maternal employment effects—questionnaires administered to mothers and to their school-age children.*

There is, however, one significant body of data which is of considerable relevance to the question of the effect of maternal employment upon infants and very young children. Maternal employment is a regular pattern of separation of mother and child: the Israeli

---

* The Burchinal-Rossman research cited previously did give special attention to employment of mothers during the child's early years. Their 7th- and 11th-grade students were divided according to when the maternal employment occurred—i.e., whether during the first three years of the child's life, second three, between the ages of 1 and 6, only within the previous 30 months or for the child's entire life. How long the mother has been working, or when in the growth of the child she began work, showed no significant effect upon the children's development: those whose mothers were working when they were under three years of age did not differ from those whose mothers began working when they were adolescents.

kibbutzim are collective settlements with several decades of experience in precisely this pattern. On the kibbutz, infants live in children's houses where their physical care and training are largely handled. During the infancy months the mother visits the house to feed the infant; as toddlers, children begin a pattern of visiting with their parents for a few hours each day, living in the children's houses for the remaining portions of their days and nights. A number of studies have been conducted to investigate the effect of this intermittent multiple mothering on the young child.[7] They all point to essentially the same conclusion; the kibbutz child-rearing practices have no deleterious effects upon the subsequent personality development of the children involved. In fact, there are a number of respects in which the kibbutz-reared Israeli children exceed those reared in the traditional farm family: the kibbutz children showed a more accurate perception of reality, more breadth of interest and cultural background, better emotional control and greater overall maturity.

Continuous mothering, even in the first few years of life, does not seem to be necessary for the healthy emotional growth of a child.* The crux of the matter appears to be in the nature of the care which is given to the child.** If a child is reared by a full-time mother who is rejecting and cold in her treatment of him, or if a child is reared in an institutional setting lacking in warmth and stimulation and with an inadequate staff, both children will show personality dis-

* There are of course other instances of infant and toddler care by persons supplementing the biological mother, notable among them being the creche and nursery school systems in the Soviet Union. What effect these early experiences of creche care have upon the subsequent personality development of Soviet young people is not known. Western observers who have visited them during the past several years have been impressed with the facilities, quality of staff personnel, and general happy mood of the children seen in them, but there is no rigorous evidence to substantiate these impressions, or assess the effect of such early separation from the mother upon personality.

** In this analysis, I am placing primary emphasis on the quality of the care given to the children. Another specification of maternal employment involves introducing the motivations and satisfactions of working and non-working mothers: many women work who do not wish to work, and many women are at home who do not wish to be at home. One recent study which took these factors into consideration found that the non-working mothers who are dissatisfied with not working (who want to work but, out of a sense of "duty," do not work) show the greatest problems in child rearing—more difficulty controlling their children, less emotional satisfaction in relationships to their children, less confidence in their functioning as mothers. Cf. Marian Radke Yarrow *et al., op. cit.*

turbances in later years. If the loving care of the biological mother is shared by other adults who provide the child with a stable loving environment, the child will prosper at least as well as and potentially better than one with a good full-time mother.* In the section below on child care and careers, I shall suggest institutional innovations which would ensure good quality care for children and ease the combination of work and child-rearing for women.

Turning now to the second question raised above: how successful has the new pattern of full-time motherhood been? Are women more satisfied with their lives in the mid-twentieth century than in the past? Does motherhood fulfill them, provide them with a sufficient canvas to occupy a lifetime? Are contemporary children living richer lives, developing greater ego strength to carry them through a complex adulthood? Are children better off for having full-time mothers?

I think the answer to all the questions posed above is a firm *no*. Educators, child psychologists and social analysts report an increasing tendency for American middle-class children to be lacking in initiative, excessively dependent on others for direction and decision, physically soft.[8] Our children have more toys and play equipment than children in any other society, yet they still become bored and ask their mothers for "something to do." No society has as widespread a problem of juvenile delinquency and adolescent rebellion

---

* This shifts the ground of the problem of maternal employment to a very different level from the one on which it is usually discussed. As a research problem, the crucial question is not whether the mother is employed or not, but what is the quality of the care given to the children—whether by the mother alone or a combination of other adults. Since full-time mothers vary from loving care to rejecting neglect, and mother substitutes may be presumed to vary in the same way, it is scarcely surprising that maternal employment *per se* shows very little effect upon the personality of children. Social scientists have uncritically borrowed the assumption of the psychoanalysts that the mental health of the child is possible only with continuous care by the biological mother. What is clearly called for is a shift in research definition from maternal employment versus full-time motherhood, to the quality of the care the child receives under conditions of full- and part-time working or nonworking mothers. There is also a need for research which is based on a clear conceptualization of the variables of both "maternal care" and "maternal deprivation." For a careful review of crucial dimensions of maternal care and their effect upon infants, see Leon J. Yarrow, "Research in Dimensions of Early Maternal Care," *Merrill-Palmer Quarterly*, 9 (April, 1963), 101–114. The same author has written a careful re-evaluation of the concept of maternal deprivation: "Maternal deprivation: toward an empirical and conceptual re-evaluation," *Psychological Bulletin*, 58 (1961), 459–490.

as the United States. Alcoholism, compulsive sex-seeking and adolescent delinquency are no longer social problems confined to the working class, socially disorganized sections of our cities, but have been on the increase in the middle-class suburb in the past twenty years, and involve more women and girls than in the past. There is a strong strand of male protest against the mother or "matriarch" in both our beatnik culture and our avant-garde literature: social and artistic extremes are seldom fully deviant from the middle range in a society, but show in an exaggerated heightened way the same though less visible tendencies in the social majority.

In a large proportion of cases, the etiology of mental illness is linked to inadequacy in the mother-child relationship. A high proportion of the psychoneurotic discharges from the army during World War II was traced to these young soldiers' overly dependent relationships to their mothers.[9] This has been the subject of much earnest discussion in the years since the war, but the focus has remained on the mother-*son* relationship, I suspect only because as a fighter, a professional man or a worker, male performance is seen to be more crucial for society than female performance. But dependence, immaturity and ego diffusion have been characteristic of daughters as well as sons. The only difference is that, in the case of daughters, this less often reaches the overt level of a social problem because young women move quickly from under their mothers' tutelage into marriage and parenthood of their own: female failures are therefore not as socially visible, for they are kept within the privacy of family life and psychoanalytic case records. It is a shortsighted view indeed to consider the immature wife, dominating mother or interfering mother-in-law as a less serious problem to the larger society than the male homosexual, psychoneurotic soldier or ineffectual worker, for it is the failure of the mother which perpetuates the cycle from one generation to the next, affecting sons and daughters alike.

Disturbing trends of this sort cannot all be traced to the American woman's excessive and exclusive involvement with home and family. We live in turbulent times, and some part of these trends reflects the impact of world tension and conflict. But there is no reason to assume that world tension is relevant to many of them. Emotional and physical difficulties after childbirth or during the menopause years, the higher incidence of college girl than college boy breakdowns, the shrunken initiative and independence of children, are clearly not explained by world conflict. Besides, vast sections of American society remain totally unmoved and unaffected by international political and military events until they directly impinge on their own daily lives. Since history is both written and produced more by men than by women, the fact that our writers are preoccupied with the relationship to the mother points to difficulties in our family system more than the course of world events.

It is a paradox of our social history that motherhood has become a full-time occupation in precisely the era when objectively it could, and perhaps should, be a part-time occupation for a short phase of a woman's life span. I suspect that the things women do for and with their children have been needlessly elaborated to make motherhood a full-time job. Unfortunately, in this very process the child's struggle for autonomy and independence, for privacy and the right to worry things through for himself are subtly and pervasively reduced by the omnipresent mother. As a young child he is given great permissive freedom, but he must exercise it under supervision. As an adolescent he is given a great deal of freedom, but his parents worry excessively about what he does with it. Edgar Friedenberg has argued that there is entirely too much parental concentration on adolescent children, with the result that it has become increasingly difficult to *be* an adolescent in American society.[10] He suggests that parents are interested in youth to the extent that they find their own stage of life uninteresting. Middle-class children are observed and analyzed by their mothers as though they were hothouse plants psychologically, on whose personalities any pressure might leave an indelible bruise. If a woman's adult efforts are concentrated exclusively on her children, she is likely more to stifle than broaden her children's perspective and preparation for adult life. Any stress or failure in a child becomes a failure of herself, and she is therefore least likely to truly help her child precisely when the child most needs support.[11] In myriad ways the mother binds the child to her, dampening his initiative, resenting his growing independence in adolescence, creating a subtle dependence which makes it difficult for the child to achieve full adult stature without a rebellion which leaves him with a mixture of resentment and guilt that torments him in his mother's declining years.

It seems to me no one has linked these things together adequately. Psychiatric counselors of college students frequently have as their chief task that of helping their young patients to free themselves from the entangling web of dependence upon their parents, primarily their mothers, and encouraging them to form stable independent lives of their own. In other words, if the patient is eighteen years old the analyst tries to help her free herself from her mother, but if the next patient is twenty-five years old with young children at home, the analyst tells her the children would suffer emotional damage if she left them on a regular basis to hold down a job. The very things which would reduce the excessive dependency of children before it becomes a critical problem are discouraged by the counselor or analyst during the years when the dependency is being formed. If it is true that the adult is what the child was, and if we wish adults to be assertive, independent, responsible people, then they should be reared in a way which prevents excessive dependence on a parent. They should be cared for by a number of adults in their childhood, and their parents should truly encourage their independence and responsibility during their youthful years, not merely give lip service to these parental goals. The best way to encourage such independence and responsibility in the child is for the mother to be a living model of these qualities herself. If she had an independent life of her own, she would find her stage of life interesting, and therefore be less likely to live for and through her children. By maintaining such an independent life, the American mother might finally provide her children with something she can seldom give when she is at home—a healthy dose of inattention, and a chance for adolescence to be a period of fruitful immaturity and growth.* If enough American women developed vital and enduring interests outside the family and remained actively in them throughout the child-bearing years, we might then find a reduction in extreme adolescent rebellion, immature early marriages, maternal domination of children, and interference by mothers and mothers-in-law in the lives of married children.

There remains one further general characteristic of our industrial society which has relevance to the question of why American society should achieve full sex equality. Our family unit is small, for the most part geographically if not socially isolated from its kin. This small family unit is possible because of the increased longevity in highly industrialized societies. In agricultural societies, with their high rate of mortality, many parents die before they have completed

* This has been argued by Eric Larrabee, though he does not suggest the employment of the mother as the way to make the older woman's life more interesting. See Eric Larrabee, "Childhood in Twentieth Century America," Eli Ginzberg (ed.), *The Nation's Children*, Vol. 3, *Problems and Prospects* (New York: Columbia University Press, 1960), pp. 199–216.

the rearing of their young. The extended family provided substitutes for such parents without disturbing the basic lines of kin affiliation and property rights of these children. In our modern family system it is an unusual event for women or men to be widowed while they have young dependent children. This also means, however, that American families must fend for themselves in the many emergencies less critical than the death of a spouse: army service, long business or professional trips, prolonged physical or emotional illness, separation or divorce often require that one spouse carry the primary responsibility for the family, even if this is cushioned or supplemented by insurance, government aid, paid helpers or relatives. The insurance advertisements which show fathers bending over a cradle and begin "what would happen if?" evoke a twinge of fear in their readers precisely because parents recognize the lonely responsible positions they would be in if serious illness or death were to strike their home. In our family system, then, it is a decided asset if men and women can quickly and easily substitute for or supplement each other as parents and as breadwinners. I believe these are important elements in the structure of our economy and family system which exert pressure toward an equality between men and women. It is not merely that a companionate or equalitarian marriage is a desirable relationship between wife and husband, but that the functioning of an urban industrial society is facilitated by equality between men and women in work, marriage and parenthood.

The conclusions I have drawn from this analysis are as follows: full-time motherhood is neither sufficiently absorbing to the woman nor beneficial to the child to justify a contemporary woman's devoting fifteen or more years to it as her exclusive occupation. Sooner or later—and I think it should be sooner—women have to face the question of who they are besides their children's mother.

A major solution to this quest would be found in the full and equal involvement of women in the occupational world, the culmination of the feminist movement of the last one hundred and fifty years. This is not to overlook the fact that involvement as a volunteer in politics or community organizations or a serious dedication to a creative art can be a solution for many women. These areas of participation and involvement provide innumerable women with a keen sense of life purpose, and women are making significant and often innovative contributions in these pursuits. A job *per se* does not provide a woman, or a man either, with any magical path to self-fulfillment; nor does just any community volunteer work, or half-hearted dabbling in a creative art.

Women are already quite well represented in volunteer organizations in American communities. However, broadening the range of alternatives open to women and chosen by women for their life patterns is still to be achieved in the occupational world. It is also true that at the most challenging reaches of both political and community volunteer work, the activities have become increasingly professionalized. Thus while many women have and will continue to make innovative contributions to these fields as volunteers, such opportunities have become limited. Furthermore, many such women often find themselves carrying what amounts to a full-time job as a "volunteer executive," yet neither the recognition nor the rewards are equivalent to what they would receive in comparable positions in the occupational system.[12] Hence, the major focus in this essay will be on the means by which the full and equal involvement of well-educated women in the occupational world may be achieved. For reasons which will become clear later, I believe that the occupational involvement of women would also be the major means for reducing American women's dominance in marriage and parenthood, and thus for allowing for the participation of men as equal partners in family life.

Of course there have already been changes in the extent and the nature of women's participation in the American labor force. Indeed, this is sometimes cited as proof that sex equality has been achieved in the United States. There are roughly twenty-three million American women in the labor force, and it is predicted that this will swell to thirty million by 1970. About three-fifths of these women are married, an increase of well over 20 per cent since 1940. It should be noted that this increase came predominantly from women between the ages of 35 and 54 years, after the child-rearing years and before the usual retirement age for workers. This is a major social change, to be sure, and people who still raise the question of whether married women should work are arguing after the fact, for such women are doing so at increasing rates. The point is, however, that most American women—65 per cent—do *not* work outside the home, and those who do are found largely in blue collar or low-skill white collar occupations. Men fill roughly 85 per cent of the very top professional and technical jobs in the United States. Furthermore, only a very small proportion of American wives work if their husbands are in the middle and top income brackets, or if they have young children. Finally, the distribution of the female labor force by age shows two major peaks of female participation, before and for a short time after marriage, and then for the fifteen years from their early forties through middle fifties. Withdrawal and re-entry many years later is now a common female work pattern in the United States. As long as this pattern continues, women will not increase their representation in the top professional and technical occupations.*

Over the past twenty years, women in many European countries have doubled or more their representation in the professional occupations. By comparison, American women constitute a smaller proportion of the professional world today than they did twenty years ago. That this reflects a lowering of ambition among American women is suggested by the fact that of all the women capable of doing college work, only one out of four do so, compared to one out of two men. This is the point at which we begin to tap a deeper root of women's motivations in the United States. Whether a woman works steadily throughout her marriage or returns to work after the child-rearing period, no significant increase of women in the professional and high-skill job categories will occur unless American women's attitude toward education and work is changed.[13] To study and to prepare for a future job "in case I have to work" is just as poor a preparation for occupational participation as the postponement of learning domestic skills "until I have to" is a poor preparation for the homemaker role. Both views reflect a digging in of the heels into the adolescent moment of a lifetime. In many ways the middle-class girl considers only the present, the here-and-now, as do most members of the working class, and not the future, as do her father, brothers and male friends. There is evidence to suggest that such an emphasis on the present is characteristic not only of the American woman at college age, but also more generally throughout her life span. Thus, Gallup's portrait of the American woman shows the same characteristic at all points during the younger half of the life cycle: young unmarried women as well as mature women with their children now entering high school give little thought to and no preparation for their life over forty years of age.[14]

The middle-class wife of a successful business executive or pro-

* Viola Klein's study of English working women shows the same pattern: withdrawal and return to work at a later age is paid for by a loss of occupational status. See Viola Klein, *Working Wives*, Occasional Papers No. 15 (London: Institute of Personnel Management, 1960), pp. 21–24.

fessional man has a special problem. To earn a salary in the occupational world, she will be judged by her own achieved merits without regard to her social position or her husband's influence. Unless she has had the education and experience necessary to hold a position of some prestige, she will experience social and personal barriers to entering the labor force. In the absence of such education and experience, she is qualified to be only the occupational subordinate of men who are her equals socially, a status incongruity few women are likely to tolerate. By contrast, no matter how menial, her service as a volunteer will be socially approved. Unless such women secure specialized training before marriage, or acquire it after marriage, there will be little increase in the proportion of working wives and mothers in the upper half of the middle class. Many such women with a flair for organization have found full scope for their independent fulfillment in volunteer work in politics, education, social welfare and the arts. Unfortunately, there are innumerable other women for whom such outlets have little attraction who realize they have missed their chance for independent self-fulfillment, and who have little opportunity for a second chance by their late forties.

It has been argued by some sociologists that the American marriage is already too fragile to sustain competition at comparable skill levels between spouses.[15] If this were true, and women are also reluctant to work at lower prestige jobs than their husbands, this would effectively freeze most middle-class women out of the occupational world. I would raise three points concerning this assumption. First, husbands and working wives are usually found in different segments of the occupational system, which makes comparison of success a difficult matter. For example, is an architect working for a large firm and earning $20,000 a year more or less successful than his wife who directs a large family welfare agency and earns $15,000 a year? Second, even were such achievements in nonfamily roles to provoke some competitive feeling between husband and wife, I think the consequences of this competition are far less potentially harmful to the marriage or to the children than the situation of the well-educated able woman who is not working and engages instead in a competition with her husband for the affections and primary loyalties of the children. If a woman is markedly more successful than her husband, it would probably create difficulty in the marriage, particularly if there are residues of traditional expectations of male breadwinner dominance on the part of either partner to the marriage. But competition does not necessarily mean conflict. It can be a social spice and a source of pride and stimulation in a marriage of equals. Last, one must face up to the fact that a new social goal exacts a price. A change toward sex equality may cause some temporary marital dislocations, but this is not sufficient reason to expect all women to remain enclosed in the past.

Institutional Levers for Achieving Sex Equality

In turning to the problem of how equality between the sexes may be implemented as a societal goal, I shall concentrate on the three major areas of child care, residence and education. Institutional change in these areas in no sense exhausts the possible spheres in which institutional change could be effected to facilitate the goal of sex equality. Clearly government and industry, for example, could effect highly significant changes in the relations between the sexes. But one must begin somewhere, and I have chosen these three topics, for they all involve questions of critical significance to the goal of equality between men and women.

1. It is widely assumed that rearing children and maintaining a career is so difficult a combination that except for those few women with an extraordinary amount of physical strength, emotional endurance and a dedicated sense of calling to their work, it is unwise for women to attempt the combination. Women who have successfully combined child-rearing and careers are considered out of the ordinary, although many men with far heavier work responsibilities who yet spend willing loving hours as fathers, and who also contribute to home maintenance, are cause for little comment. We should be wary of the assumption that home and work combinations are necessarily difficult. The simplified contemporary home and smaller sized family of a working mother today probably represent a lesser burden of responsibility than that shouldered by her grandmother.

This does not mean that we should overlook the real difficulties that are involved for women who attempt this combination. Working mothers do have primary responsibility for the hundreds of details involved in home maintenance, as planners and managers, even if they have household help to do the actual work. No one could suggest that child-rearing and a career are easy to combine, or even that this is some royal road to greater happiness, but only that the combination would give innumerable intelligent and creative women a degree of satisfaction and fulfillment that they cannot obtain in any other way. Certainly many things have to "give" if a woman works when she also has young children at home. Volunteer and social activities, gardening and entertaining may all have to be curtailed. The important point to recognize is that as children get older, it is far easier to resume these social activities than it is to resume an interrupted career. The major difficulty, and the one most in need of social innovation, is the problem of providing adequate care for the children of working mothers.

If a significant number of American middle-class women wish to work while their children are still young and in need of care and supervision, who are these mother-substitutes to be? In the American experience to date, they have been either relatives or paid domestic helpers. A study conducted by the Children's Bureau in 1958 outlines the types of child-care arrangements made by women working full time who had children under twelve years of age.[16] The study showed that the majority of these children (57 per cent) were cared for by relatives: fathers, older siblings, grandparents and others. About 21 per cent were cared for by nonrelatives, including neighbors as well as domestic helpers. Only 2 per cent of the children were receiving group care—in day nurseries, day-care centers, settlement houses, nursery schools and the like. Of the remainder, 8 per cent were expected to take care of themselves, the majority being the "latchkey" youngsters of ten and twelve years of age about whom we have heard a good deal in the press in recent years.

These figures refer to a national sample of employed mothers and concern women in blue collar jobs and predominantly low-skill white collar jobs. Presumably the proportion of middle-class working mothers who can rely on either relatives or their husbands would be drastically lower than this national average, and will probably decline even further in future years. Many of today's, and more of tomorrow's American grandmothers are going to be wage earners themselves and not baby-sitters for their grandchildren. In addition, as middle-class women enter the occupational world, they will experience less of a tug to remain close to the kinswomen of their childhood, and hence may contribute further to the pattern of geographic and social separation between young couples and both sets of their parents. Nor can many middle-class husbands care for their children, for their work hours are typically the same as those of their working wives: there can be little dovetailing of the work schedules of wives and husbands in the middle class as there can be in the working class.

At present, the major child-care arrangement for the middle-class woman who plans a return to work has to be hired household help. In the 1920's the professional and business wife-mother had little difficulty securing such domestic help, for there were thousands of first generation immigrant girls and women in our large cities whose first jobs in America were as domestic servants.* In the 1960's, the situation is quite different: the major source of domestic help in our large cities is Negro and Puerto Rican women. Assuming the continuation of economic affluence and further success in the American Negro's struggle for equal opportunity in education, jobs and housing, this reservoir will be further diminished in coming decades. The daughters of many present-day Negro domestic servants will be able to secure far better paying and more prestigeful jobs than their mothers can obtain in 1964. There will be increasing difficulty of finding adequate child-care help in future years as a result.

The problem is not merely that there may be decreasing numbers of domestic helpers available at the same time more women require their aid. There is an even more important question involved: are domestic helpers the best qualified persons to leave in charge of young children? Most middle-class families have exacting standards for the kind of teachers and the kind of schools they would like their children to have. But a working mother who searches for a competent woman to leave in charge of her home has to adjust to considerably lower standards than she would tolerate in any nursery school program in which she placed her young son or daughter, either because such competent help is scarce, or because the margin of salary left after paying for good child care and the other expenses associated with employment is very slight.

One solution to the problem of adequate child care would be an attempt to upgrade the status of child-care jobs. I think one productive way would be to develop a course of study which would yield a certificate for practical mothering, along the lines that such courses

* In one study conducted for the Bureau of Vocational Information in 1925, Collier found that 42% of the one hundred professional and business mothers she interviewed had two or more full-time domestic servants to maintain their homes and care for their children during the day; only 9 of these 100 women had no full-time servants, five of whom had their mothers living with them. Virginia MacMakin Collier, *Marriage and Careers: A Study of One Hundred Women who are Wives, Mothers, Homemakers and Professional Women* (New York: The Channel Bookshop, 1926), pp. 59 and 74.

and certificates have been developed for practical nursing. There would be several important advantages to such a program. There are many older women in American communities whose lives seem empty because their children are grown and their grandchildren far away, yet who have no interest in factory or sales work, for they are deeply committed to life and work within the context of a home. Indeed, there are many older women who now work in factories or as cashiers or salesclerks who would be much more satisfied with child-care jobs, if the status and pay for such jobs were upgraded. These are the women, sometimes painfully lonely for contact with children, who stop young mothers to comment on the baby in the carriage, to talk with the three-year-old and to discuss their own distant grandchildren. I think many of these women would be attracted by a program of "refresher" courses in first aid, child development, books and crafts appropriate for children of various ages, and the special problems of the mother substitute-child relationship. Such a program would build upon their own experiences as mothers but would update and broaden their knowledge, bringing it closer to the values and practices of the middle-class woman who is seeking a practical mother for her family. Substitute motherhood for which she earns a wage, following active motherhood of her own, could provide continuity, meaning and variety to the life-span of those American women who are committed to the traditional conception of woman's role. Such a course of study might be developed in a number of school contexts—a branch of a college department of education, an adult education extension program or a school of nursing.

A longer-range solution to the problem of child care will involve the establishment of a network of child-care centers.* Most of the

* Child-care centers would not be an entirely new phenomenon in the United States, for there were a number of municipal day-care centers established during World War II when the need for womanpower in factories engaged in war production made them necessary to free women to accept employment. There have also been continuing debates about the provision of child-care centers for other mothers, such as the ADC mother, the problem revolving about whether such women should be given sufficient money from municipal funds to stay at home and care for her children, or to establish child-care centers and thus enable such women to hold down jobs and at least partially support their children. In either case, the focus has been upon working-class women. Child-care centers as an institutional device to facilitate the combination of job and family by women in professional and technical occupations in the middle class are very rare, and are largely confined to small private ventures in the large metropoli.

detailed plans for such centers must be left for future discussion, but there are several important advantages to professionally run child-care centers which should be noted. Most important, better care could be provided by such centers than any individual mother can provide by hiring a mother's helper, housekeeper or even the practical mother I have just proposed. In a child-care center, there can be greater specialization of skills, better facilities and equipment, and play groups for the children. Second, a child-care center would mean less expense for the individual working mother, and both higher wages and shorter hours for the staff of the center. Third, these centers could operate on a full-time, year-round schedule, something of particular importance for women trained in professional or technical fields, the majority of which can be handled only on a full-time basis. Except for the teaching fields, such women must provide for the afternoon care of their nursery school and kindergarten-age children, after-school hours for older children and three summer months for all their children. Fourth, a child-care center could develop a roster of home-duty practical mothers or practical nurses to care for the ill or convalescent child at home, in much the way school systems now call upon substitute teachers to cover the classes of absent regular teachers.

A major practical problem is where to locate such child-care centers. During the years of experimentation which would follow acceptance of this idea, they might be in a variety of places, under a variety of organizational auspices, as a service facility offered by an industrial firm, a large insurance company, a university, the federal or a state government. Community groups of women interested in such service might organize small centers of their own much as they have informal pooled baby-sitting services and cooperatively run nursery schools at the present time.

I believe that one of the most likely contexts for early experimentation with such child-care centers is the large urban university. As these universities continue to expand in future years, in terms of the size of the student body, the varied research institutes associated with the university and the expansion of administrative, technical and counseling personnel, there will be increasing opportunity and increasing need for the employment of women. A child-care center established under the auspices of a major university would facilitate the return for training of older women to complete or refresh advanced training, forestall the dropping out of younger graduate married women with infants and young children to care for, and attract competent professional women to administrative, teaching or research positions, who would otherwise withdraw from their fields for the child-rearing years. It would also be an excellent context within which to innovate a program of child care, for the university has the specialists in psychology, education and human development on whom to call for the planning, research and evaluation that the establishment of child-care centers would require. If a university-sponsored child-care program were successful and widely publicized, it would then constitute an encouragement and a challenge to extend child-care centers from the auspices of specific organizations to a more inclusive community basis. A logical location for community child-care centers may be as wings of the elementary schools, which have precisely the geographic distribution throughout a city to make for easy access between the homes of very young children and the centers for their daytime care. Since school and center would share a location, it would also facilitate easy supervision of older children during the after-school hours. The costs of such care would also be considerably reduced if the facilities of the school were available for the older children during after-school hours, under the supervision of the staff of the child-care center. There are, of course, numerous problems to be solved in working out the details of any such program under a local educational system, but assuming widespread support for the desirability of community facilities for child care, these are technical and administrative problems well within the competence of school and political officials in our communities.

I have begun this discussion of the institutional changes needed to effect equality between the sexes with the question of child-care provision because it is of central importance in permitting women to enter and remain in the professional, technical and administrative occupations in which they are presently so underrepresented. Unless provision for child care is made, women will continue to find it necessary to withdraw from active occupational involvement during the child-rearing years. However, the professional and scientific fields are all growing in knowledge and skill, and even a practitioner who remains in the field often has difficulty keeping abreast of new developments. A woman who withdraws for a number of years from a professional field has an exceedingly difficult time catching up. The more exacting the occupation, then, the shorter the period of withdrawal should probably be from active participation in the labor force. If a reserve of trained practical mothers were available, a professional woman could return to her field a few months after the birth of a child, leaving the infant under the care of a practical mother until he or she reached the age of two years, at about which age the child could enter a child-care center for daytime care. Assuming a two-child family, this could mean not more than one year of withdrawal from her professional field for the working mother.

2. The preferred residential pattern of the American middle class in the postwar decades has been suburban. In many sections of the country it is difficult to tell where one municipality ends and another begins, for the farm, forest and waste land between towns and cities have been built up with one housing development after another. The American family portrayed in the mass media typically occupies a house in this sprawling suburbia, and here too, are the American women, and sometimes men, whose problems are aired and analyzed with such frequency. We know a good deal about the characteristics and quality of social life in the American suburb[17] and the problems of the men and women who live in them. We hear about the changing political complexion of the American suburbs, the struggle of residents to provide sufficient community facilities to meet their growing needs. But the social and personal difficulties of suburban women are more likely to be attributed to their early family relationships or to the contradictory nature of the socialization of girls in our society than to any characteristic of the environment in which they now live. My focus will be somewhat different: I shall examine the suburban residence pattern for the limitations it imposes on the utilization of women's creative work abilities and the participation of men in family life. Both limitations have important implications for the lives of boys and girls growing up in the suburban home.

The geographic distance between home and work has a number of implications for the role of the father-husband in the family. It reduces the hours of possible contact between children and their fathers. The hour or more men spend in cars, buses or trains may serve a useful decompression function by providing time in which to sort out and assess the experiences at home and the events of the work day, but it is questionable whether this outweighs the disadvantage of severely curtailing the early morning and late afternoon hours during which men could be with their children.

The geographic distance also imposes a rigid exclusion of the father from the events which highlight the children's lives. Commuting fathers can rarely participate in any special daytime activities at home or at school, whether a party, a play the child performs in or a conference with a teacher. It is far less rewarding to a child to report to his father at night about such a party or part in a play than to have his father present at these events. If the husband-father must work late or attend an evening function in the city, he cannot sandwich in a few family hours but must remain in the city. This is the pattern which prompted Margaret Mead to characterize the American middle-class father as the "children's mother's husband," and partly why mother looms so oversized in the lives of suburban children.

Any social mixing of family-neighborhood and job associates is reduced or made quite formal: a work colleague cannot drop in for an after-work drink or a Saturday brunch when an hour or more separates the two men and their families. The father-husband's office and work associates have a quality of unreality to both wife and children. All these things sharpen the differences between the lives of men and women—fewer mutual acquaintances, less sharing of the day's events, and perhaps most importantly, less simultaneous filling of their complementary parent roles. The image of parenthood to the child is mostly motherhood, a bit of fatherhood and practically no parenthood as a joint enterprise shared at the same time by father and mother. Many suburban parents, I suspect, spend more time together as verbal parents—discussing their children in the children's absence—than they do actively interacting with their children, the togetherness cult notwithstanding. For couples whose relationship in courtship and early marriage was equalitarian, the pressures are strong in the suburban setting for parenthood to be highly differentiated and skewed to an ascendant position of the mother. Women dominate the family, men the job world.

The geographic distance between home and the center of the city restricts the world of the wife-mother in a complementary fashion. Not only does she have to do and be more things to her children, but she is confined to the limitations of the suburban community for a great many of her extrafamilial experiences. That suburban children are restricted in their social exposure to other young children and relatively young adults, mostly women and all of the same social class, has often been noted. I think the social restriction of the young wife to women of her own age and class is of equal importance: with very few older persons in her immediate environment, she has little first-hand exposure to the problems attending the empty-nest stage of life which lies ahead for herself. It is easy for her to continue to be satisfied to live each day as it comes, with little thought of preparing for the thirty-odd years when her children are no longer dependent upon her. If the suburban wife-mother had more opportunity to become acquainted with older widows and grandmothers, this would be pressed home to her in a way that might encourage a change in her unrealistic expectations of the future, with some preparation for that stage of life while she is young.*

If and when the suburban woman awakens from this short-range perspective and wants either to work or to prepare for a return to work when her children are older, how is she to do this, given the suburban pattern of residence? It is all very well to urge that school systems should extend adult education, that colleges and universi-

* George Gallup and Evan Hill, "The American Woman," *The Saturday Evening Post,* December 22, 1962. One must read this survey very carefully to get behind the gloss of the authors' rosy perspective. Gallup reports that almost half of the married women in the sample claimed that childbirth was the "most thrilling event" in their lives. He gives two quotes to illustrate why these women were so fascinated by childbirth: one stresses the point that it was "the one time in my life when everything was right"; the other points out "you've done something that's recognized as a good thing to do, and you're the center of attention." If these are truly typical, it tells us a good deal about the underlying attitude toward the thousands of days on which no child is born: things are *not* all right, and there must be some sense of being on the sidelines, of having a low level of self-esteem, if childbirth is important because "society views it as good" and it is the only time in her life that she is the important center of attention. In other parts of the article, which generally stresses the central importance of children to women, and their high satisfaction with marriage, we learn that a large proportion of American women wish the schools would do more of the socializing of these children—teach them good citizenship, how to drive, sex education; and if these women were so satisfied with their lives, why does only 10% of the sample want their daughters to live the same lives they have? Instead, these women say they want their daughters to get more education and to marry later than they did. If marriage is the perfect female state, then why wish to postpone it, unless there are unexpressed sides of the self which have not been fulfilled?

The only strong critical point made is the following: "with early weddings and extended longevity, marriage is now a part-time career for women, and unless they prepare now for the freer years, this period will be a loss. American society will hardly accept millions of ladies of leisure, or female drones, in their 40's" (p. 32). But only 31% of the sample reported they are "taking courses or following a plan to improve themselves," a third of these involving improvement of their physical shape or appearance. The photographs accompanying this article reveal the authors' own focus on the years of youth rather than of maturity: of 29 women appearing in these pictures, only 2 are clearly of women over 45 years of age.

ties must make it possible for older women to complete education interrupted ten or more years previously or to be retrained for new fields; but this is a difficult program for the suburban wife to participate in. She lives far from the center of most large cities, where the educational facilities tend to be concentrated, in a predominantly middle-class community, where domestic help is often difficult to arrange and transportation often erratic during the hours she would be using it.

It is for these reasons that I believe any attempt to draw a significant portion of married women into the mainstream of occupational life must involve a reconsideration of the suburban pattern of living. Decentralization of business and industry has only partly alleviated the problem: a growing proportion of the husbands living in the suburbs also work in the suburbs. There are numerous shops and service businesses providing job opportunities for the suburban wife. Most such jobs, however, are at skill levels far below the ability potential and social status of the suburban middle-class wife. Opportunities for the more exacting professional, welfare and business jobs are still predominantly in the central sections of the city. In addition, since so many young wives and mothers in this generation married very young, before their formal education was completed, they will need more schooling before they can hope to enter the fields in which their talents can be most fruitfully exercised, in jobs which will not be either dull or a status embarrassment to themselves and their husbands. Numerous retail stores have opened suburban branches; colleges and universities have yet to do so. A woman can spend in the suburb, but she can neither learn nor earn.

That some outward expansion of American cities has been necessary is clear, given the population increase in our middle- to large-sized cities. But there are many tracts in American cities between the business center and the outlying suburbs which imaginative planning and architectural design could transform and which would attract the men and women who realize the drawbacks of a suburban residence. Unless there is a shift in this direction in American housing, I do not think there can be any marked increase in the proportion of married middle-class women who will enter the labor force. That Swedish women find work and home easier to combine than American women is closely related to the fact that Sweden avoided the sprawling suburban development in its postwar housing expansion. The emphasis in Swedish housing has been on inner-city housing improvement. With home close to diversified services for schooling, child care, household help and places of work, it has been much easier in Sweden than in the United States to draw married women into the labor force and keep them there.

In contrast, the policy guiding the American federal agencies which affect the housing field, such as the FHA, have stressed the individual home, with the result that mortgage money was readily available to encourage builders to develop the sprawling peripheries of American cities. Luxury high-rise dwellings at the hub of the city and individual homes at the periphery have therefore been the pattern of middle-class housing development in the past twenty years. A shift in policy on the part of the federal government which would embrace buildings with three and four dwelling units and middle-income high-rise apartment buildings in the in-between zones of the city could go a long way to counteract this trend toward greater and greater distance between home and job. Not everyone can or will want to live close to the hub of the city. From spring through early fall, it is undoubtedly easier to rear very young children in a suburban setting with back yards for the exercise of healthy lungs and bodies. But this is at the expense of increased dependence of children on their mothers, of minimization of fathers' time with their youngsters, of restriction of the social environment of women, of drastic separation of family and job worlds and of less opportunity for even part-time schooling or work for married women.

3. Men and women must not only be able to participate equally; they must want to do so. It is necessary, therefore, to look more closely into their motivations, and the early experiences which mold their self-images and life expectations. A prime example of this point can be seen in the question of occupational choice. The goal of sex equality calls for not only an increase in the extent of women's participation in the occupational system, but a more equitable distribution of men and women in all the occupations which comprise that system. This means more women doctors, lawyers and scientists, more men social workers and school teachers. To change the sex ratio within occupations can only be achieved by altering the sex-typing of such occupations long before young people make a career decision.* Many men and women change their career plans during

* The extent of this sex-typing of occupations is shown dramatically in a study of the June, 1961 college graduates conducted by the National Opinion Research Center at the University of Chicago. Although the women in this sample of college graduates showed a superior academic performance during

college, but this is usually within a narrow range of relatively homogeneous fields: a student may shift from medicine to a basic science, from journalism to teaching English. Radical shifts such as from nursing to medicine, from kindergarten teaching to the law, are rare indeed. Thus while the problem could be attacked at the college level, any significant change in the career choices men and women make must be attempted when they are young boys and girls. It is during the early years of elementary school education that young people develop their basic views of appropriate characteristics, activities and goals for their sex. It is for this reason that I shall give primary attention to the sources of sex-role stereotypes and what the elementary school system could do to eradicate these stereotypes and to help instead in the development of a more androgynous conception of sex role.*

---

the college years—only 36% of the women in contrast to 50% of the men were in the "bottom half" of their class—their career aspirations differed markedly from those of men. Of those who were going on to graduate and professional schools in the fall of 1961, only 6% of those aspiring to careers in medicine were women; 7% in physics, 7% in pharmacology, 10% in business and administration, 28% in the social sciences. In contrast, women predominated in the following fields: 51% in humanities, 59% in elementary and secondary education, 68% in social work, 78% in health fields such as nursing, medical technology, physical and occupational therapy. In a sample of 33,782 college graduates, there were 11,000 women who expected to follow careers in elementary and secondary education, but only 285 women who hoped to enter the combined fields of medicine, law and engineering. See James A. Davis and Norman Bradburn, "Great Aspirations: Career Plans of America's June 1961 College Graduates," National Opinion Research Center Report No. 82, September, 1961 (mimeographed). Davis and Bradburn report that some 40% of the graduates had changed their career plans during their college years (p. 40).

* My attention in this section will be largely on the early years of schooling. There is a great need, however, for a return of the spirit that characterized high school and college educators of women in the 1930's. It has seemed to me that there is an insidious trend at this level of education toward discouraging women from aspiring to the most demanding and rewarding fields of work and thought. Dr. Mary Bunting, noteworthy for the imaginative Radcliffe Institute for Independent Study, now urges women to work on the "fringes" of the occupational system, away from the most competitive intellectual market places. In her first public address upon assuming the presidency of Barnard College, Dr. Rosemary Park stated that in her view college education of women in the United States should have as its goal the creation of "enlightened laymen." High school and college counselors give hearty approval if women students show talent and interest in elementary school teaching, nursing, social work; their approval is all too often very lukewarm if not discouraging, if women students show interest in physics, medicine or law.

The all-female social atmosphere of the American child has been frequently noted by social scientists, but it has been seen as a problem only in its effect upon boys. It has been claimed, for example, that the American boy must fight against a feminine identification this atmosphere encourages, with the result that he becomes overly aggressive, loudly asserting his maleness. In contrast, it is claimed that the American girl has an easy socialization, for she has an extensive number of feminine models in her environment to facilitate her identification as a female.

There are several important factors which this analysis overlooks. To begin with the boy: while it is certainly true that much of his primary group world is controlled by women, this does not mean that he has no image of the male social and job world as well. The content of the boy's image of man's work has a very special quality to it, however. Although an increasingly smaller proportion of occupations in a complex industrial society relies on sheer physical strength, the young boy's exposure to the work of men remains largely the occupations which do require physical strength. The jobs he can see are those which are socially visible, and these are jobs in which men are reshaping and repairing the physical environment. The young boy sees working class men operating trucks, bulldozers, cranes; paving roads; building houses; planting trees; delivering groceries. This image is further reinforced by his television viewing: the gun-toting cowboy, the bat-swinging ballplayer, the arrow-slinging Indian. Space operas suggest not scientific exploration but military combat, the collision and collusion of other worlds. In short, even if the boy sees little of his father and knows next to nothing of what his father does away from home, there is some content to his image of men's work in the larger society. At least some part of his aggressive active play may be as much acting out similar male roles in response to the cultural cues provided by his environment as it is an over-reaction to his feminine environment or an identification with an aggressor-father.

And what of the girl? What image of the female role is she acquiring during her early years? In her primary group environment, she sees women largely in roles defined in terms that relate to her as a child—as mother, aunt, grandmother, baby-sitter—or in roles relating to the house—the cleaning, cooking, mending activities of mother and domestic helpers. Many mothers work outside the home, but the daughter often knows as little of that work as she does of her father's. Even if her own mother works, the reasons for such working that are given to the child are most often couched in terms of the mother or housewife role. Thus, a girl is seldom told that her mother works because she enjoys it or finds it very important to her own satisfaction in life, but because the money she earns will help pay for the house, a car, the daughter's clothes, dancing lessons or school tuition.* In other words, working is something mothers sometimes have to do as mothers, not something mothers do as adult women. This is as misleading and distorted an image of the meaning of work as the father who tells his child he works "to take care of mummy and you" and neglects to mention that he also works because he finds personal satisfaction in doing so, or that he is contributing to knowledge, peace or the comfort of others in the society.

The young girl also learns that it is only in the family that women seem to have an important superordinate position. However high her father's occupational status outside the home, when he returns at night, he is likely to remove his white shirt and become a blue collar Mr. Fixit or mother's helper. The traditional woman's self-esteem would be seriously threatened if her husband were to play a role equal to her own in the lives and affections of her children or in the creative or managerial aspect of home management, precisely because her major sphere in which to acquire the sense of personal worth is her home and children.** The lesson is surely not lost on her daughter, who learns that at home father does not know best, though outside the home men are the bosses over women, as she can see only too well in the nurse-doctor, secretary-boss, salesclerk-store

* Although her sample was upper-middle-class mothers of girls in progressive schools in New York City, Ruth Hartley reports that the working mothers in her sample told their children they were working out of the home because of financial need: "They express guilt about their working and appear to hold quite traditional concepts of appropriate 'feminine' behavior which they feel they are violating." An example is provided by a well-to-do working mother who obviously loves her work but told her daughter that she works because of financial necessity. When asked why she doesn't let her daughter know she enjoys her work, she answered, "well, then what excuse would I have for working?" Ruth Hartley and A. Klein, "Sex Role Concepts among Elementary School-Age Girls," *Marriage and Family Living*, 21 (February, 1959), 59–64.

** Women enhance their own self-esteem when they urge their children to "be good when father gets home" because he is tired and needs to rest. They are not only portraying an image of the father as a fragile person, a "Dresden cup" as Irene Joselyn expresses it, but by expanding their maternalism to include the father, they are symbolically relegating him to the subordinate position of the child in the family structure. See Irene Joselyn, "Cultural Forces, Motherliness and Fatherliness," *American Journal of Orthopsychiatry*, 26 (1956), 264–271.

manager, space Jane-space John relationships that she has an opportunity to observe.

The view that the socialization of the girl is an easy one compared with the boy depends on the kind of woman one has in mind as an end-product of socialization. Only if the woman is to be the traditional wife-mother is present-day socialization of young girls adequate, for from this point of view the confinement to the kinds of feminine models noted above and the superordinate position of the mother in the family facilitate an easy identification. If a girl sees that women reign only at home or in a history book, whereas outside the home they are Girl Fridays to men, then clearly for many young girls the wife-mother role may appear the best possible goal to have. It should be noted, however, that identification has been viewed primarily as an either-or process—the child identifies either with the mother or the father—and not as a process in which there is a fusion of the two parent models such that identification involves a modeling of the self after mother in some respects, father in others. It is possible that those women who have led exciting, intellectually assertive and creative lives did not identify exclusively with their traditional mothers, but crossed the sex line and looked to their fathers as model sources for ideas and life commitments of their own. This is to suggest that an exclusively same-sex identification between parent and child is no necessary condition for either mentally healthy or creative adults.

If I am correct about the significance of the father in the childhoods of those women who later led creative adult lives, then an increased accessibility of the middle-class father to his daughters and greater sharing of his ideas and interests could help to counteract the narrow confines of the feminine models daughters have. Beyond this, young girls need exposure to female models in professional and scientific occupations and to women with drive and dedication who are playing innovative volunteer roles in community organizations; they need an encouragement to emulate them and a preparation for an equalitarian rather than a dominant role in parenthood. Only if a woman's self-esteem is rooted in an independent life outside her family as well as her roles within the home can she freely welcome her husband to share on an equal basis the most rewarding tasks involved in child-rearing and home maintenance.

What happens when youngsters enter school? Instead of broadening the base on which they are forming their image of male and female roles, the school perpetuates the image children bring from home and their observations in the community. It has been mother who guided their preschool training; now in school it is almost exclusively women teachers who guide their first serious learning experiences. In the boy's first readers, men work at the same jobs with the same tools he has observed in his neighborhood—"T" for truck, "B" for bus, "W" for wagon. His teachers expect him to be rugged, physically strong and aggressive. After a few years he moves into separate classes for gym, woodworking and machine shop. For the girl, women are again the ones in charge of children. Her first readers portray women in aprons, brooms in their hands or babies in their arms. Teachers expect her to be quiet, dependent, with feminine interests in doll and house play and dressing up. In a few years she moves into separate classes for child care, cooking and practical nursing. In excursions into the community, elementary school boys and girls visit airports, bus terminals, construction sites, factories and farms.

What can the schools do to counteract these tendencies to either outmoded or traditional images of the roles of men and women? For one, class excursions into the community are no longer needed to introduce American children to building construction, airports or zoos. Except for those in the most underprivileged areas of our cities, American children have ample exposure to such things with their car- and plane-riding families. There are, after all, only a limited number of such excursions possible in the course of a school year. I think visits to a publishing house, research laboratory, computer firm or art studio would be more enriching than airports and zoos.

Going out into the community in this way, youngsters would observe men and women in their present occupational distribution. By a program of bringing representatives of occupations into the classroom and auditorium, however, the school could broaden the spectrum of occupations young children may link to their own abilities and interests regardless of the present sex-typing of occupations, by making a point of having children see and hear a woman scientist or doctor; a man dancer or artist; both women and men who are business executives, writers and architects.*

---

* In a large metropolis, resource persons could be invited through the city business and professional organizations, the Chamber of Commerce, art, music and dancing schools, etc. This could constitute a challenging program for PTA groups to handle; or a Community Resources Pool could be formed similar to

Another way in which the elementary schools could help is making a concerted effort to attract male teachers to work in the lower grades. This would add a rare and important man to the primary group environment of both boys and girls. This might seem a forlorn hope to some, since elementary school teaching has been such a predominantly feminine field, and it may be harder to attract men to it than to attract women to fields presently considered masculine. It may well be that in the next decade or so the schools could not attract and keep such men as teachers. But it should be possible for graduate schools of education and also school systems to devise ways of incorporating more men teachers in the lower grades, either as part of their teacher training requirements or in the capacity of specialized teachers: the science, art or music teacher who works with children at many grade levels rather than just one or two contiguous grade levels.* His presence in the lives of very young children could help dispel their expectation that only women are in charge of children, that nurturance is a female attribute or that strength and an aggressive assault on the physical environment is the predominant attribute of man's work.

The suggestions made thus far relate to a change in the sex-linking of occupations. There is one crucial way in which the schools could effect a change in the traditional division of labor by sex within the family sphere. The claim that boys and girls are reared in their early years without any differentiation by sex is only partially true. There are classes in all elementary schools which boys and girls take separately or which are offered only to one sex. These are precisely the courses most directly relevant to adult family roles: courses in sex and family living (where communities are brave enough to hold them) are typically offered in separate classes for

---

that the New World Foundation has supported in New York City whereby people from business, the arts and sciences and the professions work with the public schools. Many educators and teachers might hesitate to try such a project in anticipation of parent-resistance. But parent-resistance could be a good opportunity for parent-education, if teachers and school officials were firm and informed about what they are trying to do.

* Though predominantly a feminine field, there is one man to approximately every two women planning careers in teaching. In the "Great Aspirations" study, there were 11,388 women students planning to teach in elementary and secondary schools, but also 5038 men. The problem may therefore not be as great as it seems at first: schools of education could surely do more to encourage some of these men to work in the lower grades, in part or for part of their teaching careers.

boys and for girls, or for girls only. Courses in shop and craft work are scheduled for boys only; courses in child care, nursing and cooking are for girls only. In departing from completely coeducational programs, the schools are reinforcing the traditional division of labor by sex which most children observe in their homes. Fifteen years later, these girls find that they cannot fix a broken plug, set a furnace pilot light or repair a broken high chair or favorite toy. These things await the return of the child's father and family handyman in the evening. When a child is sick in the middle of the night, his mother takes over; father is only her assistant or helper.

These may seem like minor matters, but I do not think they are. They unwittingly communicate to and reinforce in the child a rigid differentiation of role between men and women in family life. If first aid, the rudiments of child care and of cooking have no place in their early years as sons, brothers and schoolboys, then it is little wonder that as husbands and fathers American men learn these things under their wives' tutelage. Even assuming these wives were actively involved in occupations of their own and hence free of the psychological pressure to assert their ascendancy in the family, it would be far better for all concerned—the married pair and the children as well—if men brought such skills with them to marriage.

This is the point where the schools could effect a change: if boys and girls took child care, nursing, cooking, shop and craft classes together, they would have an opportunity to acquire comparable skills and pave the way for true parental substitutability as adults. They would also be learning something about how to complement each other, not just how to compete with each other.* Teamwork should be taught in school in the subjects relevant to adult family roles, not just within each sex on the playground or in the gymnasium. In addition to encouraging more equality in the parental role, such preparation as school children could ease their adjustment to the crises of adult life; illness, separation due to the demands of a job or military service, divorce or death would have far less trauma and panic for the one-parent family—whether mother or father—

* Bruno Bettelheim makes the point that American boys and girls learn to compete with each other, but not how to complement each other. He sees this lack of experience in complementarity as part of the difficulty in achieving a satisfactory sexual adjustment in marriage: the girl is used to "performing with males on equal grounds, but she has little sense of how to complement them. She cannot suddenly learn this in bed." See Bruno Bettelheim, "Growing Up Female," *Harper's*, November, 1962, p. 125.

if such equivalence and substitutability were a part of the general definition of the parental role.

A school curriculum which brought boys and girls into the same classes and trained them in social poise, the healing skills, care of children, handling of interpersonal difficulties and related subjects would also encourage the development of skills which are increasingly needed in our complex economy. Whether the adult job is to be that of a worker in an automated industry, a professional man in law, medicine or scholarship, or an executive in a large bureaucratic organization, the skills which are needed are not physical strength and ruggedness in interpersonal combat but understanding in human dealings, social poise and persuasive skill in interpersonal relations.* All too often, neither the family nor the school encourages the development of these skills in boys. Hundreds of large business firms look for these qualities in young male applicants but often end up trying to develop them in their young executives through on-the-job training programs.

I have suggested a number of ways in which the educational system could serve as an important catalyst for change toward sex equality. The schools could reduce sex-role stereotypes of appropriate male and female attributes and activities by broadening the spectrum of occupations youngsters may consider for themselves irrespective of present sex-linked notions of man's work and woman's work, and by providing boys as well as girls with training in the tasks they will have as parents and spouses. The specific suggestions for achieving these ends which I have made should be viewed more as illustrative than as definitive, for educators themselves may have far better suggestions for how to implement the goal in the nation's classrooms than I have offered in these pages. Equality between the sexes cannot be achieved by proclamation or decree but only through a multitude of concrete steps, each of which may seem insignificant by itself, but all of which add up to the social blueprint for attaining the general goal.

Summary Profile

In the course of this essay I have suggested a number of institutional innovations in education, residence and child care which

---

* These are the same skills which, when found in women, go by the names of charm, tact, intuition. See Helen Mayer Hacker, "The New Burdens of Masculinity," *Marriage and Family Living*, 19 (August, 1957), 227–233.

would facilitate equality between the sexes. Instead of a more conventional kind of summary, I shall describe a hypothetical case of a woman who is reared and lives out her life under the changed social conditions proposed in this essay.

She will be reared, as her brother will be reared, with a combination of loving warmth, firm discipline, household responsibility and encouragement of independence and self-reliance. She will not be pampered and indulged, subtly taught to achieve her ends through coquetry and tears, as so many girls are taught today. She will view domestic skills as useful tools to acquire, some of which, like fine cooking or needlework, having their own intrinsic pleasures but most of which are necessary repetitive work best gotten done as quickly and efficiently as possible. She will be able to handle minor mechanical breakdowns in the home as well as her brother can, and he will be able to tend a child, press, sew, and cook with the same easy skills and comfortable feeling his sister has.

During their school years, both sister and brother will increasingly assume responsibility for their own decisions, freely experiment with numerous possible fields of study, gradually narrowing to a choice that best suits their interests and abilities rather than what is considered appropriate or prestigeful work for men and women. They will be encouraged by parents and teachers alike to think ahead to a whole life span, viewing marriage and parenthood as one strand among many which will constitute their lives. The girl will not feel the pressure to belittle her accomplishments, lower her aspirations, learn to be a receptive listener in her relations with boys, but will be as true to her growing sense of self as her brother and male friends are. She will not marry before her adolescence and schooling are completed, but will be willing and able to view the college years as a "moratorium" from deeply intense cross-sex commitments, a period of life during which her identity can be "at large and open and various."[18] Her intellectual aggressiveness as well as her brother's tender sentiments will be welcomed and accepted as *human* characteristics, without the self-questioning doubt of latent homosexuality that troubles many college-age men and women in our era when these qualities are sex-linked.* She will not cling to

* David Riesman has observed that this latent fear of homosexuality haunts the Ivy League campuses, putting pressure on many young men to be guarded in their relations with each other and with their male teachers, reflecting in part the lag in the cultural image of appropriate sex characteristics. See David Riesman, "Permissiveness and Sex Roles," *Marriage and Family Living*, 21 (August, 1959), 211–217.

her parents, nor they to her, but will establish an increasingly larger sphere of her own independent world in which she moves and works, loves and thinks, as a maturing young person. She will learn to take pleasure in her own body and a man's body and to view sex as a good and wonderful experience, but not as an exclusive basis for an ultimate commitment to another person, and not as a test of her competence as a female or her partner's competence as a male. Because she will have a many-faceted conception of her self and its worth, she will be free to merge and lose herself in the sex act with a lover or a husband.*

---

* It goes beyond the intended scope of this essay to discuss the effects of a social pattern of equality between men and women upon their sexual relationship. A few words are, however, necessary, since the defenders of traditional sex roles often claim that full equality would so feminize men and masculinize women that satisfactory sexual adjustments would be impossible and homosexuality would probably increase. If the view of the sex act presupposes a dominant male actor and a passive female subject, then it is indeed the case that full sex equality would probably be the death knell of this traditional sexual relationship. Men and women who participate as equals in their parental and occupational and social roles will complement each other sexually in the same way, as essentially equal partners, and not as an ascendant male and a submissive female. This does not mean, however, that equality in non-sexual roles necessarily de-eroticizes the sexual one. The enlarged base of shared experience can, if anything, heighten the salience of sex *qua* sex. In Sweden, where men and women approach equality more than perhaps any other western society, visitors are struck by the erotic atmosphere of that society. Sexually men and women do after all each lack what the other has and wishes for completion of the self; the salience of sex may be enhanced precisely in the situation of the diminished significance of sex as a differentiating factor in all other areas of life. It has always seemed paradoxical to me that so many psychoanalysts defend the traditional sex roles and warn that drastic warping of the sexual impulses may flow from full sex equality; surely they are underestimating the power and force of the very drive which is in so central a position in their theoretical framework. Maslow is one of the few psychologists who has explored the connections between sex experience and the conception of self among women. With a sample of one hundred and thirty college-educated women in their twenties, he found, contrary to traditional notions of femininity and psychoanalytic theories, that the more "dominant" the woman, the greater her enjoyment of sexuality, the greater her ability to give herself freely in love. Women with dominance feelings were free to be completely themselves, and this was crucial for their full expression in sex. They were not feminine in the traditional sense, but enjoyed sexual fulfillment to a much greater degree than the conventionally feminine women he studied. See A. H. Maslow, "Dominance, Personality and Social Behavior in Women," *Journal of Social Psychology*, 10 (1939), 3–39; and "Self-Esteem (Dominance Feeling) and Sexuality in Women," *Journal of Social Psychology*, 16 (1942), 259–294; or a review of Maslow's studies in Betty Friedan, *The Feminine Mystique*, pp. 316–326.

Marriage for our hypothetical woman will not mark a withdrawal from the life and work pattern that she has established, just as there will be no sharp discontinuity between her early childhood and youthful adult years. Marriage will be an enlargement of her life experiences, the addition of a new dimension to an already established pattern, rather than an abrupt withdrawal to the home and a turning in upon the marital relationship. Marriage will be a "looking outward in the same direction" for both the woman and her husband. She will marry and bear children only if she deeply desires a mate and children, and will not be judged a failure as a person if she decides against either. She will have few children if she does have them, and will view her pregnancies, childbirth and early months of motherhood as one among many equally important highlights in her life, experienced intensely and with joy but not as the exclusive basis for a sense of self-fulfillment and purpose in life. With planning and foresight, her early years of child bearing and rearing can fit a long-range view of all sides of herself. If her children are not to suffer from "paternal deprivation," her husband will also anticipate that the assumption of parenthood will involve a weeding out of nonessential activities either in work, civic or social participation. Both the woman and the man will feel that unless a man can make room in his life for parenthood, he should not become a father. The woman will make sure, even if she remains at home during her child's infancy, that he has ample experience of being with and cared for by other adults besides herself, so that her return to a full-time position in her field will not constitute a drastic change in the life of the child, but a gradual pattern of increasing supplementation by others of the mother. The children will have a less intense involvement with their mother, and she with them, and they will all be the better for it. When they are grown and establish adult lives of their own, our woman will face no retirement twenty years before her husband, for her own independent activities will continue and expand. She will be neither an embittered wife, an interfering mother-in-law nor an idle parasite, but together with her husband she will be able to live an independent, purposeful and satisfying third act in life.

REFERENCES

1. Cowles and Dietz, Myrdal and Klein, and Jean Warren have shown that there has been very little change in the past quarter century in the total working time per week devoted to homemaking activities. May L. Cowles and Ruth P. Dietz, "Time Spent in Homemaking Activities by a Selected

Group of Wisconsin Farm Homemakers," *Journal of Home Economics,* 48 (January, 1956), 29-35; Jean Warren, "Time: Resource or Utility," *Journal of Home Economics,* 49 (January, 1957), 21 ff; Alva Myrdal and Viola Klein, *Women's Two Roles: Home and Work* (London: Routledge and Kegan Paul, 1956).

2. Benjamin Spock, "Should Mothers Work?" *Ladies' Home Journal,* February, 1963.

3. See Anna Freud and Dorothy T. Burlingham, *Infants Without Families* (New York: International University Press, 1944); William Goldfarb, "Psychological Deprivation in Infancy and Subsequent Adjustment," *American Journal of Orthopsychiatry,* 15 (April, 1945), 247-255; John Bowlby, *Maternal Care and Mental Health* (Geneva: World Health Organization, 1952); John Bowlby, *Child-Care and the Growth of Love* (London: Pelican Books, 1953); and James Bossard, *The Sociology of Child Development* (New York: Harper, 1954).

4. Burchinal and Rossman found no significant relationships between any kind of employment and personality characteristics or social interaction of children in the 7th and 11th grades in school—Lee G. Burchinal and Jack E. Rossman, "Relations among Maternal Employment Indices and Developmental Characteristics of Children," *Marriage and Family Living,* 23 (November, 1961), 334-340. Nye administered questionnaires to over two thousand high school students and found no significant relationships between maternal employment and educational achievement or neurotic symptoms—F. Ivan Nye, "Employment Status of Mothers and Adjustment of Adolescent Children," *Marriage and Family Living,* 21 (August, 1959), 240-244. Using scales to tap nervous symptoms, antisocial and withdrawing tendencies, Perry found no significant differences between children with working and non-working mothers—Joseph B. Perry, "The Mother Substitutes of Employed Mothers: An Exploratory Inquiry," *Marriage and Family Living,* 23 (November, 1961), 362-367. Kligler found that employed mothers reported their maternal role suffered least from their occupations—Deborah S. Kligler, "The Effects of the Employment of Married Women on Husband and Wife Roles." Unpublished. Ph.D. dissertation, Department of Sociology, Yale University, 1954. Roy found no consistent effects of maternal employment on the social life and participation of children or their academic performance, or the affection, fairness of discipline and cooperation in the family—Prodipto Roy, "Maternal Employment and Adolescent Roles: Rural-Urban Differentials," *Marriage and Family Living,* 23 (November, 1961), 340-349. Peterson found no significant differences on employment of mothers and maternal interest in and supervision of their adolescent daughters—Evan T. Peterson, "The Impact of Maternal Employment on the Mother-Daughter Relationship," *Marriage and Family Living,* 23 (November, 1961), 355-361. In Eleanor Maccoby's reanalysis of data from the Gluecks' study of working mothers and delinquency, she shows that working or not working has little effect once the quality of child care is taken into account—Eleanor Maccoby, "Effects Upon Children of their Mothers' Outside Employment," in National Manpower Council, *Work in the Lives of Married Women* (New York: Columbia University Press, 1958), pp. 150-172. General reviews of the literature are

found in: Lois M. Stolz, "Effects of Maternal Employment on Children: Evidence from Research," *Child Development*, 31 (December, 1960), 749–782; Eli Ginzberg (ed.), *The Nation's Children*, Vol. 3, *Problems and Prospects* (New York: Columbia University Press, 1960) in the chapter by Henry David on "Work, Women and Children," pp. 180–198; and Elizabeth Herzog, *Children of Working Mothers* (Washington, D. C.: U. S. Department of Health, Education and Welfare, Children's Bureau Publication #382, 1960); and most recently, a volume of research papers on the employed mother by F. Ivan Nye and Lois W. Hoffman, *The Employed Mother in America* (Chicago: Rand McNally, 1963).

5. Marian Radke Yarrow, Phyllis Scott, Louise de Leeuw, and Christine Heinig, "Child-rearing in Families of Working and Non-working Mothers," *Sociometry*, 25 (June, 1962), 122–140.

6. Only in recent years has there been a shift in the discussion and research on maternal employment: investigators have begun to explore the *positive* effects of maternal employment. For example, Urie Bronfenbrenner has suggested that employed mothers may have a positive effect upon adolescent children by giving them a chance to develop responsibility for their own behavior—Urie Bronfenbrenner, "Family Structure and Personality Development: Report of Progress" (Ithaca, New York: Cornell University, Department of Child Development and Family Relationships, 1958 (mimeographed). Ruth Hartley has suggested that the working mother may have "stretching effects" upon a child's perceptions and social concepts—Ruth E. Hartley, "What Aspects of Child Behavior Should be Studied in Relation to Maternal Employment," *Research Issues Related to the Effects of Maternal Employment on Children* (New York: Social Science Research Center, The Pennsylvania State University, 1961), p. 48.

7. A. I. Rabin, "Infants and Children under Conditions of 'Intermittent' Mothering in the Kibbutz," *American Journal of Orthopsychiatry*, 28 (1958), 577–584; Rabin, "Personality Maturity of Kibbutz and Non-Kibbutz Children as Reflected in Rorschach Findings," *Journal of Projective Techniques*, 21 (1957), 148–153; Rabin, "Attitudes of Kibbutz Children to Family and Parents," *American Journal of Orthopsychiatry*, 29 (1959), 172–179; Rabin, "Some Psychosexual Differences between Kibbutz and Non-Kibbutz Israeli Boys," *Journal of Projective Techniques*, 22 (1958), 328–332; H. Faigin, "Social Behavior of Young Children in the Kibbutz," *Journal of Abnormal and Social Psychology*, 56 (1958), 117–129. A good overview of these studies can be found in David Rapaport, "The Study of Kibbutz Education and its Bearing on the Theory of Development," *American Journal of Orthopsychiatry*, 28 (1958), 587–599.

8. This passivity and softness in American young people has been noted in the following works: David Riesman, Introduction to Edgar Friedenberg, *The Vanishing Adolescent* (Boston: Beacon Press, 1959); Paul Goodman, *Growing Up Absurd* (New York: Random House, 1960); Marjorie K. McCorquodale, "What They Will Die for in Houston," *Harper's*, October, 1961; the *Dædalus* issue on *Youth: Change and Challenge*, Winter 1962. The White House attempt in recent years to revitalize physical education has been in part a response to the distressing signs of muscular deterioration and physical passivity of American youth.

9. Edward A. Strecker, *Their Mothers' Sons* (Philadelphia: Lippincott, 1946).

10. Friedenberg, *The Vanishing Adolescent.*

11. Numerous authors have analyzed the effect of women's focus on their children as their chief achievement: John Spiegel, "New Perspectives in the Study of the Family," *Marriage and Family Living,* 16 (February, 1954), 4–12; Bruno Bettelheim, "Growing Up Female," *Harper's,* October, 1962. The effects of such exclusive maternal focus on children upon relations with married children are shown in: Marvin Sussman, "Family Continuity: Selective Factors which Affect Relationships between Families at Generational Levels," *Marriage and Family Living,* 16 (May, 1954), 112–130; Paul Wallin, "Sex Differences in Attitudes toward In-Laws," *American Journal of Sociology,* 59 (1954), 466–469; Harvey Locke, *Predicting Adjustment in Marriage* (New York: Holt, 1951); Evelyn M. Duvall, *In-Laws: Pro and Con* (New York: Associated Press, 1954); and Frances Jerome Woods, *The American Family System* (New York: Harper and Brothers, 1959), pp. 265–266. These authors discuss the strains with mothers-in-law stemming from too exclusive a focus of women on their children and their subsequent difficulty in "releasing" their children when they are grown.

12. See Margaret Cussler's profile of the "volunteer executive" in her study *The Woman Executive* (New York: Harcourt, Brace, 1958), pp. 111–118.

13. Myrdal and Klein, *Women's Two Roles: Home and Work,* pp. 33–64; National Manpower Council, *Womanpower* (New York: Columbia University Press, 1957); Florence Kluckhohn, *The American Family: Past and Present and America's Women* (Chicago: The Delphian Society, 1952), p. 116; and Rose Goldsen et al., *What College Students Think* (Princeton: D. Van Nostrand, 1960), pp. 46–59, 81–96.

14. Florence Kluckhohn, "Variations in Basic Values of Family Systems," in Norman W. Bell and Ezra F. Vogel, *A Modern Introduction to the Family* (Glencoe, Illinois: The Free Press, 1960), pp. 304–316; and George Gallup and Evan Hill, "The American Woman," *The Saturday Evening Post,* December 22, 1962, pp. 15–32.

15. Talcott Parsons, *Essays in Sociological Theory Pure and Applied* (Glencoe, Illinois: The Free Press, 1949), pp. 222–224 and 243–246.

16. Henry C. Lajewski, *Child Care Arrangements of Full-Time Working Mothers* (Washington, D. C.: U. S. Department of Health, Education and Welfare, Children's Bureau Publication No. 378, 1959); and Herzog, *Children of Working Mothers.*

17. William Whyte, *Organization Man* (New York: Simon and Schuster, 1956); Robert Wood, *Suburbia, Its People and Their Politics* (Boston: Houghton Mifflin, 1959); John Keats, *The Crack in the Picture Window* (Boston: Houghton Mifflin, 1956); A. C. Spectorsky, *The Exurbanites* (Philadelphia: J. B. Lippincott, 1955); and Nanette E. Scofield, "Some Changing Roles of Women in Suburbia: A Social Anthropological Case Study," *Transactions of the New York Academy of Sciences,* 22 (April, 1960), 6.

18. Eric Erikson, *Childhood and Society* (New York: W. W. Norton, 1950).

ESTHER PETERSON

Working Women

IN TODAY's plethora of popular writings about the American woman the spotlight shines most brightly on the suburban housewife, the college-trained woman and the professional. Very little light is shed on the great majority of America's 25 million working women.

These women are not among the pacesetters. They lack the economic security of the highly educated professional woman and the well-to-do wife of a junior executive. To them a job is vital, and all too often economic pressures are so great that they accept whatever employment they can get with little regard to personal choice. Their fortunes fluctuate with the state of the nation's economy. If it grows rapidly enough to utilize the kinds of work they can do and to absorb their growing numbers, they will probably have some leeway in choosing a job. If the economy is sluggish, however, their prospects are bleak. For those who are unskilled the future holds very little promise, for low-skill jobs are not expanding, even when the economy is strong. At worst these women will become part of the hard core of poverty which persists in the midst of an expanding economy.

Women, of course, have always had a role in the economic productivity of the nation. Before the coming of the machine they worked in their homes to produce the food and clothing which their families needed, and they reared the children, nursed the sick and took care of the aged. Farm wives helped in the fields and barns, and tradesmen's wives were often found in the family shop. But as the country became more industrialized many home tasks were taken over by commercial enterprise. Mass production made it easier and often cheaper to purchase the family's needs than to rely on home production. This meant that the family's greatest need was cash income to buy processed foods and manufactured goods. Because the new factory system needed workers, women and even children were encouraged to seek employment.

But the greatest influx of women into the work force came in time of war. During the Civil War, for instance, women left their homes to work as teachers, nurses and seamstresses who made the clothing and other articles required by the military. World War I saw women going into factories and munitions plants, acquiring new skills such as those of assembler and inspector, and taking over some of the clerical and sales jobs formerly done by men. World War II widened the scope of women's employment even further and set a new high for the number of women employed. Women dropped out of the labor force, to some extent, when men returned to their jobs at the end of the war, but the number of working women remained greater than it had been in the prewar period and it continued to climb, as indicated by the table below:

Table 1. Women in the Labor Force
(Selected years)

Year	Women workers (14 years and over)		
	Number	*Percent of all workers*	*Percent of all women*
	RECENT HIGHLIGHTS[1]		
April 1962	24,052,000	34	36
Start of sixties (April 1960)	23,239,000	33	36
Mid-fifties (April 1955)	20,154,000	31	34
Korean war (April 1953)	19,296,000	31	33
Pre-Korea (April 1950)	18,063,000	29	32
Postwar (April 1947)	16,320,000	28	30
World War II (April 1945)	19,570,000	36	37
Pre-World War II (March 1940)	13,840,000	25	28
	LONG-TERM TRENDS[2]		
1930 (April)	10,396,000	22	24
1920 (January)	8,229,000	20	23
1900 (June)	4,999,000	18	20
1890 (June)	3,704,000	17	18

[1] "Current Population Reports" for civilian labor force.
[2] Decennial census for total labor force, including Armed Forces.
Source: U.S. Department of Labor, Bureau of Labor Statistics; and U.S. Department of Commerce, Bureau of the Census.

In the period 1947–1962 women have counted for about three-fifths of the entire labor force increase. The number of women workers rose by 7.6 million as compared to 4.1 million for men. The proportion of all women in the labor force rose from 31 to 37 per cent and the number of married women with husbands present increased from 6.7 to 13.5 million, accounting for 55 per cent of the total labor force growth. There were other trends developing in our society as more and more women became a part of the labor force. The advanced technology demanded training and skill, and women sought education in greater numbers. As their sphere widened beyond the home they became more aware of social and economic problems, and having won the vote they took more interest in politics and public life. It was inevitable that these many and varying forces should contrive new patterns of life for the American woman, patterns which contrast sharply with her way of life in the nineteenth century.

Married or single, a woman's course through life at the turn of the century was almost as sure as death and taxes, and marriage was the determining factor. Working women were, in general, single women or those who were widowed, divorced or separated from their husbands, and who had to support themselves and, in all probability, their families. Married women devoted their time to home and children and "good works" in the church or community, if there was time.

The young woman who entered the work force seldom had any intention of remaining long. As soon as "Mr. Right" came along she handed in her resignation, put the finishing touches on her hope chest and made plans for the wedding. After the honeymoon she settled down to devote her life to the physical, intellectual and spiritual needs of her family. Only the tragedy of penniless widowhood or a broken marriage could drive her back into the labor market. The woman who did not marry was apt to be an object of pity. If her family could support her, she filled in her time with cultural pursuits or volunteer work in the community. Sometimes she shared the home of a married sister or brother and helped keep the house and raise the children. If she had to be self-supporting—or preferred to be—she found a job in one or another of the few fields approved for women and worked as long as she was able.

Today there is a shifting of patterns so that a woman can no longer be sure of the course her life will take. Often she is brought up to expect that she will follow in the footsteps of her mother and grandmother, with marriage, children and homemaking filling her life, but more and more unforeseen events, new plans and ideas, new economic pressures change her expectations. As a result it is impossible to make a prediction for an individual woman. However, in current trends we can see three major patterns in women's lives.

Single women are no longer the predominant group in the female labor force. In March, 1962, only 5,481,000 or 23 per cent of women workers were single,[1] as compared to 6,710,000 in 1940.[2] Those who enter the work force before they are 20 years of age and remain unmarried will probably work for about 40 years.[3] Because the majority of single women workers are under 25 years of age, many of them employed in entry clerical positions, there are relatively more single women than women with other marital status in clerical jobs. The percentage of women in professional and technical positions also is higher for single women. This may be attributed to the fact that many single women with considerable education and work experience are more likely to qualify for these jobs than are other women. The continuity of their lives in the work force also is a factor here.

The percentage of widowed, divorced or separated women in the work force is also relatively small. This group comprised 21 per cent of the women working in 1962 and numbered 5,012,000.[4] Their work pattern is fairly comparable to that of single women.

The largest group of women in our society, of course, is made up of married women living with their husbands. Typically they work for about four years after leaving school and then quit work when they marry or when the first child is born. Many married women seek employment once their youngest child enters school. For some this means a return to the work force after an absence of eight or ten years. For others, working outside the home is a brand new venture. In either case, if they do take a job at age 30 and have no more children, they can expect to average 23 years of work. While married women workers totaled 13,485,000 in March, 1962, and made up 56 per cent of the female work force, they represented only one-third of all married women.[5] It seems clear that despite concern in many quarters over the number of wives and mothers in the work force, we are still far from a situation in which most women work outside the home during their child-bearing and child-rearing years.

An examination of the factors which have contributed to the

147

changing patterns in the lives of women reveals that they are related to other changes in the society—the change from a predominantly rural culture to an urban society, the change from simple small-scale production methods to the mass production which mechanization has made possible, the change from a society in which the home was self-sufficient and self-supporting to one in which the home is dependent upon all facets of the economy for the goods and services essential to daily living. There is another factor which has a direct bearing on the number of years which a woman may have free for activities other than homemaking; that is the tendency toward early marriage. Between 1890 and 1962 the median age of marriage dropped from 22.0 to 20.3 years for women and from 26.1 to 22.7 years for men.[6]

One development from these trends has been that as science and technology advanced, women gained not only extra hours but added years in their life span, hours and years to give to activities outside their homes. Advanced medical science has given the American woman two gifts of great import: one greater longevity for herself, the other a greater chance of survival for her children. The girl baby born in 1900 had a life expectancy of 48 years, but one born at the end of World War II could expect, on the average, to live 69 years;[7] for today's newborn girl the figure is about 73 years.[8] And so, we might say, the twentieth century has given women approximately 25 years of added living time for whatever they choose to do with it. Today the average woman faces motherhood with a sense of security for herself and her infant. Modern medical science has developed techniques for the care of both mother and child in the prenatal and postnatal periods which have taken many of the old risks out of childbirth. In 1900, 145 out of every 1,000 infants died before they were a year old.[9] Today that figure has been reduced to 25 in 1,000.[10]

Mechanization and automation have given the American woman another bonus in time. Many of the chores once done in the home are now the concern of commercial ventures ranging from giant industries to Chinese laundries. But mechanization has come to the kitchen as well, and a battery of automatic appliances do everything from warm the baby's milk to store in deep freeze a season's needs of foodstuffs. All this means extra time which the homemaker can spend in a variety of activities.

Today husbands and fathers are sharing more and more in homemaking tasks. This may be due in part to the trend which followed

World War II and which found young men, newly out of service, returning to school to finish their educations. If they married, their wives might also be students or might take jobs to help meet expenses. At any rate, with both partners away from home part of the day, it was natural for them to share household tasks. A 1962 survey by a manufacturer of stainless steel sinks, for example, revealed that almost three-fourths of America's men help with the dishes, at least occasionally.

In combination, these trends mean that women marry early, and because infant deaths are relatively rare, they complete their families and see their last child off to school while they are still relatively young women, often by the time they are 30 years of age. With the likelihood of added years in the latter part of their lives, and with their homemaking tasks lightened, these women may well have another thirty or forty healthful, vigorous years ahead of them.

The amount of formal education which women receive has a distinct bearing on the patterns into which their lives fall. Obviously, the better their education the better their job opportunities. It is also true that their education has a strong impact on their interest in working and the types of employment they seek.

It is a serious matter, then, that among today's female population less than half of all women 25 years of age and over are high school graduates. Illiteracy is also a factor to be reckoned with. In 1960 there were almost 4 million adult women with less than five years of schooling. Job opportunities for these women are severely limited, for they cannot read simple instructions or fill out necessary forms. Job training is impossible until they learn to read and write. In their homes they are handicapped by an inability to take part in the education of their children or improve their household skills through the normal channels of reading and study. Scarcely better off, as far as job opportunities are concerned, are the 11.5 million women who have started but failed to finish high school.[11]

Young women today are receiving more formal education than they did at the beginning of the twentieth century, but their record as compared to men's is better at the lower academic levels than at the higher. The 966,000 girls who graduated from high school in 1962 constituted 53 per cent of the graduating class for that year, but only 43 per cent of the college entrants in 1962 were girls.[12] Nor do as many women as men finish college. Only one in three of the bachelor's and master's degrees conferred by universities and col-

149

leges go to women, and only one in ten of the Ph.D.'s.[13] These ratios represent a significant decrease since the 1930's, when two out of five bachelor's and master's degrees and one out of seven Ph.D.'s were earned by women.[14]

While women are not keeping pace with men in the field of academic achievement, there has been a dramatic growth in the number of women going to college. From 1920 to 1960 college enrollments of women more than quadrupled. In 1920 there were fewer than one-third of a million women college students;[15] in 1960 the figure was one and one-quarter million. By 1965 we expect an increase to one and three-quarters million, and by 1970 to two and one-third million.[16] In 1920, 16,642 bachelor's degrees were earned by women;[17] in 1950 there were 104,000 and in 1960 approximately 140,000—more than an eightfold growth in 40 years. In 1970 the figure is expected to reach 276,000.[18]

Another factor which has influenced the changing patterns of women's lives has been a widening of the choice of jobs open to them. Women's earliest job opportunities were in the kinds of work they were accustomed to doing at home—nursing, tailoring and dressmaking, teaching and domestic service. Then as the country shifted from an agricultural to an industrial economy, populations shifted from rural areas to urban centers where women found employment in the cotton and woolen mills, canning and food processing plants and garment factories.

Industrial production gave rise to a growth of commerce and trade which required vast amounts of paper work, and women found ample opportunities in clerical work. The invention of the typewriter, which many predicted would reduce job opportunities, actually increased them. At the same time women found employment in sales occupations and the service industries. Many of the jobs for which women were recruited during World Wars I and II remained open to them when the wars ended, giving women an established place in such new industries as aircraft, plastics, atomic energy and many others, and in the armed forces.

The 1960 census showed that there were some women workers in each of the 479 individual occupations listed, but that is not to say that all fields were readily open to women. There is still considerable prejudice on the part of employers, educators and women themselves as to what is "men's work" and what is "women's work." The very fact that most newspapers divide their classified ads into "Help Wanted—Men" and "Help Wanted—Women" attests to this fact. When this view is held by school counselors and teachers, there is little likelihood that young women will be alerted to the new fields for which they might have aptitudes.

This attitude extends to many apprenticeship programs in the skilled occupations. In 1954 a count of female names listed among registered apprentices in seven states indicated that fewer than 1 per cent of the group were women.[19] The small number of women apprentices is attributed to the fact that few trades having apprentices hire many women, either because of physical requirements or because of the length of training required. Two exceptions are bookbinding and cosmetology. Women are sometimes apprenticed as dressmakers, dental technicians, fur finishers, fabric cutters, tailoresses and printers.

Automation, of course, is making it possible for more women to do more jobs by eliminating heavy lifting, dangerous working conditions, and other difficulties. The problem is to change the habits of thought which do not even consider women for jobs in particular industries or plants simply because women have never been employed there. As President Lyndon B. Johnson said (September 24, 1962, Washington, D. C.), "Most of our problems arise out of ignorance and a desire to avoid change. This is what is happening with the problem of equal opportunity for women. Modern technology has created new patterns of production which rely much more upon brains and nimbleness than upon brawn and endurance. We have at the same time developed a labor supply to fill that demand, but somehow we have failed to bring together the expanding needs of our productive system for intelligent and skilled workers and women with the necessary qualifications."

Most women, like most men, work because of economic necessity. This is true of the married woman worker as well as the single woman, contrary to a common belief that married women usually work to fill up their spare time or for "pin money." This nineteenth-century thinking fails to look at twentieth-century facts. The latest Bureau of the Census figures show that half of the men in the population in 1963 had incomes of less than $4,372.[20] Half of the nation's 47 million families had incomes under $5,956, including the contributions of wives and children.[21] One out of every five families had incomes below $3,000, two out of five below $5,000, and more than three out of five below $7,000.[22]

How much of this constitutes poverty? This is a difficult question because there is no absolute measure for subsistence and adequacy, but recent estimates have placed at 30 to 50 million the number of families existing in substandard living conditions. The taxable limit for income under federal tax laws taken as a criterion provides a general picture of America's low-income families. For instance, in 1959 it was estimated that almost one-fifth of the families, with nearly one-fourth of the nation's children, had low incomes—that is, less than $1,325 for a mother and child; less than $2,675 for a married couple with two children and less than $4,000 for a family of six.[23]

In terms of living, these low incomes mean a lack of nutritious food, overcrowded housing in rundown neighborhoods, school dropouts due to lack of proper clothing and books, and little or no medical care. Michael Harrington sums it up in his book *The Other America:* "The character of poverty has changed, and it has become more deadly for the young. It is no longer associated with immigrant groups with high aspirations; it is now identified with those whose social existence makes it more and more difficult to break out into the larger society." [24]

It is little wonder that one-third of the nation's married women work, accounting for over one-half of all women workers. They numbered 13,485,000 in March, 1962.[25] Married women contribute about 35 to 40 per cent of the family's total income when they work full time and about 15 to 20 per cent if they are part-time workers.[26]

It is no surprise, either, that there were 8.8 million mothers in the work force in 1962. The family's economic need has a direct bearing on whether a mother goes out to work. For example, 1962 statistics show that one in four mothers with children under six years of age worked if the husband earned less than $3,000, but only one in eight if the husband earned $7,000 or over.[27] Nevertheless, it seems evident that mothers with very young children are reluctant to work, for only one out of five mothers with children under three years of age is in the labor force.[28]

The economic reasons for which mothers work go beyond providing food, shelter and other bare necessities for their families. One is to provide a sound education for their children. Recent figures provided by the University of Massachusetts revealed that the typical income of its students' families was $7,600, including salaries of both father and mother. More than 40 per cent of the mothers reported some earnings, the average being $2,500.

There is still another aspect of the problem of economic pressures on the family, presented by the large number of young men and women who will not go on to college. The 26 million young people who are expected to enter the labor market in this decade will find fewer unskilled entry jobs and a demand for higher educational qualifications.[29] Until these young people acquire needed skills they will have difficulty finding employment, and their families will have to maintain them for longer periods of time. This may well require the combined incomes of father and mother.

I have gone, in some detail, into the economic pressures which impel wives and mothers to work. But I would not wish to imply that these are or should be the only reasons. Some women feel they can make their greatest contribution to society by using their talents in paid employment. This is particularly true of the woman who has had a good education and has, perhaps, prepared for a profession. Certainly today's homemaking chores are no great challenge to such a woman. Her sense of boredom and frustration is likely to heighten as her children go off to school and there is even less need of her in the home. Paid employment may be the solution for these women.

I cannot agree with those who would try to raise a moral issue concerning whether or not a mother should work outside the home. Surely the question here is one which she, in counsel with her family, must settle on an individual, personal basis. It is an area in which she has every right to exercise her freedom of choice. If the decision is that she should work, then the tenets of our democratic way of life dictate that her choice be respected and that she have the same opportunities and rights afforded the male worker. Actually we have, in my opinion, moved beyond that point in history where a woman has to choose between a home and a career. Today she can have both—often at different intervals in her life, sometimes simultaneously.

There are other groups of women for whom the need to work is unquestioned. Four and one-half million women are the heads of their families, and half of this group is working.[30] Many of these are married women who have been divorced or separated. Others are widows and some are single women. Most single women, once they leave school, support themselves today. In addition many support parents, younger brothers and sisters or other relatives. Because some divorced women and widows tend to list themselves as single in census reports, it is difficult to determine the exact number of never-married women supporting dependents. The 1960 Census shows 486,997 single; 701,576 divorced and 2,093,073 widowed heads of families.

While women are represented in almost every occupation one could name, most jobs that women hold are in the low-paid categories. In April, 1962, three-fifths of all women workers were in clerical, service and operative jobs. The fourth largest group was professional workers, including teachers; private household, sales and managerial workers followed in that order.

The distribution of women workers by occupation differs from that of men, as the following chart indicates:

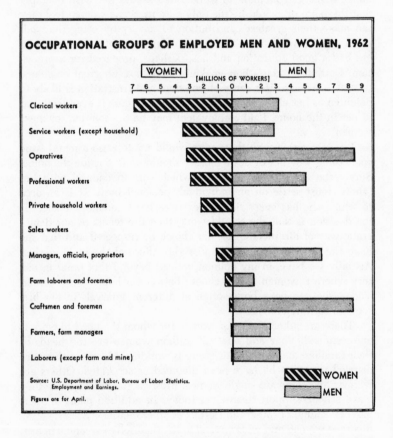

Median wages and salaries for these occupations show a marked discrepancy which indicates that women also receive less for their work than men do, as can be seen in the table below:

Table 2. Wage or Salary Income for Selected Occupations: 1960 and 1939

| | Year-round full-time workers | | | |
| | Women | | Men | |
Occupational group	1960	1939	1960	1939
Professional workers...............	$4,384	$1,277	$6,848	$2,100
Managers, officials, proprietors......	4,173	1,218	7,241	2,254
Clerical workers...................	3,586	1,072	5,247	1,564
Operatives........................	2,970	742	4,977	1,268
Sales workers.....................	2,428	745	5,755	1,451
Service workers (except household)...	2,418	607	4,089	1,019
Private-household workers..........	1,133	339	......	549

Source: U.S. Department of Commerce, Bureau of the Census: "Current Population Reports," P–60, No. 37.

In the light of these figures, it is not surprising that the median income for women workers is well below that for men. In 1962 the figure for all women workers was $1,342 as against $4,372 for all men. For year-round, full-time workers the median income of women was $3,458 and for men, $5,826.[31] This gap is partly the result of a difference in occupational patterns; the kind of work performed by women is traditionally low paid.

Recent studies made by the U.S. Civil Service Commission demonstrate a situation in federal employment that probably has parallels in many private companies. In the federal service, the number of women employees peaks in grades 3 and 4, in which pay ranges from $3,880 to $5,475 in 1964. Well over half of all women employees work at this level. In addition, almost 25 per cent work in grades 5 and 6 ($4,690 to $6,810). By contrast, the greatest number of men—about one in four—have posts in grades 9 and 11 ($7,030 to $10,650).[32] Where levels of education and years of service are comparable, women are mostly in lower grades than men. Among those in the higher grades, more women than men have a college education, and the women are somewhat older.

The future is more promising for women in the federal service. In July, 1962, federal agencies were required by presidential directive to make all appointments, and to select employees for advancement and training, without regard to the sex of the worker. There has been marked improvement since in the number of women hired from the Federal Service Entrance Examination, which is taken by many college students. In the calendar years 1962, 17.3 per cent of the appointments from that register were women as compared to 14.9 per cent in the period October, 1960 to October, 1961.[33] A survey by the Civil Service Commission revealed, however, that there is still considerable prejudice against women workers in high-grade federal jobs, and the President's Commission on the Status of Women recommended that efforts be continued to ensure that advancement of employees is based solely on merit.

The income that women receive is, of course, determined to a large extent by the amount of education they have. Of the women with income in 1961, 5,561,000 who had graduated from elementary school had a median income of only $950; 11,921,000 who had graduated from high school had a median income of $1,938. For 2,050,000 college graduates with no graduate study, the median income was $3,179, and for 741,000 with 5 years or more of college it was $4,694.[34]

The greatest expansion in women's employment over the past two decades has been in the clerical field, although the number of women employed in the 11 broad categories reported by the Bureau of the Census increased in every field except farm work. The percentage of women workers in some categories declined or remained the same. For instance the number of professional women workers increased from about 1.6 million in 1940 to 2.9 million in 1962. However, they constituted 13 per cent of all women workers in both years. The number of women operatives also increased— from nearly 2.2 million in 1940 to over 3.3 million in 1962. But in 1940 they represented 18 per cent of the female work force, and in 1962 only 15 per cent. On the other hand, clerical women workers increased from 2,530,000 in 1940 to 6,948,000 in 1962, while their percentage distribution rose from 21 to 31 per cent of all employed women. While the number of women in private household work increased slightly, the percentage of all women workers in this type of work declined from 18 per cent in 1940 to 10 per cent in 1962.[35] It is clear from the table shown below that the trend of women's employment is away from unskilled, manual jobs toward those requiring a high degree of skill and a sound educational background.

Negro women, who constitute the largest minority in the United States, are also the lowest paid and the most disadvantaged group in the labor force.

A total of 2,455,000 Negro women were employed in 1960, as compared with 1,870,000 in 1950. They made up a majority, prob-

Table 3. Occupational Trend of Employed Women

Occupational group	Number of women (in thousands)			Percent distribution		
	1962	1950	1940	1962	1950	1940
All employed women.....	22,641	17,176	11,920	100	100	100
Professional workers........	2,941	1,862	1,570	13	11	13
Managers, officials, proprietors	1,148	941	450	5	5	4
Clerical workers............	6,948	4,539	2,530	31	26	21
Sales workers..............	1,685	1,516	830	7	9	7
Service workers (except household)...................	3,364	2,168	1,350	15	13	11
Operatives................	3,290	3,215	2,190	15	19	18
Private-household workers...	2,275	1,771	2,100	10	10	18
Craftsmen, foremen.........	239	181	110	1	1	1
Farmers, farm managers.....	137	253 }	690	1 }	1 }	6
Farm laborers, foremen......	504	663 }		2 }	4 }	
Laborers (except farm and mine)..................	112	68	100	(1)	(1)	1

1 Less than 0.5 percent.
Source: U.S. Department of Labor, Bureau of Labor Statistics and U.S. Department of Commerce, Bureau of the Census.

ably 94 per cent, of the nearly 3 million nonwhite women workers in the labor force in 1960. This number, which comprises both the employed and those looking for work, represents a 35 per cent increase over the number of nonwhite women workers in 1950. One out of eight women workers was nonwhite both in 1950 and in 1960.[36]

The percentage of Negro women in the labor force has for many decades been greater than that of white women. In 1900, 41 per cent of the nonwhite women were gainfully employed, whereas only 17 per cent of the white women were in the labor force.[37] By 1963, although there were far more whites and far fewer nonwhites among women workers, the proportion of nonwhites with a job was still a fourth greater than the proportion of whites.[38] Negro mothers also tend to work outside the home to a greater extent than do white mothers. In 1960, 31 per cent of nonwhite married women living with their husbands and having children under six years of age were in the labor force. This compared with 18 per cent for white women.[39]

The President's Commission on the Status of Women called a special consultation on the problems of Negro women in April, 1963 to determine their particular problems and the place they now occupy in our American culture. It was the consensus of this group of 22 persons with special interest in the Negro that the fact of racial discrimination is basic to every problem in the life of the Negro. His lack of opportunity for education and employment is particularly pertinent to this study.

Because it is often easier for the Negro woman to secure work than it is for her husband, the Negro family tends to be matriarchal. Often the Negro woman earns more than her husband does, and sometimes she is the only wage earner in the family. Nevertheless, according to the Bureau of the Census, the median earned income of nonwhite men is higher than for nonwhite women. The following table tells the story of the differences in earnings from 1939 to 1960 between nonwhite men and women and between white and nonwhite workers:

Table 4. Median Annual Wage and Salary Incomes of White and Nonwhite Persons, 1939, 1947, 1957, 1960

	1939	1947	1957	1960
Males:				
White.........................	$1,112	$2,357	$4,396	$5,137
Nonwhite......................	460	1,279	2,436	3,075
Nonwhite as a percent of white....	41.4	54.3	55.4	59.9
Females:				
White.........................	$676	$1,269	$2,240	$2,537
Nonwhite......................	246	432	1,019	1,276
Nonwhite as a percent of white....	36.4	34.0	45.5	50.3

Source: U.S. Department of Commerce, Bureau of the Census.

It will be noted that while the earnings of nonwhite workers remain considerably below those of white workers, there has been some progress. The increases achieved by nonwhites from 1939 to 1960 were a good deal greater percentagewise than were the increases in earnings of whites. For instance, among all workers, the earnings of nonwhite men increased 568 per cent as against 364 per cent for white men. Among women the increase was 275 per cent for whites and 419 per cent for nonwhites.[40] The rate of increase for nonwhites is attributed in large part to a shift of Negro population to urban areas where higher rates are paid for unskilled and semiskilled jobs, and to the fact that the educational level of the Negro also is now higher.

Negroes as a group have shown an interest in and an appreciation for education, and they have made notable advances, especially in higher education. In 1950 only 26 per cent of the nonwhite population 25 years of age and over had attended high school or college as compared to 53 per cent of the white population, but by 1960 the percentage was about 40 per cent for nonwhites and 62 per cent for whites.

A study of Negro women by Dr. Jeanne L. Noble of Teachers College, Columbia University, gives some insight into the educational motivation of Negro women. She found that in general they based their educational choice on vocational opportunity. The Negro girl who felt she had a chance to become a teacher, majored in education. But she seldom went on to higher study if her educational and employment status threatened the status of her husband.

Negro women holding college degrees outnumbered Negro men college graduates. Latest available figures on the number of college degrees earned by nonwhites are for the year 1957–1958. They show that women received 6,878 bachelor's and 829 master's degrees. Men received 4,915 bachelor's and 502 master's degrees.[41] Because highly educated Negro women outnumber Negro men with comparable educations, the women often marry below their educational level. This situation may give rise to jealousy and insecurity on the part of the husband, particularly if the wife earns more than her husband; the family may dissolve and as a result the matriarchal family pattern is perpetuated.

The employment picture for the Negro woman is a complex one in which job opportunities are more likely to be available at the lowest economic level or at the professional level, with very few chances for employment in between. Jobs in sales, clerical work and many skilled occupations are still often closed to Negroes, and this situation, of course, discourages Negro girls from training for these fields. Nevertheless, the number employed as clerical, professional, sales and miscellaneous service workers has increased considerably since 1940, when less than one-fifth of all Negro women workers were in these occupations. In 1960 more than one-third of all employed Negro women were in these jobs.[42] The largest number of nonwhite women in 1963 was in private household work, which employed 1,026,000. The second highest number, 696,000, were service workers other than household, and in third place were the 391,000 operatives.[43]

The group consulting with the President's Commission on the Status of Women felt that steps should be taken to upgrade the occupation of household service, improving the workers' skills on one hand and improving working conditions on the other. It was suggested that facilities be made available to train household workers in such skills as using modern labor-saving devices and cleaning and caring for new types of fabrics and plastics. Such training might also develop skills and technical knowledge which could qualify workers to advance to jobs in allied service industries. The group also felt that counseling and guidance were particularly important for the Negro child. Because of old patterns of discrimination against Negro workers, parents and counselors often fail to give girls the encouragement they need to prepare for jobs other than those traditionally open to their race.

Vocational guidance for youth and the promotion of job opportunities must go hand in hand if the status of Negroes is to improve and the nation is to have the benefit of their talents and skills. Much of the driving force and motivation will come from the Negro women.

The knowledge that there is a Federal Fair Labor Standards Act which puts a floor under wages for both men and women tends to lull many into thinking that the exploitation of women workers is part of the nation's picturesque past, but no more prevalent today than the bustle.

The bitter fact is that the Fair Labor Standards Act exempts millions of workers, many of them women, who are employed in hotels, motels, restaurants, laundries, nonprofit organizations and certain retail establishments. Further, the act applies only to those engaged in interstate commerce, and an estimated 6 million women who are employed in intrastate occupations are not protected by either federal or state laws. There are minimum wage laws in 33 states, Puerto Rico, and the District of Columbia. Most of these apply primarily to trade, service and production industries. Seventeen states have no such laws,[44] and in four of the 33 states there are only token laws. In the final analysis we find that millions of low-paid workers, many of them women, who most need protection are without it and earnings of less than $1 an hour are all too common. It is estimated that federal and state minimum wage laws cover less than 10 million women workers.

It is difficult to realize that in our affluent society some persons still work for less than a living wage. But President Johnson reminded us in his State of the Union Message on January 8, 1964 that one-fifth of all American families have incomes too small to meet their basic needs. And my mail is a constant reminder. One letter was from a group of girls who worked in a restaurant and bar. Their duties included putting out the set-ups, fixing menus, taking orders, serving, cleaning up and resetting tables, cleaning the bar and, at the end of their shift, sweeping the floor. These women received nothing in wages—just tips, which were pitifully small. In the same state, which had no minimum wage law, store clerks reported earnings of from 30 to 75 cents an hour.

The Department of Labor's "Industry Wage Survey" in 1961, which covered 27 cities, revealed that 13 per cent of the pantrywomen in eating and drinking places and 19 per cent of the chambermaids in hotels and motels earned less than $1 an hour. In one city the average hourly rate for chambermaids was 46 cents; in another dishwashers also averaged 46 cents an hour. A nationwide survey by the Bureau of Labor Statistics in June, 1962 indicated that about half of the 2.5 million women in nonsupervisory jobs in retail establishments earned less than $1.25 an hour, and that about a tenth, or almost 300,000, less than $1. Of the last group, about 100,000 earned less than 75 cents an hour. With these figures before it, the President's Commission on the Status of Women recommended extension of the Fair Labor Standards Act to cover employment subject to federal jurisdiction but not now covered. It also urged raising the present minimum as rapidly as possible. At the state level it was proposed that state laws be improved to benefit workers not covered by the federal law.

The pattern of an 8-hour day and a 40-hour week for both men and women has resulted from provisions of the Federal Fair Labor Standards Act, which requires premium pay for work in excess of 40 hours. Further, most states have legal limitations on the number of hours women may work in a day or a week. However, there is no legal maximum in 7 states and Puerto Rico. In 4 states the maximum is a 60-hour week; in 14 states over 48 but under 60 hours are permitted; and in 24 states and the District of Columbia the maximum is a 48-hour week. One state permits a 44-hour week.[45] Nationwide, in early 1963 the average work week in private employment, except in agriculture and household service, was 40 hours. About 71 per cent of all employees worked 40 hours or less; but 13.5 per cent worked 49 hours or more.[46] The President's Commission on the Status of Women concluded that "the best way to discourage excessive hours for all workers is by broad and effective minimum wage coverage, both Federal and State, providing overtime of at least time and a half the regular rate for all hours in excess of 8 a day or 40 a week." [47] Until this goal is achieved, the commission recommended, state legislation protecting women workers from excessive hours should be maintained, expanded and strengthened.

Because restrictions on the hours they may work often limit employment and advancement opportunities for executive, administrative and professional women, the commission felt that this group should be exempt from maximum hours regulations. It also recommended that flexibility be maintained, under proper safeguards, in laws regulating hours of work so that additional time could be worked where there was a demonstrated need.

Considerable other legislation has been developed in the past fifty years to protect women workers. However, state laws vary widely in such areas as health and safety measures, weightlifting, night work, industrial homework and maternity benefits. The Committee on Protective Legislation of the President's Commission on the Status of Women made an extensive study of existing and needed protection. In general its consensus was that, wherever practical, legislation affecting labor standards should benefit men as well as women. It recommended re-examination of statutes regulating weightlifting by women in the light of technological changes which have made it possible to use mechanical devices instead of muscles. Similarily, it was felt that laws applying to night work might be revised in cases where they put women employees at a disadvantage or where safe transportation home is available to women.

Two committtees of the President's Commission on the Status of Women considered the problem of maternity benefits for working women. The suggestion of the Committee on Social Insurance and Taxes was incorporated in the commission's recommendation that "paid maternity leave or comparable insurance benefits should be provided for women workers; employers, unions, and government should explore the best means of accomplishing this purpose." [48] The Committee on Protective Labor Legislation suggested, further, that state legislation be enacted to assure at least six months maternity leave without loss of re-employment and seniority rights.[49]

In summing up, it might be said that the greatest weakness in this nation's system of protective labor legislation is its limited coverage—the fact that it offers little to those segments of the work force most likely to be exploited and least able to help themselves. In his book *Women and Work in America*,[50] Robert W. Smuts pinpoints the problem as it affects women:

In industry, women are more likely than men to work for marginal businesses characterized by small size, low capital investment, low profit margins, haphazard personnel practices, high employee turnover and low pay. Many thousands of women still work in such plants, making cheap clothing, costume jewelry, paper hats and party favors, inexpensive toys, picture frames, knickknacks, and similar products. Sometimes ignored by government and union alike, these are the plants where conditions are most likely to be reminiscent of the last century, even to the crudely lettered "Operators Wanted" sign on the door. Usually located in old buildings in run-down neighborhoods, they draw upon the least educated and neediest portion of the labor supply: Puerto Ricans, Negroes, Mexicans and poor white migrants from the rural South. . . . Largely because of the establishment of minimum standards, moreover, wages and working conditions in such businesses are generally not so far below average as they were in 1890. Nevertheless, women industrial workers still tend to be concentrated in the industries and occupations which pay the lowest wages.

In spite of their contributions to the national economy in periods of emergency, women have too often been considered as marginal workers and have been subjected to discriminations which have seriously hampered their advancement in the labor force.

Women's earnings have always lagged behind those of men, not only because they are more frequently employed in low-paying jobs but because they often are paid a lower rate for a job even when they are doing the same work as men.

In preparation for testimony on the Equal Pay bill the Women's Bureau of the Department of Labor made a study in 1963 of job orders filed with public employment offices in nine different cities. This survey confirmed the findings of similar studies made in different areas in 1962 and earlier. The bureau found 91 orders offering men higher wages or salaries than were offered to women for the same job. The orders covered a variety of occupations and industries. One offered $3,600 a year for a male clerk-typist and only $3,000 for a woman. Another, seeking an accounting clerk, quoted a rate of $1.80 for a man and $1.45 for a woman. Over one-half of the orders listed had wage differentials ranging from 11 to 25 per cent of the men's rate.

Other Department of Labor studies confirmed the pattern of discrimination in a wide range of jobs. In banking, for instance, it was found that men note tellers with less than five years' experience averaged from $5.50 to $31 a week more than women in the same classification.[51] In factory work average hourly rates for labelers and packers in one area were found to be $1.43 for women and $2.08 for men; hand or machine filler jobs averaged $1.45 for women and $2.14 for men. Many more instances could be quoted, but these few describe a situation which was prevalent when the Eighty-seventh Congress took up the question of equal pay for equal work.

Equal pay for women has been an issue in the United States since 1945, when the first bill seeking the same pay for men and women doing the same job was introduced in Congress. Throughout the years the equal pay principle was vigorously supported by women's organizations, church and social welfare groups, and labor organizations; but it was not until June, 1963 that legislation finally was enacted by the Eighty-eighth Congress, to become effective in June, 1964.

The Equal Pay Act of 1963 amends the Fair Labor Standards Act to require equal pay for equal work for men and women employed in establishments covered by that act. This is limited coverage, indeed, but it is a beginning, and it does establish as national policy the principle of paying a rate for the job regardless of the sex of the worker. During the nineteen years which preceded passage of the Equal Pay Act of 1963, opponents of the legislation put forth many arguments against it, arguments strong enough to convince Congress after Congress. Much of the opposition grew out of the fact that the issues were never clearly understood by the public, nor even by women themselves. And so it has taken nineteen years of public debate to bring the issues into focus.

Employers maintained that lower wages were in order for women because it costs more to employ them. They cited the cost of providing special restroom facilities for women as required by state laws; they claimed that women were absent more often and that they were in and out of the labor force more frequently than men. They maintained that women's production rates were not as great as men's, and they argued that women do not need the higher incomes received by men.

Supporters of the legislation had answers for all the objections. They pointed out that while state laws requiring sanitary and other facilities applied only to women, good labor relations practice dictated that high standards should apply equally to men and women. Complaints about women's absenteeism and "quit rates" were discounted.[52] A study by the Health Information Foundation of the University of Chicago's Graduate School of Business found that in 1960 the average days lost per person because of chronic illness were 3.1 for men and 2.6 for women.[53] The most recent Public Health Service survey found little difference between the absenteeism of men and women for illness and injury during 1960. The average for women was 5.6 days and for men 5.5 days.[54] It was pointed out that facts other than the sex of the worker entered into the problem of employee absenteeism. A Civil Service Commission study of sick leave records for federal employees in 1961 indicated that as salary and responsibility increased, the amount of time taken as sick leave diminished.[55]

In studying the overall averages of labor turnover for the period January, 1950 to January, 1955, the Department of Labor found that the average quit rates for the entire period were 24 per 1,000 women employees and 18 per 1,000 men employees. Nevertheless, here, as in the case of absenteeism, other factors were more significant in determining quit rates. Skilled, professional and managerial workers had lower quit rates than sales, service and unskilled workers.[56] Perhaps the fact that more women are employed in the less skilled jobs accounts in part for the generalization that they are less reliable as steady employees. Age was found to be another factor, with men and women 45 years of age and over more likely to remain on the job than younger men and women. Tenure on the job also was reflected in quit rates. Men and women workers with less than one year of service showed higher rates than those who had worked longer. All these variations underline the weaknesses of the generalization concerning quit rates of women workers.

It was also argued that there is no basis for the contention that women's production rates were lower than men's when jobs and working conditions were comparable. Further, it was shown that in many jobs women are more dexterous, faster and more accurate than men. In jobs where production rates count most, piece rates are usually paid so that the worker is paid for what he or she actually produces; but this should be at the same rate of pay for men and women. In the long run, of course, exploitation of women workers by paying them substandard wages tends to depress all wage rates, for men as well as women.

There are more subtle discriminations against women in the labor force, of course, and while the Equal Pay Act of 1963 may help them get more equitable pay on the jobs they now hold, it cannot assure that they will be considered on an equal basis with men for initial hiring or for promotion. In this area many of the same arguments used against equal pay are used against equality of opportunity. In addition, many employers still feel that men should play a dominant role in the economic world. The National Office Managers Association surveyed 1,900 firms and found that 65 per cent of those replying questioned the advisability of putting a woman in a supervisory position. Some felt that men would resent working for a woman, and others claimed that men would feel restricted in their actions and language.[57] Women are also denied advancement, particularly to executive positions, because employers feel that they are "too emotional." However, there is no evidence to show that a woman cries more often than a man "blows his stack."

An important deterrent to the hiring and advancement of women, particularly if on-the-job training is involved, is the fact that until they reach maturity they are likely to be in and out of the labor market as they marry and have children. It is argued that to give them training is a waste and that they are not too interested in promotion and added responsibility, particularly if they are combining homemaking and a job. It should be noted that this situation applies, for the most part, to young married women—that women who do not marry and those who return to the labor force when their families are raised tend to be interested in advancing their careers and usually remain on the same job longer than men.

The President's Commission on the Status of Women was concerned that women be afforded equal opportunity in hiring, training and promotion in private employment as well as in the federal service. It recommended that this principle be stated in an executive order and applied to work done under federal contract. It was thought that such an order would encourage employers to consider individual qualifications in hiring women rather than base judgments on outmoded attitudes about women workers.

Progress toward equal opportunity for women in employment has been slow, but there have been breakthroughs. This is particularly true in occupations where there is a shortage of skilled workers. Some employers, forced to hire women because men were not available, have found the innovation a successful one and are opening more doors to women workers. But if women are to take advantage of these opportunities, Americans are going to have to accept social changes and changes in attitudes which will make it possible for a woman to exercise the freedom of choice which should be hers by virtue of the democracy in which she lives.

New and imaginative ways must be found to adapt management practices and work schedules to make maximum use of the nation's womanpower. More and more, women are finding part-time work the solution to the problems encountered in trying to combine home-making and paid employment. In October, 1963 about 5.7 million women were working less than 35 hours a week. They constituted one-fourth of women workers in nonagricultural industries. Women most often employed part time include private household workers, farm workers, retail saleswomen, waitresses, beauty operators, practical nurses, typists, cashiers, telephone operators, teachers and professional nurses.

Greater opportunities for employment must be provided the mature woman. The number of women 45 years of age and over in the work force has more than doubled since 1947, and the average age of the working woman has risen to 41 years. However, many employers still raise barriers to their employment. The need here is twofold—to educate and train middle-aged women who seek paid employment, and to educate employers to the valuable potential of this segment of the nation's human resources.

Changes in thinking and planning are also necessary in the area of home-community relationships. The place of the employed wife and mother in the work force is well established, and as long as this country maintains its high standard of living, she is likely to remain in it. Society, then, has a responsibility, as President John F. Kennedy put it during the WGBH-TV program, "Prospects of Mankind," May 23, 1962, "to be sure that women are used as effectively as they can be to provide a better life for our people—in addition to meeting their primary responsibility, which is in the home."

This means that communities must offer more services to the family so as to ease the burden of the woman who works outside the home. "If the family is to continue to be the core institution of society, as it has been for many centuries," the report of the President's Commission on the Status of Women states, "new and expanded community services are necessary. Women can do a far more effective job as mothers and homemakers when communities provide appropriate resources and when they know how to use such resources for health, education, safety, recreation, child care, and counseling." [58]

Child-care facilities are a primary need, of course. These should be available not only for preschool children but for youngsters who need care after school hours. Tax relief also should be afforded parents who must pay for the care of their children during working hours. The President's Commission on the Status of Women recommended that the existing provisions for tax exemptions be liberalized. Family counseling, homemaker services and education in homemaking skills for inexperienced housewives are other aids which the community can provide.

Perhaps the most drastic changes in thinking and planning will be in the field of education, for women's foremost claim on society will be for educational opportunities geared to their multiple roles in modern society. The times demand a concept of education as a continuing thing, for men certainly, but for women especially. They require a revision of the conventional structure of education so that adults may resume education at whatever point they broke off their formal schooling.

The worker who trains for a particular occupation which he expects to follow all of his working life has a difficult time keeping abreast of new developments, techniques and knowledge which change the character of his work, if they do not make it obsolete. But even greater is the problem of the woman who may leave the work force for ten to fifteen years while she raises her family and then seeks to pick up where she left off in her work experience. She will find, more often than not, that her skills are rusty and her knowledge outdated unless she has had an opportunity for continuing education during her homemaking years.

Certainly she will not be able to find her way through the complexities of choosing the right education and the right job unless she has the advantage of expert counseling. She must know what the demands upon her will be, what choices she will have and what opportunities she may expect in the world of work. That is why counseling should not be confined to the young. The woman in the home looking forward to the second half of her life, when she will be free from household responsibilities, and the woman trying to combine homemaking with work away from home are equally in need of expert guidance.

Having provided women with the education and counseling they require, the nation still faces the question of how best to utilize the skills and capabilities of its womanpower. Indeed, many question the wisdom and justice of encouraging women's efforts to enter the labor force when fathers of families are without work. The answer, I believe, lies in the unmet needs of the country, the filling of which would provide a vast number of new jobs—jobs that would require the efforts of every citizen willing and able to work.

The lack of child-care facilities, health centers and recreational opportunities in many communities suggest fields of employment which might be opened up. Schools and hospitals are understaffed, and most communities have no way of supplying homemaker services for the ill, the aged and the family faced with a special emergency. Almost every area of scientific research is in need of both professional and technical workers. The electronic data processing field is expanding faster than workers can be trained in the programming and computer-operator skills that are required.

The key to the situation, of course, lies in the availability of highly developed skills, of trained workers, for in the decade 1960–1970, professional and technical jobs are expected to increase by more than 40 per cent. How far the educated woman will be able to advance will depend in some measure upon the state of the economy, but even if it does not expand as rapidly as we now anticipate she can still expect to have a good job; her skills will be the skills of the shortage occupations. Other factors also must be considered if any predictions are attempted—the availability of education, training and counseling, the willingness of employers to hire and promote on the basis of merit and capacity—but there is no denying that the educated woman will be the pacesetter for the future.

REFERENCES

1. U. S. Department of Labor, Bureau of Labor Statistics: Special Labor Force Report, No. 26, "Marital and Family Characteristics of Workers, March, 1962," table A.

2. U. S. Department of Commerce, Bureau of the Census: Current Population Reports, Series P-50, No. 11, table 2.

3. U. S. Department of Labor, Bureau of Labor Statistics: "Tables of Working Life for Women, 1950," Bull. No. 1204.

4. See note 1.

5. See note 1.

6. U. S. Department of Commerce, Bureau of the Census: Current Population Reports Series P-20, No. 122, "Marital Status and Family Status, March 1962," table C.

7. U. S. Department of Commerce, Bureau of the Census: "Historical Statistics of the United States, Colonial Times to 1957," Series B92-100.

8. U. S. Department of Commerce, Bureau of the Census: "Statistical Abstract of the United States, 1963," p. 59.

9. U. S. Department of Health, Education, and Welfare, Public Health Service, National Office of Vital Statistics: Special Report of Vital Statistics, 1900–1939, Vol. 43.

10. U. S. Department of Health, Education, and Welfare, Public Health Service, National Office of Vital Statistics: Annual Report "Vital Statistics of U. S., 1961." Vol. II, table 511.

11. *American Women. Report of the President's Commission on the Status of Women* (Washington, D. C., October 1963), p. 10.

12. U. S. Department of Labor, Bureau of Labor Statistics: Special Labor Force Report, No. 32, "Employment of High School Graduates and Dropouts," table 1.

13. U. S. Department of Health, Education, and Welfare, Office of Education: "Earned Degrees Conferred, 1961–62." Circular No. 719 (OE 54013-62).

14. U. S. Department of Health, Education, and Welfare, Office of Education: Biennial Survey of Education 1952–54, "Statistical Summary of Education," chapter I, table 32.

15. See note 14.

16. U. S. Department of Health, Education, and Welfare, Office of Education: "Projection of Total Fall and First Time Fall Enrollment to 1975." Mimeographed report, January 7, 1963.

17. See note 14.

18. U. S. Department of Health, Education, and Welfare, Office of Education: "Projection of Earned Degrees to 1975–76" (Supplemental mimeographed report: Projections as of April 1963).

19. U. S. Department of Labor: Women's Bureau and Bureau of Apprenticeship and Training joint study made in 1954.

20. U. S. Department of Commerce, Bureau of the Census: Current Population Reports Series P-60, No. 41; Consumer Income, "Income of Families and Persons in the United States: 1962," table 18.

21. See note 20, table 2.

22. See note 21.

23. U. S. Department of Health, Education, and Welfare, Social Security Administration: "Some Effects of Low Income on Children and Their Families" by Leonore A. Epstein in *Social Security Bulletin*, XXIV, 2 (February 1961), 12–17.

24. Michael Harrington, *The Other America* (New York: The Macmillan Company, 1962), p. 187.

25. U. S. Department of Labor, Bureau of Labor Statistics: Special Labor Force Report No. 26, "Marital and Family Characteristics of Workers, March 1962," table A.

26. U. S. Department of Labor, Bureau of Labor Statistics: "The Working Wife and her Family's Economic Position," *Monthly Labor Review*, April 1962.

27. See note 25, table L.

28. See note 25, table G.

29. U. S. Department of Labor, Manpower Challenge of the 1960's. 1960.

30. See note 25, table V.

31. See note 20.

32. U. S. Department of Labor, Women's Bureau: "Women in the Federal Service, 1939–59," Pamphlet 4, Revised, table 2.

33. See note 11, p. 32.

34. U. S. Department of Commerce, Bureau of the Census: Current Population Reports Series P-60, No. 39, "Income of Families and Persons in the U. S., 1961," table 27.

35. U. S. Department of Labor, Women's Bureau: "1962 Handbook on Women Workers," Bull. 285, p. 12. 1963.

36. U. S. Department of Labor, Women's Bureau: "Negro Women Workers in 1960," Bull. 287. 1963.

37. See note 7, Series D26-35.

38. U. S. Department of Labor, Bureau of Labor Statistics: "Employment and Earnings," December 1963, table A-18.

39. See note 36.

40. U. S. Department of Commerce, Bureau of the Census: Current Population Reports Series P-60, No. 37, "Income of Families and Persons in the U. S. 1960," table 37.

41. U. S. Department of Health, Education, and Welfare, Office of Education: Biennial Survey of Education 1956–58, "Statistical Summary of Education," chapter I.

42. See note 36.

43. U. S. Department of Labor, Bureau of Labor Statistics: "Employment and Earnings," May 1963, table A-21.

44. See note 35, p. 137.

45. See note 35, p. 140.

46. U. S. Department of Labor, Bureau of Labor Statistics: "Employment and Earnings," February 1964.

47. See note 11, p. 37.

48. See Note 11, p. 43.

49. *Report of the Committee on Protective Labor Legislation to the President's Commission on the Status of Women* (Washington, D. C., October 1963), p. 16.

50. Robert W. Smuts, *Women and Work in America* (New York: Columbia University Press, 1959), p. 105.

51. U. S. Department of Labor, Women's Bureau: *Economic Indicators Relating to Equal Pay, 1963,* Pamphlet 9, Revised.

52. U. S. Department of Labor, Women's Bureau: "What About Women's Absenteeism and Labor Turnover?" April 1963.

53. The University of Chicago, Graduate School of Business, The Health Information Foundation. "The Economic Costs of Absenteeism," *Progress in Health Services* (March–April 1963).

54. U. S. Department of Health, Education, and Welfare, Public Health Service Study of Worktime Lost Throughout the Economy (July 1959–June 1960).

55. U. S. Civil Service Commission: Government-Wide Sick Leave Study, 1961.

56. U. S. Department of Labor, Women's Bureau: "Labor Turnover of Women Factory Workers, 1950–55" in *Monthly Labor Review,* August 1955.

57. "Factor of Sex in Office Employment," *Office Executive* (February 1961).

58. See note 11, p. 18.

DAVID C. MCCLELLAND

Wanted: A New Self-Image for Women

COUNTLESS psychological studies have shown that woman is still perceived by both men and women as Adam's rib—despite all the efforts of feminists from Lucy Stone to Simone de Beauvoir. That is, she is defined not in terms of her self, but in terms of her relation to men: Adam's rib, Adam's temptress, Adam's helpmate, Adam's wife and mother of his children. To sharpen the point, let us consider the findings of just one psychological study in which both men and women were asked to rate adjective pairs, like *large* vs. *small*, according to how well they described words like man, woman, male, female, husband, wife, father, mother.[1] Generally speaking, the male image around the world is characterized by both sexes as strong; that is, as *large, strong, hard,* and *heavy*. Where does this leave the women? The female image is characterized as *small, weak, soft,* and *light*. In the U.S. and many countries, it is also *dull, peaceful, relaxed, cold, rounded, passive,* and *slow*. Two conclusions are immediately apparent from such studies.

First, women are perceived as the opposite of men. This is possibly the psychologist's fault because if a judge wants to describe a woman as "not strong," he must place a check mark closer to its polar opposite, *weak*. Yet a woman may obviously be "not strong" without being *weak*. In fact, the *strong-weak* dimension may simply not apply to her at all. It is useful in describing male behavior, however. So she is commonly dragged in and placed somewhere on it, not only by the psychologists, but by the man in the street. Again, Adam's rib. She is perceived in terms of where she stands on a male characteristic.

Secondly, most of the terms describing the female image have a negative tone. Who wants to be *small, weak, light* (a light-weight?), *dull?* Women must be pretty feeble creatures, pale reflections of men, by this definition. No wonder they have been dissatisfied with the image and have reacted either with open

173

resentment or secret doubts as to their real worth. The obvious reaction is simply to deny the charge, so to speak. The early feminists argued that women could be just as loud, rough, strong, ferocious, sharp and fast as men, as several proved by their own behavior. If females weren't like this very often, they contended, it was either because they were kept in subjection by men or because they were lazy and didn't want to amount to anything. Increasingly, however, modern women have been wondering if this line is really satisfactory. Do they and should they really want to be so rough and tough—so masculine? Or does accepting the issue as joined in this way in the first place concede too much to the male image? Isn't it possible to fashion a female image that is not identical with the male image, but consists of a set of quite different characteristics altogether? Then the real feminist answer to the question of how assertive a woman can be judged is: "The category doesn't apply. You simply can't stuff women into that pigeonhole."

But if you can't use male categories to describe accurately women's characteristics, what ones can you use? As we shall see in a moment, women don't like pigeonholes of any kind as well as men do. So we are playing a male game, but it may be justified here on the ground that it may help some women to entertain a higher opinion of themselves and their role in life. Fortunately, our search will not suffer for lack of facts on which to base conclusions. In psychology's short history, literally thousands of studies have been reported that show significant sex differences. Men and women, boys and girls, differ in dozens of ways—in abilities, in interests, in their reactions to various types of treatment, in the way they are "put together" psychologically. The problem is not lack of information, but making sense out of a surfeit of facts, the mere listing of which is enough to bore and confuse most people. What follows is an attempt to bring some order out of this chaos—an attempt to find dimensions that better characterize the way women actually function. There is no guarantee, of course, that we will find the ideal in the real, that we will discover how women *should* behave from the way they *do* behave. But the facts should be helpful, particularly if they can be ordered in some meaningful way that is not the mirror opposite of the male image. They will at least show clearly how women are not only not men, but something else.

To begin with an obvious male characteristic—and most male characteristics are more obvious which is why they are better understood—men are more *assertive* than women. Many studies show that boys are stronger, more active, more aggressive or pushing practically from birth on.[2] The characteristic may have some physiological basis in the dominance of the male sex hormone, but in any case, nearly all cultures (roughly 85 per cent) strengthen it by training boys more than girls in self-reliance and achievement.[3] Males get into more trouble in school,[4] in college (compare bills for furniture repair in men's and women's dormitories), and in later life (male crime rates are much higher).[5] In the words of Kagan and Moss, "Traditional sex-typed values regard some forms of aggression as critical attributes of masculinity. Thus boys who are striving to identify with a masculine ideal will be prompted to push a peer, to grab a toy, to jeer at a teacher. These behaviors may not necessarily reflect hostile needs but may be the child's way of announcing to the social environment, 'I am a boy, I am capable of executing those behaviors that help to define my role.' Thus a boy may employ a shove or verbal taunt as a way of greeting a peer—a 'hello' if you wish. This use of aggression in a girl is unlikely."[6]

These authors report the results of a long-term study in which the same people were followed from infancy to adulthood. They found that the two characteristics which were much more stable or consistent over the years for boys than for girls were aggressiveness and active interest in the opposite sex. They interpret this to mean that both of these *assertive* traits were less apt to be interfered with in boys because they are considered to be normal and proper masculine characteristics. They also found that men were much quicker at detecting aggressive scenes flashed briefly on a screen. Others have shown that even three-, four-, and five-year-old boys play more violently with dolls than girls do.[7]

Boys prefer rough games, physically strenuous, adventuresome activities (and stories about them), selling activities, showers over baths, being a racing car driver, hunting.[8] They report more often that they feel "entirely self-confident," or like picking a fistfight with someone. They much more often enter occupations which express their assertive interests, like selling, soldiering, engineering (adventurous activities), and law (which allows considerable play for aggressive interests). It is interesting that the entrants into the last two occupations have remained over 95 per cent male in the United States despite the freedom of at least a couple of generations of women to enter them.[9]

Women share much less in these assertive interests and activities. But to say they are not assertive in this way is to say very little. It is to fall into the traditional trap of explaining women as "not men." If they are not so vigorously acting on the world about them, what are they doing? All the evidence suggests that they pay more attention to what goes on around them and modify their behavior accordingly. They care more about relationships. They are *interdependent*. The characteristic shows up at the motor level just as assertiveness does for boys. Girls excel at tasks involving rapid, fine motor adjustments, as in tests of finger dexterity and clerical aptitude.[10] Their organism seems more finely tuned to make adjustments to stimulus changes. Their interaction or interdependence with the world or the environment is greater than for boys, who are more set to barge ahead assertively, no matter what is happening around them. The female concern for interdependence is most striking in the social field where interrelationships with people are concerned. Women recognize more readily scenes flashed quickly on the screen that show interdependence—as when a child is clinging to an adult's knees.[11] Findings like this are sometimes interpreted as indicating *dependence* in women, but interdependence is a better word for an obvious reason: it is not clear whether the female observer identifies with the dependent child or the nurturant parent. Overwhelmingly, the evidence points to the conclusion that women are more concerned with *both* sides of an interdependent relationship. They are more highly trained in nurturance (child care, looking after people) in 82 per cent of the cultures on which data are available,[12] and they are also more dependent on others in the sense that they are more easily persuaded by others to change their minds.[13] In one study, where couples were working together on a problem in which the success of one might mean the failure of another, a confederate at one point asked his partner to "please slow down." The girls responded to this plea by slowing down; the boys did not.[14] Child care obviously involves this kind of give-and-take or interdependence in which one's actions are continually dependent on reactions of others.

It is not surprising in view of all this to find that women disclose more of their secrets to others,[15] feel less dislike for all sorts of odd people (infidels, people with gold teeth, spendthrifts, etc.), and are most attracted to fiction and movies that deal with interpersonal relationships, sentimental stories, romances, social problem movies, etc. Many tests like the Allport-Vernon-Lindzey *Study of Values* show women as more concerned for the welfare of others and as more moralistic (e.g., women are more apt to report that "I become quite irritated when I see someone spit on the sidewalk."). In both instances they are simply expressing their social concern which covers all sorts of interrelationships of people from child care to proper social behavior, including proper dress, makeup, etc.[16]

It is not surprising, then, that they enter occupations like nursing (78 per cent female), social work (68 per cent female) or teaching (59 per cent female).[17] In fact, researchers report that female occupational interests show only one major pattern (as contrasted with several for males) which covers whatever it is that housewives, office workers, stenographers, nurses and teachers have in common. The men who did the study with the usual male bias called the factor "Interest in Male Association." Leona Tyler,[18] noting that this label doesn't cover teaching very well, rather noncommittally calls it "Typical Feminine Interests," whereas actually all these occupations fit rather nicely in the *interdependence* category we have been using to describe one of the main dimensions of female interest and actions. To summarize, women are quicker to recognize their own interdependence; they are more interested in situations where interdependence is important; they enter jobs where this characteristic is salient—from child care to teaching or office work. One can even explain their general tendency to score higher on tests of neuroticism in these terms.[19] For they are more willing to admit to concern about interpersonal problems that men are simply less aware of. Consider the following test item: "I get very tense and anxious when I think other people are disapproving of me." Women are much more apt to report "True" to such a statement than men are, and are correspondingly more likely to get a higher score for "worries" or "neurotic problems." But the fact is that for women, as we have seen, interpersonal relationships are more important and therefore it is more worrying, more necessary to make an adjustment when someone disapproves. The men may not notice or not care. To be fair, one should point out that men are just not on the interdependence dimension: they are often deaf, dumb and blind to what is going on around them because they are so busy assertively concentrating on a task. In work groups, women make more comments that relate to social and emotional relationships in the group, men make comments that relate to the task itself.[20]

To move on to a different but related characteristic difference between men and women, men are interested in *things,* women in

177

people. Such a contrast is scarcely surprising in view of what has already been reported, but it is remarkably prominent throughout life. In nursery school little boys are more apt to draw pictures with physical objects in them (toys, buildings, etc.), girls with people.[21] This interest continues throughout the school years. Twelve-year-old boys, when asked to "construct an exciting movie scene," more often chose blocks and vehicles.[22] They like mechanical and scientific activities much more, from reading *Popular Science* or radio magazines to "repairing a doorlatch" or working with a chemistry set.[8] Not surprisingly, they are much better in these activities in school, scoring higher on "mechanical-aptitude measures, such as mazes, puzzle boxes and tests calling for the assembly of small objects."[23] "In Bennett's Mechanical Comprehension Test there is not a single item for which women average higher scores than men."[23] This superiority reduces basically to a greater interest in and ability at manipulating spatial relationships or "things in space." Later in life, men enter far more often than women occupations like engineering and physical science where these interests and abilities are all-important. The girls, in the meantime, continue to show their interest in people by preferring dolls to cars, by liking dramatics, stories about love relationships, charades or just "being with one another."[8] They are also better at tests of verbal fluency—that is, they talk earlier, think of words more quickly and usually see or write more in a given period of time.[24] One can argue that this is because language is *par excellence* the means of interacting with people, of communicating with people and responding to them. Since girls care about people more, they learn the means of interacting with them better. That the interest is not in language *per se* is shown by the fact that girls are not better at tests of verbal meanings.

Ian Fleming was not a professional psychologist, but he is making use of a scientifically established fact when he has his famous detective, James Bond, say that women are apt not to be good drivers because they will more often take their eyes off the road to look at whoever is with them. In carefully controlled studies, it has been found that in small groups women typically look more often and longer at each other's faces than men do.[25] College girls are more likely to fill their imaginative stories with living creatures —animals and people—than boys are.[26] These interests, like the corresponding male interests, tend to draw women to occupations like nursing, teaching and office work where they will be satisfied.

They apparently even influence the choice of the scientific field that attracts the largest proportion of women—namely, biology, particularly, biochemistry (44 per cent female entrants), the science that is concerned with the ultimate source of life itself.

Running through these differences is another theme which contrasts the way men and women go about dealing with the world—their respective *styles*. Again, the male style is easiest to describe. It is, very simply, *analytic and manipulative*. If boys start early assertively moving things (trucks, toys, stones, etc.) about in the environment, it is scarcely surprising that they end up better able to abstract common elements out of changing situations. As already noted, they are better at tests involving restructuring of spatial relations, taking puzzles apart, or noticing what is wrong with a picture. Numbers are abstractions *par excellence* and males generally are better at tests involving the use of numbers in new combinations—so-called mathematical reasoning tests.[27] Consequently, among college males roughly two-thirds of the College Board Quantitative Test Scores are higher than their Verbal Test Scores while the reverse is true for women.[28]

Nowhere is this male ability more clearly demonstrated than in certain perceptual tasks, such as finding a simple figure hidden in a complex design[29] or trying to see apparent motion between two visual displays flashed on and off successively.[30] The men take longer to see the apparent motion than women do, maintaining a more "analytic" attitude. For the same reason they are quicker to notice that something has changed when small increases are introduced in the size of squares that are briefly presented one at a time.[30] They also make fewer errors in adjusting a rod to the vertical position when they are sitting in a tilted chair or a tilted room.[31] In short, men spend more time actively inspecting the environment, pulling things apart, taking things out of context and putting them back together in a new way. They are constantly manipulating, analyzing and restructuring and do better at tasks that require these abilities.

Women are more influenced by the tilt of the room in adjusting the rod to the upright. So they have typically been described as "field dependent" or "passive acceptant." Again, these terms have a clear, if unintentional negative connotation, based on the bias that the male mode of reacting is the right one. In this case, it happens to be more appropriate to the task requirement, but it would not be difficult to set up a situation in which compromising among conflicting cues would be the task requirement. Then women should do better because their style is *contextual* rather than analytic. As noted earlier, they have a more complex interdependent relationship with the world than men do. They are more "open" to influence, where men are "closed." It is amusing to note that such an interpretive statement is quite literally reflected in figure preferences shown by a test developed for cross-cultural use by Whiting *et al.*[32] In seventeen out of eighteen cultures so far tested, women preferred the figures in the left-hand, men those in the right-hand columns below:

Female preference   Male preference

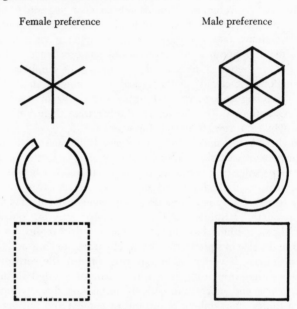

Note how much easier it is to describe the male style: it shows a preference for the simple, the closed, the direct. In contrast, women are more interested in the complex, the open, the undefined. They are quicker to see similarities or "equivalences" among objects and to observe apparent motion.[30] It is scarcely surprising, then, that they are much more interested in art and generally score higher on Art Appreciation Tests.[33] They also like the subtleties of poetry better[8]—which is not simple and direct enough for the average male. And it may be that this characteristic accounts for their superior memory, particularly for details.[34] That is, since women pay more attention to context, the *whole* picture, while men are abstracting something out of it, women should be better able to recite from memory, for example, a story which has just been read aloud—which is, in fact, the case.[35] Male bias unfortunately shows up in labeling this female superiority as "rote memory," or "memory for details," terms which make women seem to be robots recording unimportant details (to men, that is!). The contextuality label seems preferable. Women are concerned with the context, men are forever trying to ignore it for the sake of something they can abstract from it.

In trying to make this point clear to students, I have several times asked them to read Virginia Woolf's famous feminist essay, "A Room of One's Own." Her chief argument is that women have not become great and famous like men chiefly because they had little privacy and less support—either financial or emotional—for independent effort. In terms of our present analysis, she is right, though the lack of privacy may be self-generated in the sense that a woman is less able than man to *ignore what is going on around her*, to forget the context. Virginia Woolf's style in presenting her argument makes the point beautifully. Most of the students like the essay, but the boys in the class typically complain that they don't see why she is so circumstantial, so roundabout, so "literary." Why can't she get to the point? Why doesn't she lay out her argument in one, two, three order? Most of the girls (but not all, of course!) like her circumstantial, complex, contextual style.

The differences between the sexes are sufficiently important to shape their reactions in many areas of life. Psychologists have found that they lump together men and women in their experiments at their peril since women are very apt to react differently from men. To cite a few examples, I found years ago that all I had to do to get college men to write imaginative stories full of achievement themes was to tell them their intelligence and leadership qualities were at stake.[36] The same approach had no effect on the women's fantasies. They remained unmoved by all sorts of appeals of this kind which we tried in an attempt to generalize our finding to the female sex. No luck. Women were just "different." When another investigator used a technique we had employed to arouse affiliation thoughts in men on women, he found that it increased their achievement thoughts. The technique involved asking a person to stand up in a group while the rest rated him or her on various traits (which had favorable and unfavorable connotations). This made men feel lonely and possibly rejected so that they filled their stories with themes of love and interpersonal support. But the same experience made the women think about achieving since *interpersonal relations* define their self-image just as assertive leadership does for men.[36]

Or consider some of the findings reported by Kagan and Moss in their study of the long-term development of men and women. They wanted to know what types of upbringing produced what types of adults and so they correlated child-rearing practices with adult characteristics. They often found no relationships at all until they separated the boys from the girls for the simple reason that the same treatment had opposite effects on the two sexes.[37] Take maternal hostility, for example. If mothers had been hostile to their girl babies during the first three years of life, the girls were much more apt to grow up into tough, assertive, "masculine" women. If mothers were hostile to their boys during the same period in life, the boys became shy, withdrawn and non-aggressive. The reverse was true of maternal protectiveness. Protected girls became shy and quiet; protected boys tough and extroverted. The simplest explanation would seem to be in terms of whether the mother liked girls or boys—since her hostility or protectiveness showed up before the child had had much chance to deserve one or the other. If she rejected the female role as shown by her hostility to a girl infant, the girl was more likely to grow up "unfeminine"—to reject the role herself and become assertive like a man. If the mother rejected the male role, the boy grew up to be "unmanly" or non-assertive. Protectiveness, on the contrary, could be interpreted as acceptance of the contrasting sex roles so that girls grew up to be like other girls and boys like other boys. But obviously the polarization along sex lines is so important a fact of life that the same treatment had very different effects. Not only psychologists but parents ignore it at their peril.

The last example has to do with how the sexes have learned to get what they want. The male procedure is simple and straightforward. He asserts himself. He sees life as a series of episodes in which he attacks the environment, works on a problem, brings it to a successful or unsuccessful resolution, stops and goes on to something else. The approach can be illustrated from a study which contrasted the way college men and women told stories about a picture of a male and female acrobat in the midst of a trapeze act.[38] The following is a typical male story:

This picture suggests a dynamic, intimate relation between the man and woman—hence the light is around their bodies and the rest is dark. This picture is a climax to a period in which they have come to understand each other. Both are completely lost in the thought of their union. They are totally occupied. From such heights they can only go down.

Note that the acrobats have reached a climax from which "they can only go down." Sixty-one per cent of the male stories, vs. 30 per cent of the female stories, were of this type in which the acrobats worked themselves up to some peak and then some letdown, often a fall, occurred. Professor Murray has dubbed this psychological theme in its more extreme form the Icarus Complex, since Icarus flew high on his wings toward the sun, but the wax melted and he fell into the sea.[39] This is the male image of achievement, the straight line projecting upward to a peak of glory until his assertiveness fails—perhaps just with old age—and he falls.

No such simple approach is available to a woman who lives in a far more complex interpersonal world where she is more constantly aware of *all* that is going on and modulates her reactions accordingly. The following story manages to catch the flavor of her approach rather well:

Mary is learning to do a change between trapezes. She is about to swing to the next and her teacher, old Mr. Picken, is going to become instantly ill, and she is going to catch him from falling by a lucky chance. He will then train her to circus stardom.

Note that the relationship is an *interdependent* one where the teacher helps the pupil and the pupil helps the teacher, but beyond that a difficulty—a fall—is portrayed as the means to eventual success. In 70 per cent of the girls' stories, as contrasted with only 32 per cent of the boys' stories, the same sequence occurs: problems, often falls, occur but they lead on to greater happiness and success in a manner which is almost the reverse of the male sequence. It is as if women have learned that going without, suffering, or difficulties may often be the means or at least the road that one must pass through to happiness. This is scarcely surprising in view of the complex interdependence of the world in which a woman lives. If she is to respond to all of it, she cannot ignore most of it as a man can, but she must often postpone responding to one part while she is responding to another. Is it any wonder that she says "True" much more often to the assertion "Sometimes I feel that I am about to go to pieces"? She is pulled in various directions—toward the tilted room as well as to the instructions to set the rod straight—and she learns that this makes for troubles which can best be handled by mediation—giving up a little of each to get a happy result.

But must women be like this? Or are they simply under-privileged men—human beings who, because of society's fixed rules, are forced into a shape they need not assume? Few women like to think in our age that "anatomy is destiny," that they cannot become truly great because of an accident of birth. If women are the way they are largely because of social rules and expectations, why not change the rules? As in most things human, a good case can be made for the effect of both biological and social factors in producing sex differences. That the genes play a role is suggested by such facts as (1) sex hormones differ and are known to affect character-istics like assertiveness in other animals; (2) sex differences in motility and sensitivity show up in neonates before culture could have had much effect;[40] (3) some of the differences, such as the ease with which apparent motion is seen, appear to be unrelated to any of the usual types of sex role expectations or training; (4) practically all cultures train their boys in one way—for assertive-ness—and their girls for another—interdependence. If there were no biological biasing in these directions, wouldn't it be more likely that the differences in training would be randomly distributed between the two sexes?

On the other hand, it is easy to demonstrate the importance of training. After all, a few cultures can and do reverse the usual sex-typing, as Margaret Mead demonstrated long ago in reporting how the Tchambuli women are assertive and the men timid, artistic, and dependent. In Whiting's picture preference test, one of the eighteen cultures did not show the normal sex-typing of responses. The Kagan and Moss findings already reported show, in fact, just how a woman can be brought up to behave assertively like a man. What she needs is a mother who "dislikes girls" and rejects femininity with all its sex-typed correlates. That this does not happen more often can be attributed to a bias introduced by certain sociological and biological "facts of human existence." On the sociological side, it can be argued that if the family is to survive as a unit, someone must be assigned the role of bringing outside supplies into the unit and protecting it against attack. Because the male is usually stronger, he gets assigned this assertive role in most societies. On the other hand, relationships within the unit must be the responsibility of someone, or fights will break out, supplies will not be properly divided, the weak will not be cared for, etc.[41] Women are normally assigned this role because they are not strong enough to play the male role. The needs of a functioning society, plus one biological factor (greater male strength), are sufficient to account for the sex-typing that exists. Obviously, according to such a theory, as the need for male strength decreases in a technologically modern society, the basis for sex-typing disappears—particularly since no biological basis for the female superiority in interdependent relationships is assumed.

Anatomy, or the body image, is also one of the facts of existence which shapes the learning of boys and girls. Every boy experiences the phallic tumescence-detumescence cycle literally thousands of times from birth onward. The association between rise-pleasure-assertion should be firmly fixed by this recurrent experience. It might well be the anatomical basis of the Icarus complex mentioned earlier. Girls, on the other hand, learn early that they are penetrated in the sexual act, that the often painful experiences of menstrual flow and childbirth are difficulties that lead to pleasure and happiness, that to bear a child—the purpose for which their body is obviously constructed—they must relate to another, who will support them during childbirth and their somewhat dependent state thereafter, etc. So there may be common learning experiences based on anatomical facts that help create some of the psychological reactions observed more often among women—their interest in interdependence, their idea that they must give up one thing to get another, etc.[42]

But again, nothing is absolutely foreordained about these learnings. Women can learn the male patterns; men can fail to learn them. All anatomy does is to make some associative patterns *more likely* in one sex than the other if nature takes her course, and if nothing is done to change what would normally be learned. So, unfortunately, the facts of science cannot dictate what women should be and do. In fact, many women on most of the traits mentioned are more masculine than the average man. Science certainly cannot assert that women can't behave like men or vice versa. Nature leaves society a choice, but it does bias the outcome if nothing is done to reverse normal learning.

185

Despite the general favor with which male characteristics are viewed in our society, there is little evidence that most women want to reverse the normal pattern and abandon the traditional feminine role altogether. They *like* being women for the most part, but they wish it didn't seem to mean that they had to be so "unsuccessful." They don't want to feel—quite rightly—that being a woman dooms them to a kind of second-class existence—with lesser potentialities. So let us consider the plight of these women, recognizing that there is nothing in nature or society which prevents a woman from adopting the male assertiveness pattern if she wants to. Her lot won't be an easy one because of the habits of thought and responding of most of the women and men in our society, but we can still respect her—and perhaps even see in her the harbinger of a new day when men and women will become psychologically indistinguishable from each other, at least on the average. In that day there would only be individual differences in behavior which would be unrelated to sex.

But let us consider further what some younger college women have been calling "femininism"—a kind of militant femininity which glories in the differences between the sexes and insists that to be a woman more or less as defined by the characteristics reported above is a wonderful thing. In fact, according to their point of view, to adopt the male pattern is to "sell out"—to admit that the masculine approach to life is better. The difficulty with this feminine protest movement has been that it has lacked a very clear idea of the distinction between the male and female images. Thus, it often is little more than the emotional feeling that "we don't want to be men," combined with a kind of shamefaced admission that "we're not sure what that means except that we are probably admitting we won't amount to much." One of the main purposes of this paper has been to give distinctive content to the female image as it emerges from psychological findings to date so that women may have a clearer idea of what they are opting for or against (and quite obviously I am playing the male analytic game in trying to give them a clear choice when their more natural reaction would be to say "it depends"!). What is debilitating and anxiety-producing is lack of self-respect, a feeling of unimportance. Yet the two images, as we have defined them both, should command respect and obviously complement each other. They should make it easier for a woman to feel that the male single-minded assertive attacks on objects has its real limitations and is not for her. Instead, she might with pride prefer the feminine interest in interdependent relationships in which context and giving up here to get there are so much more important.

There are two consequences of opting for a full-fledged femininity that need to be made explicit, however. First, it means insisting on the importance of traditional feminine strengths—working with people, taking account of context, doing many things at once, all part-time. Obviously, individual women are already choosing careers that maximize opportunities for using these skills and interests—in nursing, teaching, homemaking, office work—but what they need often is a more explicit justification for what they are doing—more pride in their work. In a sense, in most of these situations, males have been taking too much credit for what happens because often their contribution is easier to describe. Yet the sociological theorists are obviously right. If men in most societies play the instrumental, assertive role, they could not possibly succeed unless women were managing the interpersonal and emotional relationships which hold the society together. It is safe to predict that a society would quickly collapse into anarchy or the war of all against all unless some people were actively concerned with problems of interdependence and social cohesion. Why is this functional role, which has been traditionally a feminine responsibility, so undervalued in our time?—particularly when the world is getting so complex that such skills are going to be even more in demand to keep it from literally blowing up. One could make a good case for the fact that the world is suffering from an overdose of masculine assertiveness right now and needs above all a realization of the importance of interdependence in all human affairs. Who could play a more effective part in creating this realization than the women for whom such interests and skills come naturally?

But more is involved than simply placing a higher value on typical feminine skills. I suspect the real problem for many educated women is not that, but the difficulty they have in recognizing whether they have been a success. Again, the male has the advantage. With his pinhole vision he both wants to concentrate on one thing at a time and is encouraged to by society. So his success is easily measured by how much insurance he sells, how many people he knocks out in the ring, how great a book he writes, or whether he makes a basic discovery in science or not. Most women by inclination and by force of circumstance will do many more things in the course of a lifetime. The phrase "part-time" catches a lot of the essence of the feminine style of life in a very practical sense. Women will be part-time daughters, part-time mothers, part-time wives, part-time cooks, part-time intellectuals, part-time workers. They may spend part of their lives being wholly wives and mothers and another part being wholly intellectuals. But their psychology permits this degree of alternation more easily than for a man who will often blindly follow a single course. A woman's success is less easily visible, by the same token, because it consists of the sum of all these activities rather than the result of a single-minded pursuit of one. When scholars point out that even the best cooks have been men, the proper answer is, "But what man has been not only the second-best cook, but the third-best parent, the seventh-best typist, the third most considerate child and the tenth best community leader?" In other words, if there were awards in life for the all-around sum of successes—a kind of pentathlon— women would win them all. Instead, it is as if we keep noting that the men win the javelin throw, the 100-yard dash, etc., and give no accolades for the best all-around athletes.

Nowhere is this more evident than in the study of the lives of outstanding women. Consider the scholars at the Radcliffe Institute for Independent Study. They are selected for intellectual excellence, but what is surprising about them—to the male, anyway, who can accomplish something only by concentrating—is *how many different things* they do well.[43] Theirs is not a success that has come about by shutting family and community responsibilities out of their lives. Most of them have pursued their many interests with vigor and enthusiasm, whether in their own work, or in their community, or in their husband's careers or in their children's lives, alternating capably from one to the other, ready always to take context into account, to give up one interest for the other if need be. One gets the impression that for these women the more they did, the more they were able to do. Their capacity for giving was not exhausted but stimulated by demands—just like the pot of honey that kept renewing itself whenever any was taken from it. For instance, pregnancy, which might be considered an excuse for giving up most activities, actually served to stimulate several of them to do even more than before.

In other words, these women seem to have accepted and thrown themselves vigorously into the feminine role. Because they respected themselves and what they could do well, they seemed to be able to do a great deal more than the average person of either sex. They had decided to swim vigorously *with the tides of life,* rather than lie helplessly tossed about bemoaning their handicaps as women, or rather than try to "rise above" the pressures on them in the typical male fashion. Such a strong embrace of the female life style would seem to offer a promising way of life to the "femininist" who wants to stay feminine and yet leave her mark. Men may build greater monuments—particularly to themselves—but how long do monuments last *sub specie aeternitatis?*

REFERENCES

1. The generalizations in the text are drawn from very extensive research findings reported by Professor Osgood and his associates. See for example his recent report on constancies in ratings of such concepts across cultures and language groups, C. E. Osgood, "Semantic Differential Technique in the Comparative Study of Cultures," *American Anthropologist* (1964), 66, No. 3, Part 2, 171–200.

2. Cf. L. M. Terman and L. E. Tyler, "Psychological Sex Differences," and K. C. Pratt, "The Neonate." In L. Carmichael (Ed.), *Manual of Child Psychology* (New York: Wiley, 1946).

3. H. A. Barry, M. K. Bacon, and I. L. Child, "A Cross-Cultural Survey of Some Sex Differences in Socialization." *Journal of Abnormal and Social Psychology* (1957), 55, 327–332.

4. H. D. Williams, "A Survey of Predelinquent Children in Ten Middle-Western Cities." *Journal of Juvenile Research* (1933), 17, 163–174.

5. Cf. L. Tyler, *The Psychology of Human Differences.* Chapter 10 on "Sex Differences" (New York: Appleton-Century-Crofts, 1956).

6. J. Kagan and H. A. Moss, *Birth to Maturity* (New York: Wiley, 1962), p. 274.

7. P. S. Sears, "Doll Play Aggression in Normal Young Children: Influence of Sex, Age, Sibling Status, Father's Absence. *Psychological Monographs: General and Applied* (1951), 65, No. 6.

8. Whenever preferences of this sort are described in the text, they are drawn from standard test instruments developed to measure "Masculinity-Femininity" of interests. That is, the items have been selected from a large pool of such items according to the extent to which they show distinctive preferences by men or women (largely in the U.S.). An early study in this field was carried out by L. M. Terman and C. C. Miles and reported in their book *Sex and Personality: Studies in Masculinity and Femininity* (New York: McGraw, 1936). Items are drawn from their study and also from Strong's *Vocational Interest Test* and the Masculinity-Femininity Scale of the *California Personality Inventory.*

9. J. A. Davis and N. O. Bradburn, *Great Aspirations: Career Plans of America's June 1961 College Graduates* (Chicago: National Opinion Research Center, 1961).

10. Cf. Tyler, *op. cit.*, p. 254.

11. Kagan and Moss, *op. cit.*, Chapter 8.

12. Barry *et al.*, *op. cit.*

13. I. L. Janis and P. B. Field, "Sex Differences and Personality Factors Related to Persuadability." In I. L. Janis *et al.*, *Personality and Persuadability* (New Haven: Yale Univer. Press, 1959).

14. E. L. Walker and R. W. Heyns, *An Anatomy for Conformity* (Englewood Cliffs, N.J.: Prentice-Hall, 1962).

15. S. M. Jourard, *The Transparent Self* (Princeton, N.J.: Van Nostrand Insight Book, 1963).

16. Cf. topics covered in women's magazines, also Tyler, *op. cit.*

17. Davis and Bradburn, *op. cit.*

18. *Op. cit.*, p. 260.

19. Cf. for example, Tyler, *op. cit.*, p. 262, or G. Gurin *et al.*, *Americans View Their Mental Health* (New York: Basic Books, 1960).

20. Cf. R. V. Exline, "Need Affiliation and Initial Communication Behavior in Problem-Solving Groups Characterized by Low Interpersonal Visibility." *Psychological Reports* (1962), 10, 79–89. See also F. L. Strodtbeck and R. D. Mann, "Sex Role Differentiation in Jury Deliberations." *Sociometry* (1956), 19, 3–11.

21. E. W. Goodenough, "Interest in Persons as an Aspect of Sex Differences in the Early Years." *Genetic Psychology Monographs* (1957), 55, 287–323.

22. E. H. Erikson, "Sex Differences in the Play Configurations of Pre-Adolescents." *American Journal of Orthopsychiatry* (1951), 21, 667–692.

23. Tyler, *op. cit.*, p. 253.

24. *Ibid.*, p. 252.

25. R. V. Exline, "Explorations in the Process of Person Perception: Visual Interaction in Relation to Competition, Sex and Need for Affiliation." *Journal of Personality* (1963), 31, 1–20.

26. I am indebted to one of my students, Mrs. Ruthanne Cowan, for this finding based on the coding of a representative sample of Harvard and Radcliffe Freshman protocols.

27. Tyler, *op. cit.*, p. 252.

28. The same superiority of performance over verbal subscales is evident in various intelligence tests.

29. H. A. Witkin, H. B. Lewis, M. Hertzman, K. Machover, P. B. Messner, and S. Wapner, *Personality Through Perception* (New York: Harper, 1954).

30. R. Gardner, P. Holzman, G. Klein, H. Linton, and D. P. Spence, "Cognitive Controls." *Psychological Issues* (International Univer. Press, 1959), vol. 4.

31. Witkin *et al., op. cit.*

32. I am indebted to Professor Whiting for making these unpublished findings available to me.

33. Tyler, *op. cit.*, p. 261

34. *Ibid.*, p. 254.

35. *Ibid.*, p. 254.

36. Cf. D. C. McClelland, J. W. Atkinson, R. A. Clark and E. L. Lowell, *The Achievement Motive* (New York: Appleton-Century-Crofts, 1953).

37. *Op. cit.*, Chapter 9.

38. This is part of a forthcoming study by Robert May carried out under my direction and supported by a grant from the National Institute of Mental Health.

39. Cf. H. A. Murray, "American Icarus." In A. Burton and R. E. Harris (Eds.), *Clinical Studies of Personality* (New York: Harper, 1955), Vol. II.

40. Cf. for example, L. S. Hendry and W. Kessen, "Oral Behavior of Newborn Infants as a Function of Age and Time since Feeding." *Child Development* (1964), 35, 201–208.

41. This argument follows traditional sociological lines. Cf. M. Zelditch, "Role Differentiation in the Nuclear Family." In T. Parsons and F. Bales (Eds.), *Family, Sociological and Interaction Process* (Glencoe, Ill.: The Free Press, 1955).

42. Obviously the interpretation given here of sex differences and of their origin in body experiences is very similar to Erik Erikson's as described in an earlier chapter. Rightly or wrongly, two psychologists reasoning independently from quite different empirical data have come to a similar conclusion as to how the sexes differ. Probably even Alice Rossi might agree that this is a fair summary of the way matters stand now. On the other hand, she feels that the difference is largely created by society—by nurture, not nature—and that in the world of tomorrow it ought to and can be made to disappear. She may be right—certainly human nature is wonderfully flexible—but I have to confess to some lingering doubts as to how easy it will be to change these natural "biases." I can illustrate my doubt with an anecdote. I have a very feminist eleven-year-old daughter who, when I asked her if she could wire up a complex electric fixture her younger brother had been working on, replied, "Yes, of course. I can do it as well as he can." But the fact is that it had been lying there

191

for a week; she knew he hadn't been able to fix it, but had passed it a dozen times a day without stopping to work on it. She just wasn't really interested. Her brother had spent hours in intense and frustrated concentration working on it. And he is certainly not doing it to follow me as a role model since I have very little skill or interest in things electrical. It is hard for me to believe that his intense interest and her disinterest (which duplicates dozens of statistical studies) come from sex-typed activities or beliefs they have picked up on TV or in school or in the home. It looks as "built in" as the difference in their passion for lighting matches —he taking every chance he can get to light a match, she indifferent. Of course she could be trained to get interested in matches or wiring fixtures, but my own conclusion is that it would be harder *on the average* to develop such interests in girls than boys, because of certain biases nature has built into the psychological makeup of the sexes. But even from such a conclusion we cannot argue that it shouldn't be done!

43. I am indebted to Dr. Alice Ryerson for sharing with me the results of her study of some of these women.

CARL N. DEGLER

Revolution Without Ideology:
The Changing Place of Women in America

IF FEMINISM is defined as the belief that women are human beings and entitled to the same opportunities for self-expression as men, then America has harbored a feminist bias from the beginning. In both the eighteenth and nineteenth centuries foreign travelers remarked on the freedom for women in America. "A paradise for women," one eighteenth-century German called America, and toward the close of the nineteenth century Lord Bryce wrote that in the United States "it is easier for women to find a career, to obtain work of an intellectual as of a commercial kind, than in any part of Europe."

Certainly the long history of a frontier in America helps to account for this feminist bias. In a society being carved out of a wilderness, women were active and important contributors to the process of settlement and civilization. Moreover, because women have been scarce in America they have been highly valued. During almost the whole of the colonial period men outnumbered women, and even in the nineteenth century women remained scarce in the West. As late as 1865, for example, there were three men for each woman in California; in Colorado the ratio was as high as 20 to 1. Such disparities in the sex ratio undoubtedly account for the West's favorable attitude toward women as in an Oregon law of 1850 that granted land to single women and, even more significant for the time, to married women; or in the willingness of western territories like Wyoming (1869) and Utah (1870) to grant the suffrage to women long before other regions where the sex ratio was more nearly equal.

Another measure of women's high esteem in American society was the rapidity with which the doors of higher education opened to women. Even without counting forerunners like Oberlin College, which admitted women in 1837, the bars against women came down faster and earlier in America than anywhere. The breakthrough came during the Civil War era, when women's colleges like Elmira, Vassar and Smith were founded, and universities like Michigan and Cornell became coeducational. The process was later and slower in Europe. Girton College, Cambridge, for example, which opened in 1869, was the sole English institution of higher education available to women until London University accorded women full privileges in 1879. Heidelberg, which was the first German university to accept women, did not do so until 1900. More striking was the fact that at its opening Girton provided six places for young women; Vassar alone, when it opened in 1865, counted some 350 students in residence. Another indication of the American feminist bias was that at the end of the century girls outnumbered boys among high school graduates.

But if the frontier experience of America helped to create a vague feminist bias that accorded women more privileges than in settled Europe, the really potent force changing women's place had little to do with the frontier or the newness of the country. It was the industrial revolution that provided the impetus to women's aspirations for equality of opportunity; it was the industrial revolution that carried through the first stage in the changing position of women—the removal of legal and customary barriers to women's full participation in the activities of the world.

Today it is axiomatic that men work outside the home. But before the industrial revolution of the nineteenth century, the great majority of men and women were co-workers on the land and in the home. Women worked in the fields when the chores of the home and child-rearing permitted, so that there was not only close association between work and home for both sexes, but even a certain amount of overlap in the sexual division of labor. The coming of machine production changed all that. For a time, it is true, many unmarried women and children—the surplus labor of the day—were the mainstay of the new factory system, but that was only temporary. By the middle of the nineteenth century the bulk of industrial labor was male. The coming of the factory and the city thus wholly changed the nature of men's work. For the first time in history, work for most men was something done outside the family, psychologically as well as physically separated from the home.

The same industrial process that separated work and home also provided the opportunities for women to follow men out of the home. For that reason the feminist movement, both socially and intellectually, was a direct consequence of the industrial changes of the nineteenth century. Furthermore, just as the new industrial system was reshaping the rural men who came under its influence, so it reshaped the nature of women.

The process began with the home, which, in the early years of industrialization, was still the site of most women's work. Because of high land values, the city home was smaller than the farm house, and with less work for children, the size of the urban family was smaller than the rural. Moreover, in the city work in the home changed. Machines in factories now performed many of the tasks that had long been women's. In truth, the feminist movement began not when women felt a desire for men's jobs, but when men in factories began to take away women's traditional work. Factory-produced clothing, commercial laundries, prepared foods (e.g. prepared cereals, canned vegetables, condensed milk, bakery bread) were already available in the years after the Civil War. Toward the end of the century an advanced feminist like Charlotte Perkins Gilman, impressed by the accelerating exodus of women's chores from the middle-class home, predicted that the whole kitchen would soon be gone. She was wrong there, but even today the flight continues with precooked and frozen foods, TV dinners, cake mixes, special packaging for easy disposal, diaper services and the like.

Middle-class women were the main beneficiaries of the lightening of the chores of the home; few working-class or immigrant women could as yet take advantage of the new services and products. These middle-class women became the bone and sinew of the feminist movement, which was almost entirely an urban affair. They joined the women's clubs, organized the temperance crusades and marched in the suffrage parades. With an increasing amount of time available to them in the city, and imbued with the historic American value of work, they sought to do good. And there was much to be done in the raw, sometimes savage, urban environment of the late nineteenth century. For example, public playgrounds in the United States began in Boston only in the 1880's, when two public-spirited middle-class women caused a cartload of sand to be piled on an empty lot and set the neighborhood children loose upon it. Many a city and small town at the turn of the century owed its public library or its park to the dedicated work of women's clubs. The venerable giant redwood trees of northern California survive today because clubwomen of San Francisco and nearby towns successfully campaigned in 1900 to save them from being cut down for lumber. The saloon and prostitution were two other prevalent urban blights that prompted study and action by women's organizations.

More important than women's opposition to social evils was the widening of women's knowledge and concerns that inevitably accompanied it. What began as a simple effort to rid the community of a threat to its purity often turned into a discovery of the economic exploitation that drove young working girls into brothels and harried working men into saloons. Frances Willard for example, while head of the Women's Christian Temperance Union, broadened the WCTU's reform interests far beyond the liquor question, causing it to advocate protective legislation for working women, kindergartens and training programs for young working girls. Jane Addams, at Hull-House in Chicago's slums, quickly learned what historians have only recently discovered, that it was the urban boss's undeniable services to the immigrants that were the true sources of his great political power and the real secret of his successful survival of municipal reform campaigns.

The most direct way in which industrialization altered the social function of women was by providing work for women outside the home. Production by machine, of course, widened enormously the uses to which women's labor could be put once physical strength was no longer a consideration. And toward the end of the century, as business enterprises grew and record-keeping, communications and public relations expanded, new opportunities for women opened up in business offices. The telephone operator, the typist, the clerical worker and the stenographer now took places beside the seamstress, the cotton mill operator and the teacher.

As workers outside the home, women buried the Victorian stereotype of the lady under a mountain of reality. After all, it was difficult to argue that women as a sex were weak, timid, incompetent, fragile vessels of spirituality when thousands of them could be seen trudging to work in the early hours of the day in any city of the nation. Nor could a girl who worked in a factory or office help but become more worldly. A young woman new to a shop might have been embarrassed to ask a male foreman for the ladies' room, as some working girls' autobiographies report, but such maidenly reticence could hardly survive very long. Even gentle, naïve farm girls soon found out how to handle the inevitable, improper advances of foremen. They also learned the discipline of the clock, the managing of their own money, the excitement of life outside the home, the exhilaration of financial independence along with the drudgery of machine labor. Having learned something of the ways of the world, women could not be treated then, nor later in marriage, as the hopeless dependents Victorian ideals prescribed.

In time work transformed the outer woman, too. First to go were the hobbling, trailing skirts, which in a factory were a hazard and a nuisance. Even before the Civil War, Amelia Bloomer and other feminists had pointed out that women, if they were to work in the world as human beings, needed looser and lighter garments than those then in fashion. Until working women were numbered in the millions, no change took place. After 1890 women's skirts gradually crept up from the floor, and the neat and simple shirtwaist became the uniform of the working girl. A costume very like the original bloomer was widely worn by women factory workers during the First World War. Later the overall and the coverall continued the adaptation of women's clothes to the machine.

The most dramatic alteration in the image of woman came after the First World War, when there was a new upsurge in women's employment. The twenties witnessed the emergence of the white-collar class, and women were a large part of it. Over twice as many women entered the labor force that decade as in the previous one; the number of typists alone in 1930 was three-quarters of a million, a tenfold increase since 1900. And woman's appearance reflected the requirements of work. Except for some of the extreme flapper fashions, which were transient, the contemporary woman still dresses much as the woman of the 1920's did. In the 1920's women threw out the corset and the numerous petticoats in favor of light undergar-ments, a single slip, silk or rayon stockings, short skirts and bobbed hair. So rapid and widespread was the change that an investigation in the 1920's revealed that even most working-class girls no longer wore corsets, and the new interest in bobbed hair resulted between 1920 and 1930 in an increase of 400 per cent in the number of women hair dressers.

The physical freedom of dress that women acquired during the 1920's was but the superficial mark of a new social equality. The social forces behind this new equality are several. Some of these forces, like the growing number of college-trained women and the increasing number of women in the working force, go back far into the past; others, like the impact of the war and the arduous cam-paign for women's suffrage, were more recent. But whatever the causes, the consequences were obvious. Indeed, what is generally spoken of as the revolution in morals of the 1920's is more accurately a revolution in the position of women. Within a few short years a spectrum of taboos was shed. For the first time women began to smoke and drink in public; cigarette manufacturers discovered and exploited in advertising a virtually untouched market. As recently as 1918 it was considered daring for a New York hotel to permit women to sit at a bar. In the twenties, despite prohibition, both sexes drank in public.

Perhaps most significant, as well as symbolic, of the new stage in the position of women was their new sexual freedom. The twenties have long been associated with the discovery of Freud and a fresh, publicly acknowledged interest in sex. But insofar as these attitudes were new they represented changes in women, particularly those of the middle and upper classes. Premarital and extramarital sexuality by men had never been severely criticized, and discussion of sexual matters was commonplace wherever men gathered. Now, though, middle-class women also enjoyed that freedom. For the first time, it has been said, middle-class men carried on their extramarital affairs with women of their own social class instead of with cooks, maids and prostitutes.

An easier sexuality outside of marriage was only the most sensational side of the revolution in morals; more important, if only because more broadly based, was a new, informal, equal relationship between the sexes, culminating in a new conception of marriage. The day was long since past when Jennie June Croly could be barred, as she was in 1868, from a dinner in honor of Charles Dickens at a men's club even though her husband was a member and she was a professional writer. (Indeed, so thoroughly has such separation of the sexes been abandoned that the new Princeton Club in New York City has closed all but one of its public rooms to any man who is not accompanied by a woman!) And at least in the gatherings of the educated middle class, talk between the sexes was often free, frank and wide-ranging. The same mutual acceptance of the sexes was visible in the prevalent talk about the "new marriage," in which the woman was a partner and a companion, not simply a mother, a social convenience and a housekeeper.

The reality of the new conception of marriage was reflected in the sharp increase in the divorce rate. Because marriage, legally as well as socially, in the nineteenth century was more confining for women than for men, the early feminists had often advocated more liberal divorce laws. And even though divorce in the nineteenth century was more common in the United States than in any European country, the divorce rate in the 1920's shot up 50 per cent over what it had been only ten years before. One sign that women in the 1920's were seeking freedom from marriage if they could not secure equality in marriage was that two thirds of the divorces in that decade were instituted by women.

By the close of the twenties the ordinary woman in America was closer to a man in the social behavior expected of her, in the economic opportunities open to her and in the intellectual freedom enjoyed by her than at any time in history. To be sure there still was a double standard, but now its existence was neither taken for granted nor confidently asserted by men.

In truth, the years since the twenties have witnessed few alterations in the position of women that were not first evident in that crucial decade. The changes have penetrated more deeply and spread more widely through the social structure, but their central tendency was then already spelled out. Even the upsurge in women's employment, which was so striking in the twenties, continued in subsequent years. Each decade thereafter has counted a larger number of working women than the previous one. During the depression decade of the 1930's, even, half a million more women entered the labor force than in the prosperous twenties. By 1960 some 38 per cent of all women of working age—almost two out of five women—were employed outside the home.

The movement of women out of the home into remunerative work, however, has been neither steady nor unopposed. Undoubtedly one of the underlying conditions is an expanding economy's need for labor. But something more than that is needed to break society's traditional habits of mind about the proper work for women. Certainly here the feminist demands for equality for women played a part. But a social factor of equal importance was war. By their very disruption of the steady pulse of everyday living, wars break the cake of custom, shake up society and compel people to look afresh at old habits and attitudes. It is not accidental, for instance, that women's suffrage in England, Russia and Germany, as well as the United States, was achieved immediately after the First World War and in France and Italy after the Second.

At the very least, by making large and new demands upon the established work force, war draws hitherto unused labor into the economic process. During the Civil War, for example, young women assumed new roles in the economy as workers in metal and munitions factories, as clerks in the expanded bureaucracy in Washington and as nurses in war hospitals. Moreover, when the war was over women had permanently replaced men as the dominant sex in the teaching profession. Furthermore, since many women found a new usefulness in the Sanitary Fairs and other volunteer work, the end of hostilities left many women unwilling to slip back into the seclusion of the Victorian home. It is not simply coincidental that the women's club movement began very soon after the war.

When the First World War came to the United States, feminist leaders, perhaps recalling the gains of the Civil War, anticipated new and broad advances for their sex. And the demand for labor, especially after the United States entered the war, did open many jobs to women, just as it was doing in contemporary Great Britain and Germany. All over the United States during the war customary and legal restrictions on the employment of women fell away. Women could be seen doing everything from laying railroad ties to working in airplane factories. The war also brought to a successful climax the struggle for the suffrage. Pointedly women had argued that a war for democracy abroad should at least remedy the deficiencies of democracy at home.

If politically the war was a boon to women, economically it failed to live up to feminist anticipations. The First World War, unlike the Civil War, did not result in a large permanent increase in the number of working women. Indeed, by 1920 there were only 800,000 more women working than in 1910. But as a result of wartime demands, women did get permanent places in new job categories, like elevator operators and theater ushers. (But women street car conductors disappeared soon after the armistice.) Certain traditional professions for women, like music teaching, lost members between 1910 and 1920, while professions that required more training and provided steadier income, like library and social work and college teaching, doubled or tripled their numbers in the same period.

The Second World War, with its even more massive demands for labor and skills, brought almost four million new women workers into the nation's factories and offices. Once again jobs usually not filled by women were opened to them. For example, the number of women bank officers rose 40 per cent during the four years of the war and the number of women employees in finance has continued to rise ever since. Furthermore, unlike the situation after the First

World War, the female work force after 1945 not only stayed up but then went higher.

Measured in the number of women working, the changes in the economic position of women add up to a feminist success. Twenty-four million working women cannot be ignored. But weighed in the scales of quality instead of quantity, the change in women's economic status is not so striking. It is true that women now work in virtually every job listed by the Bureau of the Census. Moreover, the popular press repeatedly tells of the inroads women are making into what used to be thought of as men's jobs. Three years ago, for example, a woman won a prize as the mutual fund salesman of the year. Women are widely represented in advertising and in real estate, and even women taxicab drivers are no longer rare. Yet the fact remains that the occupations in which the vast majority of women actually engage are remarkably similar to those historically held by women. In 1950 almost three quarters of all employed women fell into twenty occupational categories, of which the largest was stenographers, typists and secretaries—a category that first became prominent as a woman's occupation over a half century ago. Other occupations which have traditionally been women's, like domestic service, teaching, clerical work, nursing and telephone service, are also conspicuous among the twenty categories. Further than that, the great majority of women are employed in occupations in which they predominate. This sexual division of labor is clearly evident in the professions, even though women are only a small proportion of total professional workers. Two thirds of all professional women are either nurses or teachers; and even in teaching there is a division between the sexes. Most women teach in the primary grades; most men teach in high school. Women are notoriously underrepresented in the top professions like law, medicine, engineering and scientific research. No more than 7 per cent of all professional women in 1950 were in the four of these categories together. Only 6 per cent of medical doctors and 4 per cent of lawyers and judges were women. In contrast, almost three quarters of medical doctors are women in the Soviet Union; in England the figure is 16 per cent. In both France and Sweden women make up a high proportion of pharmacists and dentists; neither of those professions attracts many women in the United States.

One consequence as well as manifestation of the sexual division of labor in the United States has been the differences in pay for men and women. That difference has been a historical complaint of feminist leaders. In 1900 one study found women's wages to be, on the average, only 53 per cent of men's. The reason was, of course, that women were concentrated in the poorer paying jobs and industries of the economy. The disparity in pay between the sexes has been somewhat reduced today, but not very much. In 1955 among full-time women workers of all types the median wage was about two thirds of that for men. In short, women are still supplying the low-paid labor in the economy just as they were in the last century. (In substance, women workers and Negroes of both sexes perform a similar function in the economy.) The willingness of women to supply cheap labor may well account for their getting the large number of jobs they do; men often will not work for the wages that women will accept.

Today, there does not seem to be very much disparity between men's and women's wages for the same work, though the sexual division of labor is so nearly complete that it is difficult to find comparable jobs of the two sexes to make a definitive study.

There has been no improvement in women's position in higher education; indeed, it can be argued that women have failed to maintain the place reached much earlier. As we have seen, the United States led the world in opening higher education to women. This country also led in broadening the social base of education for women. No other country educated such a large proportion of women in its universities and colleges as did the United States. At the close of the nineteenth century, one third of American college students were women; by 1937 women made up almost 40 per cent of the students in American institutions of higher learning. In Germany, just before Hitler took power, no more than one out of ten university students was a woman; in Swedish universities in 1937 only 17 per cent of the students were women; in British universities the ratio was 22 per cent.

But since the Second World War the gap between American and European proportions of women in higher education has narrowed considerably. In 1952–1953 women constituted only 35 per cent of the American college population, while France counted women as 36 per cent of its university students and Sweden 26 per cent. The *number* of women in American colleges, of course, is considerably greater than it was in the 1920's and 1930's, but in proportion to men, women have lost ground in America while gaining it in Europe.

A further sign of the regression in the educational position of women in the United States is that in the early 1950's women earned about 10 per cent of the doctoral degrees in this country as compared with almost 15 per cent in the 1920's.

How is one to explain this uneven, almost contradictory record of women in America? How does it happen that a country with a kind of built-in feminism from the frontier falls behind more traditional countries in its training of college women; that a country with one of the highest proportions of working women in the world ends up with such a small proportion of its women in medicine, in law and in the sciences? Perhaps the correct answer is that the question should not be asked—at least not by Americans. For like so much else in American society, such contradictions are a manifestation of the national avoidance of any ideological principle, whether it be in feminist reform or in anything else. To be sure there has been no lack of feminist argument or rationale for women's work outside the home, for women's education and for other activities by women. But American women, like American society in general, have been more concerned with individual practice than with a consistent feminist ideology. If women have entered the labor force or taken jobs during a war they have done so for reasons related to the immediate individual or social circumstances and not for reasons of feminist ideology. The women who have been concerned about showing that women's capabilities can match men's have been the exception. As the limited, and low-paying, kinds of jobs women occupy demonstrate, there is not now and never has been any strong feminist push behind the massive and continuing movement of women into jobs. Most American women have been interested in jobs, not careers. To say, as many feminists have, that men have opposed and resisted the opening of opportunities to women is to utter only a half truth. The whole truth is that American society in general, which includes women, shuns like a disease any feminist ideology.

Another way of showing that the historical changes in the status of women in America bear little relation to a feminist ideology is to examine one of those rare instances when women did effect a social improvement through an appeal to ideology, for instance, the struggle for the suffrage. By the early twentieth century the feminist demand for the vote overrode every other feminist goal. Once women achieved the vote, it was argued, the evils of society would be routed, for women, because of their peculiar attributes, would bring a fresh, needed and wholesome element into political life. In form, and in the minds of many women leaders, the arguments for the suffrage came close to being a full-blown ideology of feminism.

In point of fact, of course, the Nineteenth Amendment ushered in no millennium. But that fact is of less importance than the reason why it did not. When American women obtained the vote they simply did not use it ideologically; they voted not as women but as individuals. Evidence of this was the failure of many women to vote at all. At the end of the first decade of national suffrage women still did not exercise the franchise to the extent that men did. Nor did many women run for or hold political offices. The first woman to serve in Congress was elected in 1916; in 1920, the first year of national women's suffrage, four women were elected to Congress, but until 1940 no more than nine women served at one time in the House of Representatives and the Senate together. That we are here observing an American and not simply a sexual phenomenon is shown by a comparison with European countries. In non-feminist Germany, where the ballot came to women at about the same time as in the United States, the first Reichstag after suffrage counted forty-one women as members. In 1951 seventeen women sat in the British House of Commons as compared with ten in the United States House of Representatives. Twice the number of women have served as cabinet ministers in Britain between 1928 and 1951 as have served in the United States down to the present.

Another instance in which social change was effected by feminist ideology was prohibition. The achievement of national prohibition ran second only to the suffrage movement as a prime goal of the organized women's movement; the Eighteenth Amendment was as much a product of feminist ideology as the Nineteenth. Yet like the suffrage movement, prohibition, despite its feminist backing, failed to receive the support of women. It was *after* prohibition was enacted, after all, that women drank in public.

In the cases of both suffrage and prohibition, women acted as individuals, not as members of a sex. And so they have continued to act. It is not without relevance that the women's political organization that is most respected—the League of Women Voters—is not only nonpartisan but studiously avoids questions pertaining only to women. To do otherwise would be feminist and therefore ideological.

One further conclusion might be drawn from this examination of the non-ideological character of American women. That the changes that have come to the position of women have been devoid of ideological intent may well explain why there has been so little opposition to them. The most successful of American reforms have always been those of an impromptu and practical nature. The great revolution of the New Deal is a classic example. The American people, like F. D. R. himself, simply tried one thing after another, looking for something—anything—that would get the nation out of the depression. If lasting reforms took place too, so much the better. On the other hand, reforms that have been justified by an elaborate rationale or ideology, like abolition, have aroused strong and long-drawn-out opposition. By the same token, when women became ideological in support of suffrage and prohibition, they faced their greatest opposition and scored their most disappointing triumphs.

The achievement of the suffrage in 1920 is a convenient date for marking the end of the first phase in the changing position of women, for by then women were accorded virtually the same rights as men even if they did not always exercise them. The second phase began at about the same time. It was the participation of married women in the work force. During the nineteenth century few married women worked; when they did it was because they were childless or because their husbands were inadequate providers. Even among the poor, married women normally did not work. A survey of the slum districts in five large cities in 1893 revealed that no more than 5 per cent of the wives were employed. Only Negro wives in the South and immigrant wives in big northern cities provided any significant exceptions to this generalization.

Before the First World War, the movement of wives into the working force was barely noticeable. During the 1920's there was an acceleration, but as late as 1940 less than 17 per cent of all married women were working. Among working women in 1940, 48 per cent were single and only 31 per cent were married. The Second World War dramatically reversed these proportions—another instance of the influence of war on the position of women. By 1950 the proportion of married women living with their husbands had risen to 48 per cent of all working women while that of single women had fallen to 32 per cent. In 1960 the Census reported that almost 32 per cent of all married women were employed outside the home and that they comprised 54 per cent of all working women. No industrial country of Europe, with the exception of the Soviet Union, counted such a high proportion. Today, married women are the greatest source of new labor in the American economy. Between 1949 and 1959, for example, over four million married women entered the labor force, some 60 per cent of *all* additions, male and female.

Such a massive movement of married women out of the home

was a development few of the early feminists could have anticipated. That it has taken place is at once a sign and a yardstick of the enormous change in women's position in society and in the family. In the nineteenth century work outside the home was unthinkable for the married woman. Not only were there children to care for, but there were objections from husbands and society to consider. That is why the convinced feminist of the nineteenth century often spurned marriage. Indeed, it is often forgotten that the feminist movement was a form of revolt against marriage. For it was through marriage, with the legal and social dominance of the husband, that women were most obviously denied opportunities for self-expression. Even after the legal superiority of the husband had been largely eliminated from the law, middle-class social conventions could still scarcely accommodate the working wife. To the woman interested in realizing her human capabilities, marriage in the nineteenth century was not an opportunity but a dead end. And it was indeed a minor scandal of the time that many of the "new women" did in fact reject marriage. The tendency was most pronounced, as was to be expected, among highly educated women, many of whom felt strongly their obligation to serve society through careers. Around 1900 more than one fourth of women who graduated from college never married; more than half of the women medical doctors in 1890 were single.

Like other changes in the position of women, the movement of married women into the work force—the reconciliation of marriage and work—must be related to the social changes of the last three decades. One of these social changes was the increase in contraceptive knowledge, for until married women could limit their families they could not become steady and reliable industrial workers. Information about contraceptive techniques which had been known for a generation or more to educated middle-class women did not seep down to the working class until the years of the Great Depression. In 1931, for instance, there were only 81 clinics disseminating birth control information in the United States; in 1943 there were 549, of which 166 were under public auspices. As the number of public clinics suggest, by the end of the 1930's birth control was both socially and religiously acceptable, at least among Protestants. And a method was also available then to Roman Catholics, since it was in the same decade that the rhythm method, the only one acceptable to the Roman Catholic Church, was first brought to popular attention with the approval of ecclesiastical authorities.

Another social force underlying the movement of wives and mothers in the work force was the growing affluence of an industrial society, especially after 1940. Higher health standards, enlarged incomes of husbands and a better standard of living in general permitted a marked alteration in the temporal cycle of women's lives. Women now lived longer, stayed in school later and married earlier. In 1890 half the girls left school at 14 or before—that is, when they finished grammar school; in 1957 the median age was 18—after graduation from high school. The girl of 1890, typically, did not marry until she was 22; the age of her counterpart in 1957 was 20, leaving no more than two years for work between the end of school and marriage. Among other things this fact explains the fall in the proportion of single women in the work force in the United States as compared with other industrial societies. Few other countries have such an early median age of marriage for girls.

Early marriages for women produce another effect. With knowledge of contraceptive techniques providing a measure of control over child-bearing, women are now having their children early and rapidly. When this tendency is combined with a younger age of marriage, the result is an early end to child-bearing. In 1890 the median age of a mother when her last child was born was 32; in 1957 it was 26. A modern mother thus has her children off to school by the time she is in her middle thirties, leaving her as much as thirty-five years free for work outside the home. And the fact is that almost half of working women today are over forty years of age. Put another way, 34 per cent of married women between the ages of thirty-five and forty-four years are gainfully employed.

Unquestionably, as the practical character of the woman's movement would lead us to expect, an important force behind the influx of married women into the work force is economic need. But simple poverty is not the only force. Several studies, for example, have documented the conclusion that many women who work are married to men who earn salaries in the upper income brackets, suggesting that poverty is not the controlling factor in the wife's decision to work. A similar conclusion is to be drawn from the positive correlation between education and work for married women. The more education a wife has (and therefore the better salary her husband is likely to earn) the more likely she is to be working herself. Many of these women work undoubtedly in order to raise an adequate standard of living to a comfortable one. Many others work probably because they want to realize their potentialities in the world. But that women are so poorly represented in the professions and other careers suggests that most married women who work are realizing their full capabilities neither for themselves nor for society.

Over sixty years ago, in *Women and Economics,* the feminist Charlotte Perkins Gilman cogently traced the connection between work and the fulfillment of women as human beings. In subsequent writings she grappled with the problem of how this aim might be realized for married women. As a mother herself, raising a child under the trying circumstances of divorce, Gilman knew first hand that work outside the home and child-rearing constituted *two* full-time jobs. No man, she knew, was expected or required to shoulder such a double burden. Gilman's remedies of professional domestic service and kitchenless apartments never received much of a hearing, and considering the utopian if not bizarre character of her solutions, that is not surprising. Yet the problem she raised remained without any solution other than the eminently individualistic and inadequate one of permitting a woman to assume the double burden if she was so minded. Meanwhile, as the economy has grown, the problem has entered the lives of an ever increasing number of women. Unlike most of her feminist contemporaries, who were mainly concerned with the suffrage and the final elimination of legal and customary barriers to women's opportunities, Gilman recognized that the logic of feminism led unavoidably to the working mother as the typical woman. For if women were to be free to express themselves, then they should be able to marry as well as to work. Women should not have to make a choice any more than men. To make that possible, though, would require that some way be found to mitigate the double burden which biology and society had combined to place only on women.

As women moved into the second stage of their development— the reconciliation of work and marriage—the problem which Gilman saw so early was increasingly recognized as the central issue. Virginia Collier, for example, in a book *Marriage and Careers,* published in 1926, wrote that since so many married women were working, "The question therefore is no longer should women combine marriage with careers, but how do they manage it and how does it work." Interestingly enough, her study shows that what today Betty Friedan, in *The Feminine Mystique,* has called the "problem that has no name," was already apparent in the 1920's. One working wife explained her reasons for taking a job in these words, "I am burning up with energy and it is rather hard on the family to use it up in angry frustration." Another said, "I had done everything for Polly for six years. Suddenly she was in school all day and I had nothing to do. My engine was running just as hard as ever, but my car was standing still." A year after Collier's book appeared, President William A. Neilson of Smith College observed "that the outstanding problem confronting women is how to reconcile a normal life of marriage and motherhood with intellectual activity such as her college education has fitted her for." That the issue was taken seriously is attested by an action of the Board of Trustees of Barnard College in 1932. The board voted to grant six months' maternity leave with pay to members of the staff and faculty. In announcing the decision, Dean Virginia Gildersleeve clearly voiced its import. "Neither the men nor the women of our staff," she said, "should be forced into celibacy, and cut off from that great source of experience, of joy, sorrow and wisdom which marriage and parenthood offer."

With one out of three married women working today, the problem of reconciling marriage and work for women is of a social dimension considerably larger than in the days of Charlotte Gilman or even in the 1930's. But the fundamental issue is still the same: how to make it possible, as Dean Gildersleeve said, to pursue a career or hold a job while enjoying the "experience . . . joy, sorrow and wisdom" of marriage and parenthood. The practical solutions to this central problem of the second stage in the changing position of women seem mainly collective or governmental, not individual. Child-care centers, efficient and readily available house-keeping services, and emergency child-care service such as the Swedes have instituted are obviously a minimal requirement if women are to have the double burdens of homemaking and employment lightened. The individual working woman cannot be expected to compensate for the temporary disabilities consequent upon her role as mother any more than the individual farmer or industrial worker can be expected single-handedly to overcome the imbalance between himself and the market. Today both farmers and workers have government and their own organizations to assist them in righting the balance.

But as the history of farmers and industrial labor makes evident, to enact legislation or to change mores requires persuasion of those who do not appreciate the necessity for change. Those who would do so must organize the like-minded and mobilize power, which is to say they need a rationale, an ideology. And here is the rub; in pragmatic America, as we have seen, any ideology must leap high hurdles. And one in support of working wives is additionally handicapped because women themselves, despite the profound changes in their status in the last century, do not acknowledge such an ideology. Most American women simply do not want work outside the home to be justified as a normal activity for married women. Despite the counter-argument of overwhelming numbers of working wives, they like to think of it as special and exceptional. And so long as they do not advance such an ideology, American society surely will not do so, though other societies, like Israel's and the Soviet Union's, which are more ideological than ours, obviously have.

Perhaps the kind of gradual, piecemeal advance toward a feminist ideology that Mrs. Rossi proposes in other pages of this book may contain the seeds of change. But a reading of the past reminds us forcefully that in America the soil is thin and the climate uncongenial for the growth of any seedlings of ideology.

EDNA G. ROSTOW

Conflict and Accommodation

MODERN MARRIAGE is a relation into which husband and wife are expected to pour major amounts of energy, time, and feeling, while each is now also expected to look to the world outside for satisfaction and recognition. The free woman of today operates increasingly in two worlds, as her husband does. Both do so in a society which provides images and ideals of how marriage should be lived, but few if any rules. The couple is free to find its own way—free, and burdened by freedom.

In modern western history, the marriage of aristocrats offered freedom of a kind to husband and wife. The aristocratic view of marriage, however, was not romantic. In this country, at least, the prevailing idea of marriage has been a romantic one, combining the values of love and freedom. The freedom was freedom to choose a partner: American society never accepted arranged marriages. These two values have acquired new dimensions: love has been endowed with post-Freudian intensities and the requirement of an all-embracing intimacy. As for freedom, it is expected that the partners who have chosen each other freely will as free men and women permit each other to seek a greater or lesser degree of success and identity in work.

There is, therefore, an inherent if rarely acknowledged contradiction between the traditional idea of marriage and the "emancipation" of women. In a future not yet conceived, this freedom could even be a threat to marriage as we now know it, for the freedom of women implies major choices, stresses, and risks largely unknown in western societies until recently. Thus far, men and women have both sought an accommodation of these conflicts within traditional forms. Despite the increased availability of divorce, marriage itself is an immensely strong social institution, perhaps more universally accepted than ever before. But the substance of marriage has changed greatly in this country, especially during the last half century. Perhaps it is not too much to suggest that as the openness of freedom is experienced, the need to enhance the marriage relationship increases.

What the young woman of today seeks and hopes for in her marriage combines classic themes into a pattern of some novelty and flexibility. For most young middle-class women in their twenties —the third generation of emancipated American women—their ideal of self emphatically includes early marriage, children, higher education, and some interesting work outside the home. Their idea of marriage implies a husband who would be a sympathetic partner, not a master. In present circumstances, their idea of work implies jobs rather than careers. There is a widespread self-consciousness about marriage, individual identity, and life routines. Romance is not dead, but there is an awareness that love as an impulsive feeling is not enough; that marriages may be made in heaven, but have to be lived on earth.

The ideal is rarely met in the real world. Occasionally, however, one does meet the young woman who seems to approximate in actual life the pattern that many, perhaps most, of her contemporaries regard as their goal. One such example recently commented on her life. Intelligent and charming, good-looking and well dressed, she had married (and married well) immediately after graduation from an excellent college. She had small children and was pursuing part-time graduate study in a leisurely way. Her attitude toward work was not so dedicated as that of men graduate students for whom success in their studies is the key to their future, but it was not that of a dilettante either. Her interest was serious, even though at this stage it was secondary to her personal life. She anticipated part-time work after she received her doctorate, and when her children were older, a full-time job.

Yet she knew, too, that her situation seemed more nearly perfect than it was. Her husband was able and successful. She did not know where his career would lead them. Her own ability was strong, as was her intellectual interest. Attaining what she wished for in the marriage relation as well as in mothering required not only love, but thought and perception, sympathy and consideration, self-knowledge and self-control. In talking about her life and her view of herself she struck two themes of the chorus on the Woman Question in which many of her contemporaries would join. "Loving," she said, "is hard work." And later she added that although she often found the flow of books and articles on the problems of women rather tiresome, being a woman in today's world "is never dull."

The pattern of combining some work outside the home with marriage and a family of four, five or even six children does not correspond to the earlier vision of how women, once liberated, would use higher education and professional training. It had seemed clear to an embattled generation that "advanced" women should complete their professional training and start careers before marrying at all. But the young American middle-class women of the present day live in a world colored by Freud as well as by Pankhurst. Their problem is not to win freedom, but how to use it. They take the equality of women for granted. And they take equally for granted the right, perhaps even the obligation, of the individual to find identity and fulfillment primarily through his own existence and through personal relationships given new significance by our culture, rather than through membership in a clan or in collectivities like "Women." When young women study law or medicine, they are not trying to prove that women can breach one more wall of resistance. They are seeking to find in a life that combines marriage and work outside the home a satisfactory means of expressing their own needs and strengths and developing their own personalities. Hence their frequent indifference to the literature on the status of women and their preoccupation—often exhilarated as well as earnest—with the challenge of a life which encourages them to be and do so many things, inside the home and outside of it.

Changes in society and in its atmosphere have intensified for many people the individual search for meaning in personal life. One effect of that process seems to be visible in the way marriage is approached. New perspectives for individual fulfillment and intimacy have been added; new mores have developed which require husband and wife to share tasks and forms of social and recreational activity previously the province of either one alone. By the same token, new stresses have been introduced into the marriage relation. The idea of marriage and of married life which seems to be emerging is one in which central importance is attached to a relation of all-embracing intimacy with another person. There is wide acceptance, almost a fervent belief, that to be completely intimate few areas of behavior, thought, or feeling can be excluded. Yet work outside the home can pull each partner toward routines and relationships which may conflict, or may be imagined to conflict, with the marriage itself. Each spouse is required to accommodate his needs, and the complications of his situation outside the home, to the needs and situation of the other. Some of these conditions may not be easily reconcilable—or may, at least, be less easily reconcilable than was the case when the wife's world was more confined.

It is hardly news that a successful marriage is a creative accomplishment involving effort. In one sense, this is "What Every Woman Knows"—or knew! For even though a successful marriage has always involved two people, it was customary to think of success as depending primarily on the woman's effort, because accommodation to the needs, routines, desires, and talents of the man was taken to be her job. But the dimensions of present-day marriage, with its high standards of sharing, understanding, and accomplishment, and with its expectation that middle-class women will function regularly in "masculine" spheres as well as in "feminine" ones, add up to a large order—and not just for the wife. It is characteristic of American optimism that we expect ambitious targets to be attained, and feel the guilt of personal failure when they are not.

Indeed, there is risk that this standard for woman's performance may become a stereotype, foisted on the American female, as rigid as those she has kicked over. And women who wish not to be ruled by it can be in difficulty—beset by guilt if they give themselves over full time to childrearing and homemaking.

The expectations and aspirations young people now bring to their individual lives, and especially to marriage, may seem beyond reach. Yet the young men and women who can be observed as they engage in the pursuit of these high goals are hardly wide-eyed, earnest dreamers. Most often they are practical, articulate, "goal-directed," active, zestful, and even possessed of humor. They live with novel conditions, ahead of experience and of the literature. But they have a singular advantage. For the young man accepts his wife's freedom as the order of nature, and both know that accommodation follows this fact. Moreover, the environment recognizes the magnitude of their task and is finding ways to favor their efforts.

Implicit in the previous section is the suggestion that a fairly distinctive ideal exists in the minds of most educated middle-class American women as the model or standard for their behavior as people and as women—a benchmark by which each woman judges her own success or failure, and that of her fellows. The prevailing notion of the ideal is quite different from that of an earlier time, at least as a standard for a large proportion of the population, rather than for a tiny group of unusual individuals among the leisured classes.

It is impossible to say how widely the community at large accepts the ideal of middle-class women of superior education for a woman's performance and for marriage. The middle classes are being rapidly enlarged, and the proportion of young people exposed to higher education, at least as a social and emotional experience, is rising steeply. At the same time the magazines of mass circulation, television, paperbacks, movies, and the other instruments by which attitudes are influenced propagate images which used to be familiar only to readers of *Vogue* or the *New Yorker*—whose subscription lists in turn have extended far beyond the happy few in recent years. The speed with which ideas from learned journals are now popularized and transmitted may not make for quick basic changes in people, but they probably do affect the goals and images toward which they turn. It is not fanciful to hypothesize that in modern American society leadership groups constitute models shared by large segments of the population. Consider the speed with which Holden Caulfield has become almost a folk figure. And Diana Trilling has just reported that a few years ago the slick popular magazines had to make a decision to strengthen their mass appeal or to raid the *Partisan Review*. Those which enticed the writers of *Partisan Review* have drastically increased their circulation. The others have gone noticeably downhill.

The ideas and feelings with which we are concerned here may be experienced primarily—or only—in so-called leadership or elite groups, but it is our hypothesis that they articulate what is felt by many others in the population—perhaps less intensely, perhaps only less articulately. Furthermore, greater numbers of women may be expected to share those ideas and ideals as higher education becomes even more widespread than it is, and the purely physical demands of housekeeping and childrearing diminish.

It is not easy to assign even an order of statistical magnitude to the term "educated middle-class woman" as we use it here. One would expect that the patterns of thought and behavior which are the subject matter of this paper are more generally found in some parts of the middle class than in others: more among intellectuals and artists than among business groups; among the wives of high governmental officials or leading professional men, or academicians, or in metropolitan centers. But it is now commonplace to meet variations on these themes in less obvious areas. The effect of freedom and education for women on the expectations men and women bring to their lives is remarkably pervasive. The manner of expressing these ideas may differ in the different parts of what is becoming a more and more unified culture. But the essence of the matter does not. A college student from an unsophisticated milieu can describe the discomfort she experiences when conflicting feelings arise about who she is, and what she wants to find in marriage and in life. A Radcliffe student in the same predicament is likely not only to describe, but to identify and label her feelings, easily commanding psychological references. Both girls have similar feelings and hold approximately the same views about the ultimate life pattern they would like to realize.

There is little reliable documentation on the relation between change in the status of women and change in attitudes towards the rightful roles of men and women. Middle-class groups have sustained the greatest effect of the emancipation of women. Although it is difficult to be categorical, one cannot escape certain impressions about the consequences of this new freedom on a husband's authority, and his wife's submissive restriction to household, church, and children. It is quite as rare nowadays to see workingmen congregate of an evening in the corner saloon as it is to see wealthier men spending evenings regularly in their clubs.

These cautions being stated and stressed, one should add that the primary milieu from which the observations of this paper derive is that of an eastern university community. That community embraces students from all parts of the country, and from varied economic backgrounds. For many of them the society is familiar in style and manner; for many others, the institution is a vehicle of mobility in a large society that is still open for those with brains, energy, and the ability to educate themselves not only intellectually but in nuances of custom and manners. The graduates of the institution permeate the world into which they emerge. They are represented in all areas of activity and at different levels—usually at the middle and upper end of the middle class spectrum. Within the university, men and women students in the various schools give evidence of contemporary modes of thought and feeling. The faculty represent various areas geographically, and various socio-economic backgrounds, as do the graduates dispersed throughout the nation. One has therefore a perspective through layers of time as well as the obvious and more subtle differences of ranges within class and country.

One may well debate the extent to which educated middle-class men and women provide others in the society with their ideals or norms of conduct. That enquiry is not, however, our purpose here. Our purpose, rather, is to consider some of the forces which shape the life-view of the young American woman who graduates from a first-class college, and usually becomes part of the higher reaches of the American middle class. It is the view of this writer that these women are a feminine elite, and the wives, by and large, of a male elite. They are part of a vanguard, self-conscious and articulate in thought and feeling, purposeful and active, whose behavior and attitudes are not only intrinsically important, but are of interest to men and women throughout American society, and, indeed, throughout the world. For although much of what takes place here does not accord with the values or social patterns which prevail on other continents, America is still the prototype (to be accepted or rejected) of what life offers—or becomes—under conditions of affluence and social freedom.

The model life-pattern for the young woman of this class mirrors the social and intellectual forces which make our culture distinctive: the pervasive influence of the Freudian revolution; the changing social and economic status of women; the altered structure and atmosphere of family life; and the rising standard of living, the prevalence of labor-saving products and routines, and the disappearance of domestic servants.

The "Woman Question" of today, as it appears in the eyes of college students, their sisters in graduate and professional school, and those in their late twenties and early thirties who are married and have children, is largely one of accommodation. By the time girls reach college they are fully aware that society prepares them for two conflicting goals. They are told that they are members of an elite. As members of this group, they are to be wives of the important men in the society and find their greatest fulfillment in marriage and motherhood. Their education, however, follows terms set by men's education and aims at self-realization in work. Parents and teachers wish to see young women get as much education as possible under their belts before "embarking on life." For some teachers the overriding motive is for women to win leading places in business, politics, and the professions. For parents, involved with the insecurities of practical living, education is also insurance for the future and a protection in the present. The idea that women should have an active part in the world outside the home—still largely a world of men—is pressed on these girls, and it is widely accepted.

Accepting both these goals has meant conflict for many if not most educated women, and it inevitably still presents difficulties. For education does not mean postponement of social experience. The acceleration of social experience witnessed in our society, where dating can and often does begin in the early teens, brings into the foreground challenges to feelings and to the management of feeling. Questions arise about who one is and how to live life. These feelings and questions cannot easily be postponed or ignored. How, therefore, can young women reconcile all their ambitions, fulfill all their drives and dreams, within the boundaries of circumstance? No matter how much energy they have, or how much discipline in organization or skill in the art of eating their cake and having it, there are choices to be made.

A great deal has been written about the frustration and misery which is thought to have resulted from this conflict. A great deal has also been said on the subject of how girls attempt to deal with the conflict, and how they make their choices. Margaret Mead has expressed the view of her generation that a girl in this dilemma learns to be successful, but not too successful: that she must display "enough ability to get and keep a job, but without the sort of commitment that will make her either too successful, or unwilling to give up the job entirely for marriage or motherhood." In our culture, Miss Mead has commented, boys are unsexed by failure, girls by success. She suggests that girls actually "quest for failure" in the working world of men as their adaptation to the conflicts involved in combining a career with marriage and motherhood.

But is this really the way in which most girls now see the choice before them? And is the outcome of their choice as they now attempt to exercise it as destructive as Margaret Mead feared it would be? For those whose goals admit no compromise in the way women pursue work in a man's world, any adaptation spells failure. But the view of young women today seems to be that accommodation itself is their goal—that they would be "failing" in Miss Mead's sense if they failed to make the accommodation. The conflict between work and marriage does not in itself require them to "fail" in work in order to "succeed" in marriage. It requires them instead to discover empirical compromises between the two ideas

which many of them are in the process of doing rather effectively
and cheerfully.

To a degree often galling to members of another generation, this
accommodation acquiesces in the continued inequality of women in
the working world. But acquiescence in discrimination seems to be
a transitory element in the evolution of our changing attitudes
toward women. Our culture is reacting to this inequality—as it
reacts to others—perhaps too slowly, even grudgingly, but it is
reacting nonetheless. In this way society has responded to other
needs of women when they became manifest—or could no longer
be ignored: relief from drudgery, part-time education, employment,
and the like.

A "solution" of this order can be accepted without the kind of
protest some would wish to see because of qualities inherent in the
present state of society, and its climate of thought and values.
Enough women are exercising the franchises of opportunity to keep
them open in all areas for some time to come. Men and women
both now seek many satisfactions from life other than through
work, and they value many of these functions and duties as highly
as they value their work. The conditions of modern life, often so
threatening in its larger atmosphere and in the structures within
which work is conducted, in its mobility and in its tempo, provide
a setting in which individuals welcome belief in the ideas which
have been identified loosely as the Freudian revolution.

Freud was not the first to describe the paradox of man's discon-
tent with the world as it advanced in culture and wealth. His consideration of individual striving for expression and fulfillment in a
world that found new ways to limit individuality struck echoes
which reached into the lives of innumerable people. The popu-
larizers of his ideas and the ideas of others bolstered individual
yearning in numberless ways. If man is to be ruled by law, his
aggressions must be channeled into acceptable acts. If he is to be
monogamous, the needs which would lead him elsewhere should
be answered in marriage. Intimacy and sharing then become magic
words for those who believe they provide magic answers. If infancy
and early childhood govern the development of ultimate personality, then a mother's role should be regarded as a creative act of
social worth and personal meaning. If individual dreams and wishes
and feelings have value, then time given to them is not always a
waste. The overall question posed by civilization is not new—how
man can accommodate himself to the demands of group life at the

same time that he strives to answer individual ones which may not always be compatible. The pulls of both worlds are believed by some to be inevitably conflicting. It is certain that the opposing pulls are now most striking in women's lives; it is debatable, however, that these conflicts are beyond resolution.

It is inherently difficult for all modern youth to find tasks and causes worthy of their enthusiasm—tasks that can satisfy high standards of craftsmanship, and causes which satisfy the need for an ideal. Freedom from the doom of destiny to preordained callings imposes the burden of choice. Men protested at the old monotony which condemned most of them to their father's farm or craft, and at the slavery which made them accept marriages arranged for them. Now they find the necessity to decide almost as vexing. More, they find the search for their own identity—which each person must carve out for himself from the bewildering opportunities offered by the society—a complicated process beset by needs and feelings which often conflict. For educated women the search for identity and for their rightful place in the society involves finding the rightful means of achieving satisfactions through clouds of conflicting values, needs, feelings, and situations. Their satisfactions must be found primarily in two areas—for to succeed in relation to one of these goals alone seems to leave a sense of frustration and failure. Despite conflict, therefore, young women are committed, more noticeably than was the case even thirty years ago, somehow to rationalize the conflicts and to incorporate both the goal of marriage and the goal of work outside the home into the pattern of their lives. Dealing with that conflict is a task this generation faces knowingly and consciously, a fact which seems to be crucial to its view of the roles of men and women.

This is not to suggest that the two goals are of equal value in the minds and feelings of these women, or that a conflict between them is in any sense an equal contest. Its outcome is rarely in doubt. But it may well leave scars nonetheless. Experience with women in graduate and professional schools—young women of exceptional ability and strong motivation in their work—testifies that it is rare for one to hesitate if the necessity for choice arises between the demands of her graduate training and those of her marriage—or between choosing training against marriage. At least at that stage of life, marriage almost invariably comes first.

The persistent primacy of marriage among the aims of a woman's life is hardly a surprising finding, although the fact goads some surviving members of the old feminist orthodoxy to protest against the "mystique" of femininity. Attitudes based on millennia of experience could hardly have been expected to vanish in a couple of generations. Women are not storming the professions or providing leaders for industry and government in large numbers—a condition which disappoints the hopes projected by the suffragettes and their crusading daughters. But this is not because women are all sheep, at the mercy of soothsayers who have led them astray down the path of least resistance. Most educated women want to participate in the world's work, but principally in ways which do not imperil their fulfillment in traditional roles as wives and mothers.

Thirty and forty years ago, intelligent women, touched with zeal for women's rights, treated maternity with reserve and hoped to keep childbearing and childrearing to an aseptic minimum. They grudged the concessions to nature which interfered with their new freedom to pursue careers or the pleasures of idle afternoons. At that time, as a pediatrician remarked, the nursing mother was a museum piece, and the idea of natural childbirth was considered barbaric.

Today, manifestly, there have been changes in attitudes toward love, marriage, and motherhood. The instinctual life of men and women is not deplored, even verbally and ritually, but taken to be the base of life, to be enjoyed and cultivated—sometimes, be it said, cultivated with a solemnity bordering on pathos. The cult of sexuality has for many people overloaded the sexual element in life, so that achieving sexual fulfillment according to prescribed standards becomes a source not of health but of anxiety. Sexual fulfillment is part of a highly demanding idea of love. The meaning of love is widely questioned, especially in prolonged relationships when time tempers impulsive and naïve feeling. An increasing number of young men and women are lucid about what they want from love and marriage. They are willing to confront their feelings and undertake sustained examination of them. Their articulateness, their perceptions are more than intellectual exercises, for they do accept the central place of feeling in the relationship of married love, and have varying degrees of awareness of the demands made on individuals beyond the realm of spontaneous feeling. As many say—loving means work—it doesn't just happen. Motherhood, like love and marriage, becomes a more self-conscious task—rarely underestimated, sometimes exaggerated. The view of the mother's function as it has emerged in the literature influenced by Freud's work is more carefully delineated and articulated than it had previously been. By its detailed consideration of the many ramifications and effects of the mother-child relationship, it imposes on women an almost awesome responsibility. For those who are influenced by these ideas—and they are inescapable, especially for the highly educated—fulfillment of self in marriage and motherhood is to be won through loving and nurturing in anything but narrowly defined ways.

Freudian ideas gained momentum, in this country at least, when the First World War broke many shackles and freed people from the habit of automatic acceptance of existing custom. The fight for women's freedom progressed in both individual and collective ways as part of the total change. Women won the vote and began to take part in the business and professional life of the community. They also took to smoking and drinking in public places, traveling without escorts, managing their own business and legal affairs, and living alone, apart from the family. Attack was intensified on the last surviving traces in the law of old rules which deny a wife legal identity apart from that of her husband. For women the new freedom meant freedom to go out into the world—freedom from home. That freedom implied her conscious control over certain of the circumstances of her life: conception, for example, and closely related to it, the nursing of babies. Now, after many years, the wheel has turned. Women have recovered from the first shock of their reaction to the extremely powerful implications of birth control and bottle-feeding. As with other changes which once were crusading issues, they can view birth control now not as an end in itself but as a means toward having an ample, but not an oppressively ample, family. And nursing is regarded, in a setting of popularized psychoanalytic ideas, not as a degrading nuisance but as an important part of the physical aftermath of childbirth, and of the physical and emotional relationship between mother and child.

The conviction that a young woman's first fulfillment is as a wife and mother, now more comfortably accepted in its traditional pre-eminence, does not, however, mean that her life is to be lived traditionally. Higher education has given many intelligent young mothers interests which are not wholly satisfied by their domestic activities as wife, mother, housekeeper, chauffeur, gardener, decorator, hostess, and nurse. One distinctively contemporary feature of the model life pattern women now contemplate is that they expect to have roles in the world outside the home. It is not novel for women of exceptional talents to play several roles in life. Many have done so for centuries. But in previous periods only a minute number have had roles in the world of men. One consequence of the feminist victories of the last century, and of their acceptance and consolidation, is that the theater of activity has been extended for all women who choose to act in it, and that many elect to do so.

Thus a girl who marries in the middle of her college experience or immediately after it—even more clearly, one who marries in graduate school—is not necessarily ignoring the question of work, even the possibility of serious long-term work, at some point in her life. When she marries, she is usually "in love"—that is, she is dominated by strong feelings and drives—and she assumes that she will be able to work out later whatever other roles in life she will want to undertake. Because society agrees that marriage should be her first goal, it is now beginning to help her to implement her other ambitions when she emerges from her total absorption in answering the needs in regard to that side of her life which asserted themselves through her marrying. Individuals and the society have both suffered from the fact that until recently it was difficult if not impossible after the age of late adolescence to remedy lacks in education or to obtain training for a vocation. Failure to follow the prescribed order of educational experience was punished by not being given another chance—at least not easily or freely. This situation is changing rapidly, and the dropout (male and female) is being taken more regularly into account in educational planning.

For many, perhaps even for most educated young women, the ambition to do well at a job in the world of men at some stage of life is now a strong emotional need, concededly subordinate to the demands of her primary goal, but not to be ignored on that account. Her motives for working outside the home tend to be pragmatic and personal rather than those of a crusade. But her drive for work is a real one, even if she tends to be content with a job rather than a career. M. M. Hunt has listed the needs of women which may be met by work as those for "money, identity, achievement, status, personal pride, inner joy, and for many a woman, whether she realizes it or not, a means of achieving a lasting peace rather than a cease-fire within marriage." Both men and women, he asserts, have a need for work as a means of absorbing aggressive energy and directing it "from destructive and hostile acts into deeds and objects of value, thus at one and the same time serving the economy of the society and the individual psyche."

In this respect women's life becomes somewhat more like that of men, and in turn this adds a new dimension and a new demand to the marriage relation. For a woman to perform in two worlds, as men do, her marriage must countenance her dual goals and support her in seeking them. The marriage relation is seen more and more consciously as a process in which husband and wife cooperate on many levels in order to permit each separately and both together to achieve a number of goals and satisfy a number of needs—not the least of them the need to control or eliminate destructive elements between them. It has always been taken for granted that men often have to meet the obligations of several functions simultaneously—as breadwinner, father, citizen, husband, hobbyist, and member of a series of formal and informal social groups. As one man recently remarked, they have been able to do this, by and large, because women have made it possible for them to do so. By concentrating on the home and on the minutiae of child-rearing, the women enabled the paternal role to be tailored to other demands in a man's life. For a woman to accept from her husband the kind of help that man has traditionally taken as his due from his wife, however, can be an emotionally complicated experience for both.

This new demand often made of contemporary husbands is characteristic of some of the novel sources of what can be pressure and tension as well as pleasure and satisfaction in marriage for young people of the present day. The demand is for action and understanding—or for the acceptance (without complicated forms of understanding) of sharing in certain of the traditional household jobs of women, so that the wife can work outside the home. The demand is also for acceptance and approval of the strivings which lead her to want to do so. Success depends to a considerable extent on having a husband who is as willing as his wife to do battle against the inner and outer forces which divide men from women, and to join her in seeking the rewards of an extended partnership.

Some of the novel perspectives (and sources of tension) in modern middle-class marriage arise from changes in social structure; others are intellectual and moral. Taken together, these changes in the internal and external life of society have affected the model for marriage in people's minds and have greatly increased its emotional meaning in the lives of both men and women. For contemporary America is now a more self-conscious culture than ever before, suffused with the insights and preoccupations which have spread throughout society from the corpus of Freud's work and the literature which has built upon it. This is not to say that self-consciousness is new to the world. But as an articulate mass phenomenon it is new, if for no other reason than the extent of education and the character of communication in our time. Those who communicate their feelings do so to millions: those who can be observed are viewed by millions, and those who speak are heard by millions. The millions, in turn, become aware (or take for granted) that their feelings are shared, are not unique, and have value.

Art, music, and literature reflect the stress on private and unconscious responses to life, to what the artist feels as the atomization of society. The individual is the focus. Only he and his few relationships genuinely exist, and they are often described in almost private language, or in symbols having private and deliberately limited reference. The problem of the existence of the individual has been the theme of one of the most influential schools in modern philosophy. And there has been generally increasing awareness of the challenge to the individual—a challenge which often becomes a threat—inherent in the choices put before each person in a mobile, dynamic society. He has to choose among goals, among modes and kinds of work, among places to live, among possible marriage partners, and even the number of marriages as well, for divorce is part of the social environment. The individual is acutely conscious of the nature of his involvements with himself and with others. Accepting psychoanalytic awarenesses, society encourages the individual to devote a great deal of his energy to those involvements and to his feelings about them. It is not remarkable, in this connection, that we have recently witnessed such an assertion of the primacy of private feelings in the action of a prominent political figure who judged that the society would tolerate his self-concern, even at the expense of breaking up two families, without much risk to his high political ambition.

Second, lingering traces of conflicting ideas about the proper position of women often add distinct strains to marriage. While the equality of women is now accepted as an abstraction, that acceptance is hardly uniform or consistent. The revolution in the attitudes of men and women toward the role of women outside the home is not fully realized. Older attitudes, often contrary ones, coexist uneasily with prevailing doctrine. Everyone is the child of his past. This generation, like its recent predecessors, has been struggling with stages in the process of liberating woman and transforming the subordinate social and personal status she had for so long. Even

225

the present generation of college students has not reached the point of handling the freedom and equality of women in a completely consistent and comfortable way. Thus the process of accommodation in marriage, inherently and inevitably complicated under the best conditions by the interacting personalities of husband and wife, and then of children, is complicated further by the intrusion of antithetical ideas about the rights, duties, and privileges of husband and wife, man and woman. Young men and young women often try to live by precepts which do not correspond to the dynamic forces within themselves or to the claims and preachings of society —sometimes, indeed, by precepts which contradict those forces and each other.

Third, some changes in social life have weakened many older bonds defining an individual's membership in groups, or relatively coherent communities.

Physical and social mobility has greatly affected the individual's relationship to the community in which he lives. The huge masses of people who migrate from many parts of the country to California or Florida, to boom towns, to new industrial and military complexes or great metropolitan areas, can hardly be expected easily to reproduce the sense of belonging characteristic of small, stable, established communities. Such physical movements of people in themselves attenuate family bonds.

That process of attenuation is furthered also by the trend to smaller families, smaller houses, and the disappearance of the practice of having an enlarged family group live together—grandparents, maiden aunts, orphaned cousins and so on.

The conditions under which many people now work, and their increased mobility in employment, have weakened another set of emotionally meaningful links—those ties of loyalty, of pride in work, and of comradeship which used to make the work relation—even the relation between worker and employer—one of strong, positive meaning in the lives of a great many men, perhaps the majority of men.

Social transformations affect middle-class marriage in another way—by requiring husband and wife to share in all sorts of domestic labor and in decisions affecting domestic organization. Servants have virtually disappeared. At the same time, the end of the custom of having enlarged family groups live together has had a similar effect: fewer hands for domestic tasks. The high cost of craftsmen of all sorts, and the need to express oneself in a form of work which has a beginning, a middle, and an end, have led many families to "do-it-yourself" in plumbing and carpentry, as well as in gardening, cabinet work, and other kinds of hand work. The net result is that in its sharing of tasks at home, the modern middle-class family begins to approximate some of the atmosphere of an old-fashioned farm family, where everyone participated in activities of meaning to the group as a whole. For the most part these activities now do not seem to have the constricting effect that many experienced on farms. Instead, people seem to find relaxation and release in the activity and the companionship involved in these varied operations.

Social transformations have not only affected the activities of husband and wife inside the home but outside it as well. Just as men are expected to help their wives, so wives are expected to help their husbands. While these social changes may enlarge the sphere of wifely action, they can also curtail her freedom to hold jobs or pursue careers. However cooperative the relation between husband and wife, there is usually the tacit assumption that the household is basically the wife's responsibility. If she can cope with that and another job, fine, but the domestic burden is primarily hers. The domestic sphere may be enlarged to include participation in her husband's work role—extending her horizons, but limiting her freedom and taxing her time and energy. For the job descriptions of many leading positions presuppose the active participation of a wife. No couple—ambassadorial or company president—is paid a double salary, although the wife may give as much in her part as her husband in his.

The increasing movement of people; the greater impersonality in the conduct of work; the sense of the overwhelming impersonal threat implied by the fact that a careless accident could trigger an annihilating war, have meant an increased reliance for satisfaction on the narrower and more personal relationships in life, such as those between friends, and between husband and wife, rather than on the fixed and accepted relationships, however shallow or neutral, of family or tribal life, or of life in the more stable and more feudal communities of the last century. One consequence, as has been noted, is that the marital relation and other restricted personal relations, like that of parent and child, must often sustain expectations and burdens which might in earlier times have been diluted and shared in a variety of ways without emotional cost, or at a lower emotional cost than now seems to be the case.

Social changes of this order surely have emotional consequences, but their nature and extent are debatable. Concentrating on social change as such may tend to conceal more basic questions. The process of personal development is a unity, although it has more or less distinct somatic, psychological, and sociological elements. Each person's life is a uniquely patterned conjuncture of experiences determined in part by innate forces and in part by the way he develops in response to outside events. In studying that pattern, or a configuration of such patterns common to many, it is difficult if not impossible to draw a clear line between the social and the dynamic psychological aspects of the result. In contemplating the model or ideal for marriage which some young people now accept, it is relevant, for example, to note the significance of changes in the size and structure of the middle-class family, and the disappearance of servants, as well as the other social and intellectual factors just mentioned. But we do not in fact know how deeply elements such as these, and their impact on our manner of living, affect the inner lives of young adults. We have not yet sorted out which is the chicken and which the egg. It is obvious, to take the example just mentioned, that a whole series of economic, social, and political events have eliminated domestic servants for all intents and purposes from the labor market. People have reacted to this trend by sharing domestic work within the family, not by organizing cooperatives or undertaking to live in colonies or communes where work would be shared. Should we say that the disappearance of servants has added another dimension of sharing to the domestic routine of middle-class families, or that the strong social tradition of family life, reinforced by psychoanalytic and other influences in modern thought, has dominated our response to this particular feature of social change, as has been the case in other instances? Or, to take another example, we say that personal relationships seem to be more freighted with emotional meaning than ever before. Is that because social, industrial, and political transformations have left man lonely and unprotected, save in a few remaining sanctuaries of privacy and intimacy, or because our culture teaches us to seek solutions of privacy and intimacy more and more insistently? Some studies report that in the kibbutzim of Israel, where parents are relieved of a large part of the work of child-rearing, there seems to be less need for privacy and less concentration of feeling and expectation on the small family unit. Which kind of hypothesis can one consider to account for this fact, if it is a fact?

The effect of social changes of this kind should be considered in several contexts; they should be viewed as factors superimposed upon and inextricably mixed with those arising from within the individual. They provide a framework within which he seeks social adaptations for the developmental stages through which he grows. The foregoing is an attempt to sketch the model for marriage in the minds of at least a given group of American middle-class women, and their husbands, as the framework within which they seek rather pragmatically to realize their quest for a full marriage, and for sustained and interesting work outside the home as well. Like all models, it has a considerable effect in turn on behavior.

It is one thing for a young woman to adopt a model as an idea, quite another to live by it. I do not intend to suggest that all's well in the best of all possible worlds, because the main problems of women these days seem to be not the old cliches of marriage versus career, but difficulties in accommodating high and demanding standards of homemaking, marriage, and childrearing to equally high standards by which they judge themselves as citizens, friends, and workers in the "outside world."

At this stage in the evolution of women's social role, the task of reconciling the goals of work and marriage is a strenuous one. The goals themselves are often and necessarily in conflict. Conciliation of the forces involved requires energy and flexibility as well as understanding, and the ability to tolerate a great deal that falls short of perfection, both in oneself and in others. The task has psychological, social, physical, and intellectual facets. Under the best of circumstances, it is fraught with uncertainty and must be dealt with by trial and error. The large and small adjustments required to maintain a balance of forces among husband, wife, and children (and within each one) call for discipline of a kind which can be exceedingly difficult to attain and to sustain. These efforts to reach and hold equilibrium tend to encourage change in the relationship between husband and wife—change, that is, in the sense that is opposed to the relationship being static. The movements in their relation push them toward more conscious awareness, if they are capable of achieving awareness of this order. It is hardly remarkable that it has become increasingly common in our culture for people to seek professional help in working out these relationships.

Among the issues which recurringly express or symbolize the concerns of young women, none is more crucial than the choice of a husband. For the girl in college, the subject of men is the center of much discussion. As girls grow older and continue their education, the topic does not lose interest, but experience gives some substance to their dreams and talk. There is more consideration of the need to fill a womanly function—a confrontation that may become a fear that a man will not appear to help make this possible. Will a man appear? What kind of man? The questions increase in importance and become more insistent and specific as most young women pursue work and study. What manner of man, and, within the range of possibilities, which particular man offers the best chance to achieve all the goals desired in marriage and through marriage?

The question is not always one which is posed in consciously recognizable terms until marriage is imminent or has already happened. And it is usually articulated most clearly by young women who have reached high levels of education. These young women, sophisticated in their recognition of social facts and able to classify all sorts of ideas and data, wish, like others, to marry men who will satisfy their instinctual needs, men whom they can regard as "strong" and "masculine," both sexually and socially. At the same time, they want husbands who will sympathize with their wishes for themselves, and who will be willing to make adjustments in their own activities so as to facilitate their wives' advanced training and the satisfaction of their ambition to do some work outside the home. This kind of expectation can range from having the husband share in household chores, or keep a schedule which would permit his wife to do a modified medical interneship, to deciding to pursue his career in a particular place because it offers the wife a chance to finish college, do special work, or go to graduate school.

It is not unusual, however, for a young woman to find that her intellectual view of things does not coincide with the way she feels when she gets into actual situations. A young man who impresses her as strongly masculine can seem too dominating and aggressive. She may conclude with mixed feelings that as a husband he may be more "interested in her body than her mind," and suspect or fear that he may not be very flexible in response to her needs. On the other hand, men who strike her as sympathetic and adaptable often also seem dubiously masculine.

The troubles which revolve around this issue may represent elements deep in the personality of the young woman, and elements as well of the social climate in which she has developed.

In the first place, there is a problem of cultural lag: the common and prevailing images and stereotypes of masculinity and femininity derive from periods which differed from ours, and they do not always correspond to many of the commonplace present-day distributions of function between men and women. The young men who move into dormitory rooms bringing vacuum cleaners as part of their baggage are automatically incorporating into their routines, as "manly" activities, chores which were once considered to be the work only of women. It is, therefore, easier for them and for the girls they marry to contemplate shared household tasks. But both young men and young women grow up in families and in a social environment where men are still generally the support of the family and a symbol of strength. When girls find themselves competing successfully with men in college and graduate schools, or in the performance of jobs, the experience may be disconcerting for them, even seriously disturbing. Rationality does not easily dispel the symbols and emotional realities of the past. They may conjure up feelings in women which interfere with the process of developing relations with men and thus of achieving the kind of marriage to which they aspire in principle.

If one has been encouraged to compete with men on equal terms from childhood, it is not easy to stop competing at will in courtship and marriage. Because marriage is such a desired goal, young women begin to sense the danger of their strengths to themselves and to their prospects of marriage. Their strengths in study and in work are in a sense "masculine," more than acceptable when doing "men's" work—working toward high educational goals. But they can become negative rather than positive, destructive rather than constructive, if the relation is felt, in one student's phrase, as "a power struggle between men and women."

Intellectual success and achievement often bring women confidence about their power in relation to men. Through it they prove to themselves and to others their competence in the world of work. At this stage of their lives, they may or may not feel competent in sexual behavior. Whether they do or do not feel so competent, they want to establish an emotional relationship with a man, but the man has to be a man in order to help them to be women. What seems to be meant most often by this formulation is that the women are afraid of their own strength, afraid that it will lead them to become hen-pecking wives; to dominate their men; to select dependent men; or to reduce the ones they marry to weak, acquiescent, withdrawn figures. Such fears may be reinforced by the image of one or both parents and their marital history.

This is not a new desire of women in relation to men, nor yet a new fear. *The Taming of the Shrew* was a power struggle for Kate, but today's highly trained woman has a new test to pose her Petruchio. He has to best her in his own world as well as in the domestic world. Her feelings about her own strengths have been made concrete for her. And Petruchio has to be better than she in achievement as well as strong enough to satisfy her instinctual needs and to help her control her destructive impulses. The tests thus posed are difficult both for the men and for the women who put them. For if the man fails to match the woman's stereotype of what a manly man ought to be, he is scorned—as he has been scorned since Xantippe—even when, in fact, she would have no other. But in scorning a man for being less than she in some ways, the young woman of today gives vent to her strength bitterly, aware that she is behaving in ways damaging to her self-image and to her image of the marriage she knows she wants.

Confusion about the symbols and the realities of masculine and feminine roles in life clouds thought and feeling and adds to the stress in this kind of testing. People tend still to be identified by what they do: it is often assumed that a man who engages in "manly" activity—boxing or hunting, to take classical examples—is masculine. Furthermore, our notions of masculine and feminine activity are still greatly influenced by persistent association with older, sex-determined functions. In addition, discrepancies between the actual and the ideal may have been better concealed in a social organization which placed a high value on ritual and form and tried to protect the image of the man's role. The middle-class father works in a world where the family does not see his performance. His effectiveness outside the house is often reflected back to the family by his wife. In the past, the wife was bolstered by a set of other people helping to uphold certain façades, whether there was "reality" behind them or not. The "master" might be aloof with the aloofness of a ruler whose wife exercised his authority as a deputy; or he might be aloof with the aloofness of a nonentity—a humble subject in his wife's kingdom. What comes through to the children may be confused, but the fact that there has to be a "master" is usually not.

Sorting out the real from the myth in any set of relations is a process which can engage people for long periods of time, whether they are aware of it or not. In late adolescence and early adulthood the process is most active and the effort to discover the "truth" most intense. It may be obvious to adults of insight that violence may not be synonymous with strength, but to those caught in the grip of strong childhood memories, and even of older myths, this kind of distinction may be unavailable. Many men and women know that both strength and weakness, masculine and feminine, can appear in unanticipated forms, and they know too that the idea of strength in a person is not necessarily the same as the factors which make for strength in a personal relationship. Awareness of these truisms is part of the natural equipment of many men and women. Intensive training in intellectual pursuits does not ensure such recognition or knowledge. Despite their principles, despite their theoretical formulations, all too many young women find it hard to work out the terms of the relationship between themselves and young men with ease, without "power" being held by either one or the other.

When one notes how these questions recur in the life histories of young women in both college and graduate training, one wonders about their relation to maturity; in what their sense of identity consists at this stage of their lives; how nearly ready they are for adulthood. "Maturity," in this context, is nearly as slippery a concept as "strength." We say that girls "mature" earlier than boys, but what do we mean? The full maturity of the adult personality is another matter. In one of the most useful connotations of the word, maturity means that the individual has successfully come through what Erikson calls "the major crisis of adolescence, the identity crisis," and forged for himself "some central perspective and direction, some working unity," bringing the effective remnants and hopes of his childhood into sensitive combination with "what he has come to see in himself and what his sharpened awareness tells him others judge and expect him to be."

People develop at different rates in different areas of their lives. Unusually precocious intellectual development, for example, can represent a number of things psychologically: a defense or a resolution, as Anna Freud and Erikson have taught us. Intellectual success can mask, often for long periods of time, an individual's failure to grow from one stage of his psychological development to another. And it may well be that the individual's concentration on his intellectual performance, or his performance in work, may have allowed his emotional development to be postponed, encapsulated, or impaired.

For success in study and work means quite different things to different young women, just as does their recurring conflict about women's choices. For some girls, success in work may be a way of pleasing their fathers. Others pursue education in order to be like their mothers or because they are dominated (sometimes reluctantly) by their mothers' wishes. For still others it may well be neither, but a means of using their own abilities in ways which do not impair and may even help other aspects of their development. As Hartmann has commented, where achievement of this order fits into the socially determined value hierarchies which an individual accepts, and through which "he becomes part of 'a world in which men have put a law over themselves,'" fulfilling such values may provide "an appropriate way to cope with libidinal and aggressive impulses."

In late adolescence or early adulthood, young women, like young men, experience a certain amount of turbulence, which often expresses itself in rebellion against the constriction of intellectual work for those who have been following the long path to graduate education. They are concerned with the fact that they may be different from other girls—especially in the view of men. It is not uncommon for a young woman to see herself as a "phony," in one girl's phrase, as a "freak," in another's, for excelling in academic work. Trying to live in the world of the scholar or the professional person, another found, was living in "an existentialist vacuum." At this point in their life satisfaction in work does not in any way equal their accomplishment.

It would seem, then, that a basic hazard to a young woman's equilibrium may be the task of achieving balance in the relative weight of work and marriage in her life. Once this is done, with or without help, more practical problems can fall into place—how many children to have and when; education and/or professional training before or after marriage; career versus job; part-time versus full-time work. These decisions seem to be comparatively easy for the young women who have genuinely accepted the idea of compromise between marriage and work as the foundation of their lives. For those still troubled by that issue, conflict may also reflect deeper difficulties. The necessity to make such decisions will loom up not as practical details in life, but as revivals of unresolved aspects of growth and development.

Since each situation depends on its own special combination of elements, varying with the nature of each participant's history, there can be no one solution which will be "right" for everyone, but there can be patterns within which appropriate solutions can be found by many if not most people. And it is such patterns that young men as well as young women are seeking in the marriage relation. The overall requirement is flexibility to accommodate the needs of each—in relation to one another and in relation to what is necessary for the success of each in the world's work.

Marriage has been called a "social contract." It is still a contract, not so much a business contract settling property rights, or a religious sacrament establishing eternal bonds, but a personal contract in which each undertakes to do his best to make the relationship meaningful—a contract defining the "rights" of each to realize his hopes and desires for himself with the help of the other. If there is earnestness about it, there is also honesty. If there is naïveté, there is also purpose in the view that although there are always ways of escape from difficulties, one would prefer to avoid them.

There are dangers in this demanding contract. For when strenuous efforts are made to reach high goals in partnership, stress must inevitably be reckoned with—stress on the individuals, and on the ideal itself. Disappointment can be bitter, if not shattering. The old view that one made the best of what was probably far from ideal left less room for illusion. Disappointment was built into expectation. A partnership bound by high expectation and free choice limits flexibility. Failure is not failure of a system or of a moral code or of a social class. It is the failure of a person—or of two people. Hence, chagrin and divorce. The present attitude toward marriage as a personal contract is a hopeful one—at least for the period of early family life. It may give new meaning to monogamy. And perhaps this is one reason why secular marriage counseling services are springing up in such diverse social environments as London, Paris, and San Juan as well as all over the United States.

We have indicated here some of the responses that are now occurring to the opportunity and the threat of freedom for women. As is implicit in the view of marriage we have portrayed, young men and women do not regard the Woman Question as a struggle for women alone.

LOTTE BAILYN

Notes on the Role of Choice in the
Psychology of Professional Women

CONCERN about the problem of the woman in America currently takes two rather distinct forms: on the one hand, it centers on the continuing quest for social legislation to ensure that any woman who *must* work can do so and be fairly compensated for it;[1] on the other hand, the emphasis is on an attempt to redefine social attitudes in such a way that any woman who *wants* to work can do so without an excessive burden of guilt.[2] Each of these problems has its own dimensions: in the one case, work is a matter of necessity and economic considerations are primary; in the other, work is a matter of choice and the difficulties are mainly social and psychological.

Generally, these two approaches are concerned with women from different strata of society. On the one hand is the large majority of women, on the other is an elite minority. In dealing with professional women, this paper is limited to the latter: it deals with the psychological situation of a small group of highly trained women who are put into a situation of having to choose what to do with this training. More particularly, it deals with those of this group who have chosen to make use of their training by engaging in occupations that require for their successful pursuit something more than regular attendance at a place of business and a sense of responsibility about one's activities while there.*

We are dealing, then, with a particular solution to the "tragic dilemma" of the educated housewife. In the many writings on this subject that have appeared during the past few years, one answer to her problems has increasingly emerged: do everything—be a

* Creative artists are excluded from the discussion because of the uniqueness of their work situation.

mother, be a housewife, and have a career too. For the fifties have
shown, this argument goes, that it is not sufficient for the educated
woman to be a mother and a housewife only; there is too much
frustration in that, and obviously too much waste. By including professional work in their lives, these women will regain the identity
they lost in the years when the exclusive role of "housewife" was
fashionable, and at the same time the professions will get badly
needed personnel.

This argument is based on so many sound assumptions that it is
sometimes hard to understand why it should be either new or debatable. In reaffirming the premise of the feminist movement that
women have as much ability and creative potential as men, and
share with them a desire and need for achievement, it is obviously
constructive. By denying that the job of housewife is the one occupation most suitable to the needs of women, it rests on sound psychological grounds: surely it is not reasonable to assume that
women form such a psychologically homogeneous group that one
type of endeavor is fully satisfactory to all. The argument also reflects and contributes to a new approach to child rearing, an approach that is less permissive and less child-centered than that of
the immediate postwar period, and which is coming to be accepted
as psychologically superior.

Yet, despite the soundness of these assumptions, the argument is
not wholly realistic, for it underestimates the complexity of the situation facing the educated woman. Difficulties do exist in the attempt
to combine family and work. And though the presence of such complications does not invalidate the contention that women should be
seriously involved in work, it does impose the necessity of recognizing these problems for what they are, if they are to be dealt with
intelligently. They must at least be understood, if not solved, if the
new-style feminists or the recruiters for the professions or the various
programs now operating to help educated women enter, or re-enter,
the professional world are to have the impact they deserve to have.

A woman's goal, like that of men, is to develop a life style that
uses her energies and capabilities in such a way that she functions
in her various roles efficiently and productively, with sufficient integration among these roles to give her at least some personal satisfaction in each. The probability that a man with a professional career
will reach such a goal is high in our society. But for a professional
woman it is not, since work has a different meaning and plays a dif-

ferent role in her life than it does in a man's. This difference is crucial. It may be explained, I believe, in terms of the role of choice in the educated woman's life.

In making decisions about a style of life, a woman must choose in ways that men do not choose. And, as far as work is concerned, the pattern of her basic decisions is the obverse of that of a man. For most men there is no basic choice as to whether or not to work. That a man will spend at least one third of his adult life in gainful work is a premise on which the plans for his life are based. But for a woman, society creates not a decision but the necessity for a choice. She must decide whether to include work in her plans and, if so, how much of her life she should devote to it. If the answer is that she will include work in a serious way, she then arrives at the point at which the career thinking of men begins. And at that point she meets another distinguishing characteristic of her pattern of choice. For, in most cases, the choice of work available for the educated man is wide, and society supports him in his desire for training and for mobility if these are necessary to enable him to fulfill his choice. But for a woman, once the basic decision is made, the range of choice is severely restricted. This restriction is only secondarily the result of employment discrimination against women. Primarily it results from the attitudes that surround a woman's behavior in her family role, for it is the expectation of society and of women themselves that no matter what else they may do, they will also, ideally, have a family.*

It seems, therefore, that the educated woman, in the process of planning her life, has a wide basic choice but narrow instrumental ones, whereas the reverse situation holds for men. And the woman's basic choice is wide even when the options of not getting married, or of getting married but not having children, are eliminated. (These

---

* The working-class wife who works only in order to make ends meet in the family is not beset by these problems. There may be unfortunate consequences of her working—her children, for instance, may be neglected—but she herself, because her working is not a matter of choice, is not faced with the dilemmas described here. Neither, for very different reasons, is the woman at the highest stratum of American society. Her endeavors, even though they are not often professional work, may well take up as much time and involvement as professional work, but her role in the family and her image of this role are different and conflict less with other activities. It is the educated woman in the middle range of society, therefore, who is most centrally involved in these problems.

exist in principle, of course, but today's pressures are such that they do not often exist psychologically—their occurrence is usually the result of regrettable circumstance.)

The consequences of this pattern of choice are of the greatest importance for a woman's performance and satisfaction in her work and family roles.* The fact that a woman functions in a situation in which she may or may not work decreases the likelihood that the choice to work, when made, will be definitive. Commitment may be seriously undermined. All serious work entails drudgery and unrewarding effort, and there are times when anyone—regardless of sex —would welcome a legitimate excuse to stop. Such excuses are near at hand for the professional woman. When faced with discouragement in her work it is not difficult for her to discover that her children really do need her all of the time, or that dilletantism is quite as acceptable as the serious intellectual effort that has bogged down. And, as a matter of fact, a decision to desist would surely have strong social support.

Not working, however, does not necessarily imply the end of all intellectual endeavor. On the contrary, a woman's choices would seem to give her the unique opportunity to pursue her professional interests by reading and reflection, without having to do the many trivial and irrelevant things necessary to hold a specific job and advance from it. Such a prospect, however, despite its immediate appeal, is not the final answer to the problem of the professional woman: it ignores both personal and institutional complications.

To begin with, such a view makes it difficult to justify professional training for women. Training facilities are limited, and "the production of cultured and enlightened mothers—desirable as this may be —can only be regarded as a by-product, not as the main aim of university education." [3] How natural, then, that graduate admission boards "discriminate" against women. Nor is such a use of professional training easily justified from a psychological point of view. A large percentage of professional women—or men, for that matter— would find it difficult to retain their professional commitment under

---

* In tracing some of these consequences here I obviously do not mean to imply that all of them occur in all women, or even in any one woman. Rather they form the dimensions of the problem of the professional woman. The extent to which they actually occur and the conditions that exaggerate or mitigate them is an empirical question to which there is, so far, no answer. Some of the factors that would have to enter into such an empirical investigation are discussed below.

conditions of "unattachment." * And yet, under other conditions, these same people could do work that would have value for society and be satisfactory to them.

But even under conditions of "attachment" the professional woman faces a series of frustrations that are unique to her. At her job she encounters difficulties that result from the second aspect of her choice situation, the narrowness of her instrumental choices. Because of the lack of geographical mobility of the professional married woman she cannot follow the opportunities in her field but must make the most of those that exist wherever she happens to be. Such a situation leads to exploitation—exploitation not merely in the sense of lower salaries for equal work (though that occurs) but in the more general sense of an inferior work situation created by her availability and lack of autonomous force in the competitive job market. She will, for she must, accept conditions that her male counterpart would not. This sometimes has advantages for the woman: conditions such as part-time work allow her the flexibility in her arrangements that she needs and so all the more willingly accepts. But though this sort of exploitation often occurs with the knowledge and even with the approval of the woman, it impedes her professional advancement and hence increases the likelihood that she will find herself in a situation where she is superior—in ability, training, or seniority—to the requirements of her job and to the men classified as her equals or even as her immediate superiors. The problems and frustrations resulting from such a situation are obvious, and they affect the quality of her work as well as the state of her mind.

The woman, therefore, is given freedom of choice at a point that leads to confusion and is not given this freedom where it is necessary in order to ensure a satisfactory work situation. And this same pattern of choice also introduces complications into her family role.

The mother's relation to her children is particularly sensitive to the pressures created by the decisions that she must face. For though the assumption that the children of working mothers are emotionally deprived is, at least in the case of professional women,

* Constance E. Smith, Director of the Radcliffe Institute for Independent Study, uses this term to describe the lack of institutional affiliation of many professional women. She reports the complaint of some of the Institute Fellows that this condition is particularly complicated because it provides no external measure of accomplishment.

more often than not invalid, the situation does tend to increase the concern felt by the mother when a child's behavior deviates from what she considers to be acceptable. Just as a woman's wide basic choice produces problems in her work role, so too it tends to undermine her confidence in her maternal role. Given present social attitudes it is unlikely that she can escape the feeling at some time that a difficulty of her child is directly or indirectly the result of her working. Minor crises remind her of choices she has made and make her less sure in her handling of them. Such an attitude will surely be reflected in the child, who will therefore be different than he would have been had his mother not been working. Available evidence indicates that these differences are not easy to describe, and are neither all bad nor all good.[4] But is it not reasonable to assume that a mother's sensitivity to the effect of her life style on her child may on the whole be no worse for him than the uncritical assumption by the full-time mother that what she does is right? Whatever the effect on the child, however, the professional mother must cope with strain in her maternal role.

Her family role in general is similarly affected. She must justify her choice of style of life, and the locus for this justification lies in the family rather than in her professional work. In our society it is her ability to run a house, have a happy family life, and bring up well-behaved and interesting children that serves as the justification for her life rather than her success and satisfaction in her profession. "Grandmother Becomes Professor" is the way a recent appointment of a woman professor was announced in the newspapers. As a result, the woman engaged in a combination of career and family often finds herself attempting to develop all possible aspects of her family role rather than abstracting the essentials from it and ignoring or allocating to others everything else. It is often more difficult for her, for example, to say "no" to the PTA chairman when asked to participate in a project than it is for the woman who fulfills only the family role.

The attempt by the professional woman to include in her life the widest possible range of home activities exaggerates the difficulties that exist in the combination of disparate life roles and introduces basic contradictions in her self-image. A woman who is centrally involved in her family but who also undertakes volunteer activities or many social enterprises experiences no less pressure of time or physical energy than one who attempts to combine work with family. But psychologically the pressures are different. Volunteer or social activities fit within the image of the housewife-mother; they have even been encouraged, some have said, in order to fill out this role. There is an accepted value structure to comprehend all of the activities of such a woman. But the professional woman with a family meets requirements in her work that are covered by values quite different from those that organize her home life, and she is faced with the necessity of learning to tolerate such contradictions or of extemporizing an integration of her own.

The meaning and use of time are an example. For the housewife-mother, typically, time is a purely additive phenomenon. She needs enough to get things done, but any given task can be and characteristically is interrupted a number of times without detriment to the quality of the completed task. As a matter of fact, vis-à-vis children—especially when they are young—instant availability without continuous presence is probably the best role a mother can play. For the professional, however, time follows a very different principle: uninterrupted time is crucial, and little snatches of it taken here and there are not additive.

In view of such contradictory demands, how does the professional woman manage the logistics of her situation, how does she arrange her household? Characteristically she does it minimally: she gets help only to cover those times in which she must work and in which competing family demands are always present.* But such a situation continually produces conflict. A child with a cold on a school morning saved for work can lead in the miniature to the necessity of remaking the original decision about one's life plan. Similarly the professional self-image must be very strong and stable indeed to survive under the condition in which the requirements of work become secondary to the whims of a babysitter.

Compare, here, the situation of the professional man. He too is faced with different values in his work and his family, and some degree of conflict along the same lines exists for him also. His situation is eased, however, by the existence in his environment of a hierarchy of values which precludes, for the most part, the necessity of conscious decision. Unless family needs reach crisis proportion,

---

* Financial considerations are not the sole reason for this. Hanna Papanek suggests that attitudes toward the value of time and money are important: since there is not enough work in the modern American home to keep a housekeeper busy full time, it is not "worth" paying her merely to be around in case she is needed, even if one can afford it.

the demands of his work come first. And neither he nor his wife is faced with problems of choice in a condition of crisis.

These are some of the psychological consequences of the process of choice in which the woman who seeks to combine a family with a professional career is involved. It is a process that may be described at a high level of generality as revokable, irrational, and discontinuous.

It is revokable in a very basic sense. "Occupation: housewife" is an ever-present alternative, and the possibility exists at almost any time of reversing, or at least of stopping one's advance along a given professional path. It is this characteristic of revokability that makes modern woman's problem more complicated than the either-or choice earlier feminists faced.

The process is irrational because it necessitates making occupational decisions in a situation in which realistic opportunities can neither be evaluated nor freely followed up. Opportunities can of course never be evaluated with complete accuracy; but the common lack of freedom to follow up considered evaluations is unique to the situation of women, and the degree to which opportunities can be foreseen is a great deal less for them than it is for men.

Finally, the process is discontinuous because each stage in a woman's life introduces new factors which she must take into account when she plans her life—factors whose implications for such a plan are often contradictory to those of a previous stage.*

Some analysts feel that this last factor—discontinuity—must be deliberately made an integral part of every educated woman's life plan, and that it suggests a solution to the problems discussed above. The solution they have in mind might be called the "seriatim" ap-

---

* In contrast, Eli Ginzberg, Sol W. Ginsburg, Sidney Axelrad, and John L. Herma, *Occupational Choice: An Approach to a General Theory* (New York: Columbia University Press, 1951), p. 198, reach the following conclusions on the basis of their study of occupational choices of educated men:

First, occupational choice is a process which takes place over a minimum of six or seven years, and more typically, over ten years or more. Secondly, since each decision during adolescence is related to one's experience up to that point, and in turn has an influence on the future, the process of decision-making is basically irreversible. Finally, since occupational choice involves the balancing of a series of subjective elements with the opportunities and limitations of reality, the crystallization of occupational choice inevitably has the quality of a compromise.

243

proach: educated women should drop their professional work after the initial, basic training has been accomplished in order to devote themselves to their families, and resume it when their children are grown up, or at least well advanced in school.[5]

This solution deserves careful evaluation. Such an evaluation, however, cannot be done merely on the basis of a general analysis. Empirical studies are required to make clear what the satisfactions and difficulties are likely to be for women of various skills in various immediate situations to drop and resume their work at certain stages. And though it is not the purpose of this paper to present a research proposal, it is perhaps appropriate here to indicate some of its implications for research by suggesting two characteristics of a professional woman's life that should enter into the design of such investigations.

First, it must be kept in mind that for a professionally trained woman the amount of continuity between her professional and her private life can greatly alter the configuration of her situation. One form of such overlap is provided by the circumstance of a woman's working professionally in the same field as her husband. Such a situation would seem to be peculiarly suited to the "seriatim" solution: it reduces the burdens of keeping up with the field, of maintaining contact within it, and decreases the need for an independent institutional affiliation. Some psychological and institutional problems are no doubt created by this situation; but the burdens of the lack of integration in a woman's life are reduced.

A different form of overlap occurs when a woman's work lies in what might be called "feminine" fields. By this I mean professional work devoted to problems and concerns that the woman herself faces in her private capacity within the family. Pediatrics, certain forms of psychiatry, social work—or the study of the psychology of women—are examples of what I have in mind. Continuity of this sort provides in itself a special form of integration in a woman's life. By lessening the distance between her two roles and hence reducing the contradictions in her self-image it would be expected to ease her problems. It might also lead to a weakening of her intellectual force by blurring the distinction between work and family life, and create special disturbances in her family role by introducing a degree of external authority incommensurate with the natural conduct of that role. But, like identity in field between husband and wife, the circumstance of work within these "feminine" fields is important because it alters the probability that a woman will achieve a satisfactory integration in her life.* In both cases, there is a decrease in the necessity to have an independent commitment to work. This makes the discontinuity implicit in the "seriatim" approach less problematic and, in general, eases some of the strain in a woman's professional role.

But no amount of success in her work will ensure a satisfactory life style if there is strain in the woman's role in her family and community. And here the attitude of her immediate environment to her participation in professional work is crucial. The most important potential source of support or hostility is the husband, and his attitude must be a central factor in any empirical study of professional women. Less obvious, but also important, are the attitudes of contiguous groups such as neighbors, husband's colleagues, or the parents of one's children's friends, for these are groups to whom one's work role is highly visible and who serve as a constant reference for comparison and evaluation.

Both the continuity between a woman's professional and private life, and the support she receives from those around her in the decision to do professional work will affect the success with which she pursues her double life. And it is only when such factors are, for purposes of study, held constant that it makes sense to pose such research questions as what personality or other characteristics differentiate professionally trained women who do work from those who do not, and to assess the actual impact of the problems of choice on the lives of professional women.

REFERENCES

1. See, for instance, *American Women: Report of the President's Commission on the Status of Women, 1963* (Washington, D. C.: United States Government Printing Office) and the article by Esther Peterson in this issue.

2. Betty Friedan, *The Feminine Mystique* (New York: W. W. Norton and Co., 1963) represents this point of view. See also the article by Alice S. Rossi in this issue.

3. Alva Myrdal and Viola Klein, *Women's Two Roles: Home and Work* (Lon-

* This discussion points out the difficulty of using only the objective description of a person's field (such as is used in most career studies) in the study of professional women. By ignoring the role that a given field plays in a woman's life situation, the usual field designations are unlikely to be fruitful in such investigations.

don: Routledge & Kegan Paul [International Library of Sociology and Social Reconstruction] 1956), p. 153.

4. Results depend on the mother's attitude toward her work, the sex of her child, and other factors. For a summary of the few research findings on the effect on her children of an educated mother's employment see Lois M. Stolz, "Effects of Maternal Employment on Children: Evidence from Research," *Child Development*, XXXI (1960), 749–782, and F. Ivan Nye and Lois Wladis Hoffman, *The Employed Mother in America* (Chicago: Rand McNally & Co., 1963).

5. For an example, see Myrdal and Klein, *Women's Two Roles*, p. 154.

JILL CONWAY

Jane Addams: An American Heroine

Two GENERATIONS of middle-class American women from 1880 to the close of the 1920's were dominated by aspirations of a nature now quite alien. They desired a public life of restless activism, and saw fulfillment for these desires only in terms of extreme individualism. It would have been inconceivable for Jane Addams or Lillian Wald to fulfill this desire for a public role through the career of a husband, just as Eleanor Roosevelt, perhaps the last legatee of this tradition, found it necessary to create a public life of her own apart from that of the President. Three problems of the period were the basis of this drive to acquire a public life. They were not exclusively feminine problems, but all were perceived with particular acuteness by educated women of the middle class.

The first was a sense of mission. Women of their day, they believed, had a special position in history and a special duty to posterity. They were the first group of women in the United States to receive education at the college and graduate level, and they had to bring all this enlightened and disciplined femininity to bear upon the improvement of their world. A sense of mission is a painful burden if undirected, and consequently the second problem of their world was an oppressive sense of unreality. They had a total belief that a trained and well-stocked mind would fit them for new roles in life. Yet they found none immediately. They needed problems to solve in order to justify these providential gifts of knowledge and leisure, and there were too few of these to satisfy their compulsive desire to be useful. The third difficulty was sociological. If pioneer societies set no bounds on human achievement by the confining patterns of the past, they also supply no models to aspire to except masculine ones. The class societies of the old world did have definite public roles for women of birth, education and leisure, such as the life of the political salon, the literary circle or the chatelaine of estates. In Chicago achievement for an aspiring woman lay in Mrs. Potter Palmer's world of conspicuous consumption until Jane Addams set out to define new roles for women in the hitherto masculine preserve of public life. A mobile society had no recognized activities which a lady of wealth and leisure might pursue except bigger and more grandiose versions of what all American women were expected to do.

This drive to activism and participation in a masculine world was reinforced by the dominant philosophies of the day. Knowledge and truth for Americans of these generations were not objects of contemplation but means to successful action. Experience was almost the only guide to perceptions of reality. It followed that an education which did not lead to an active life was meaningless. The value of knowledge lay in its social utility to an era that accepted the Spencerian vision of society. Education was a positive aid in raising the race and it was to be assessed by the degree to which it allowed the recipient to participate in the struggle for survival. This utilitarian notion of the education they had received added to the burden of guilt of post-Civil War American women. Every powerful force in their culture urged that they should pursue active and socially beneficial careers, yet their society provided no such outlet. Their predicament was exacerbated by the persistence of certain of the Victorian notions of femininity even though the Victorian social restraints had been removed. They believed, for instance, that women were custodians of race morality, were exempt from the baser human passions, and, because of their maternal instincts, were less prone to violence than men. Thus all Victorian notions of feminine delicacy had become concentrated in the notion of the refinement of women's moral perceptions, and it seemed that they should redeem public life from the baser masculine passions.

No woman of this generation more clearly represents the predicament and its resolution than does Jane Addams. She had a mind whose brilliance and driving power made her acutely responsive to the intellectual and cultural forces of nineteenth-century America. Her personality was characterized by an extreme drive to power which she recognized and strove to discipline from early youth. Intellect made it impossible to accept the achievement of a philistine Chicago, while her complex personality demanded exceptional performance in any task she chose. Since Chicago was the milieu in which she chose to work out her demanding predicament, her solution was one of activism of epic proportions. Yet she was by nature an intellectual, and much of her impact on her society comes from the lucidity of her published reflections on her life and its meaning.

Her remarkable personality, her exceptional intellectual endowment and her very real achievement in public life do not, however, explain completely the kind of national response she evoked. Its actual dimensions are mythical, and she is remembered pietistically in the education of succeeding generations of American children. It is curious that only she should be remembered in this fashion when many other women of her generation equalled her in terms of any public achievement which posterity can measure. Lillian Wald in New York began settlement work at approximately the same time, and in the course of her career she was instrumental in the professionalization of nursing as a career for women and in the foundation of the Federal Children's Bureau. She was active in politics and as successful in raising money for good causes. Mary Richmond as a social worker probably outshone all her contemporaries. Women like Florence Sabin and Alice Hamilton developed careers of tireless public service in the medical profession. Florence Kelley probably displayed greater administrative genius in masterminding the campaigns of the National Consumers' League for social reform for over forty years and providing the legal mind necessary to pursue endless minutiae of evidence to swing some final campaign for social legislation. In hours traveled and speeches made in these causes, she surely exceeded Jane Addams. The same might be said of Julia Lathrop as head of the Federal Children's Bureau and of her career in Washington. Finally, as guardians of immigrant groups and systematizers of philanthropy, Grace and Edith Abbott might be said to excel her achievement. Yet none of these women of national reputation and significance played the kind of charismatic role for two generations which Jane Addams did. The impact of this charismatic personality is remarkable and can be detected from her early youth. One of her contemporaries described its impact in personal relations. "There was, despite her affectionate warmth and sympathy and understanding, something impersonal about that relation, akin to sharing in some blessing of nature, that like the sunlight, shone alike on the just and the unjust. One shared the gift gladly and gratefully, and without a personal stake in it exactly."[1] Such an impact came from the quality of discipline about her personality. Unlike her fellow women public figures whose public lives were a natural expression of their personalities, Jane Addams, by an act of will, conformed herself to an American model of excellence. A potential expatriate, like Gertrude Stein or Henry James, she chose to return after years of fascinated pleasure in a European world. She chose Chicago and her deepest roots, rather than the attenuated loyalties of the East Coast, and she deliberately became the model of feminine excellence in the American terms which she understood so perfectly. It was no easy choice, and it was this struggle triumphantly surmounted which gave her a genuine air of secular sanctity.

For her contemporaries it seemed logical that Jane Addams, and she alone, should second the nomination of Theodore Roosevelt at the Progressive convention of 1912 on behalf of all American women. It seemed logical to them, and to Jane Addams also, for she wrote an article shortly afterwards explaining why one woman should perform this symbolic act of participation in national politics on behalf of all her sisters.[2] As a political campaigner she was believed by the organizers of the Progressive party to be a vote-getter without equal. She toured the country from Maine to California speaking on T. R.'s behalf, and wrote tirelessly for Progressive press releases. In all sections of the country, during the campaign, speakers at rallies could have the assistance of Jane Addams Choirs singing selections from the Jane Addams song book, which sold well at a few cents a copy to raise campaign funds. Within the Progressive National Committee there is no question of her influence. She coached the Rough Rider on social issues and instructed him in feminism, and explained about moral equivalents to war, and he listened attentively. Such a position was held by Lillian Wald in the Democratic machine in New York from the time of the 1912 Wilson campaign to Al Smith's campaign in 1928, yet none of these activities seemed to involve the mystical participation of all women in the United States, or to provoke a lyrical response from Democratic choirs.

Her impact on American life was not confined to politics. It was felt at all levels of intellect and emotion throughout the nation. Jane Addams wrote very well on education, on women's problems in an urban society, on the social meaning of democracy, on prostitution, on faith, on what reflection had led her to believe was the meaning of her life at Hull-House. She was probably the most gifted of her contemporaries as a popular writer, though she was not a systematic thinker like the Abbott sisters, nor did she have the incisive mind of Florence Kelley. Yet her correspondence with William James suggests that he placed immense value upon her ideas. Hers, he said, was the most gifted mind of his generation. She "inhabited reality,"

said the great pragmatist, and in her *being* summed up the experience of his America.[3] John Dewey wrote gratefully of learning much
from visits to Hull-House and conversation with Miss Addams. She
had helped, he felt, in the elaboration of his ideas on education, and
in defining a democratic society. On every issue of public life she
was urged to write for the *Atlantic Monthly* by William Ellery
Sedgwick, as a universally accepted popular conscience.

This kind of adulation was national. Internationally, before her
involvement in the peace movement during the First World War,
she was well known also, although in a circle confined to social
workers and intellectuals in England and feminists in Europe. Frequent visits to Europe, proficiency in languages and tireless attendance at conventions in part explain this kind of reputation. Yet there
was more to it than that. People wished to introduce her abroad as a
perpetual exhibition of what was good about America and modern
American women. Aylmer Maude was anxious that she should meet
Tolstoy for this reason, and her legendary journey across Russia to
converse with the great Russian sage on questions of democratic
morality was the product of this kind of urge on the part of her contemporaries. In this way she came to be well known in London and
Paris, long before her pacifism made her famous during the First
World War.

What was it about her life that it should symbolize American
womanhood and the best aspirations of the American world of her
time? From 1889 her winters were generally spent in Chicago in a
life of administrative social work. Her genius, as she herself recog-
nised while still cloistered in Rockford Seminary, was administrative.
After the pioneer years at Hull-House, when she had captured the
support of Chicago society through the all-powerful Chicago
Women's Club, her days were spent in conferences with the powerful and wealthy, arranging the financing of ever increasing projects
for Hull-House, acquiring more real estate, discussing investments,
soliciting donations, and most efficiently of all, directing publicity.
Hers was the organizational genius which brought into being the
ideas of her gifted associates, but inevitably this left her less and
less time for close contact with the urban slum world which she had
first sought. She had sought it in a curiously Victorian way which
must be elucidated to explain her impact on her generation. Her
childhood in a small-town rural world had been the epitome of
second-generation life on the frontier. Standards had slipped a little.
She called her father and stepmother Pa and Ma, and for years her

grammar and spelling were a little shaky. Schooling remedied formal errors and gave her the desire to "go East, and become a cultivated person." She had plans to attend Vassar or Smith which were all firmly denied. She could form no estimate of them as educational institutions. She wanted to meet sophisticated people and encounter another world outside the comfortable barbarities of Cedarville, Illinois, and she knew dimly the formal way to get there. It never became open to her, and so, almost a generation later, traveled, educated and independent, she created an equivalent in Hull-House. Europe had been her education in a brilliantly enlarging sense. Paris, Dresden, Rome, Florence, Assisi allowed her to form a notion of the kind of excellence she had once hoped to find "back East." But for her the life of the expatriate was impossible. Her roots were solidly in small-town Illinois. Wealth, leisure and intellect must be disciplined to the active service of an American ideal. This service she found by an inspired combination of her European world of intellect and beauty and the Puritan ethic. She went home to found a salon in a slum. It was to be a beautiful house created by her acquired taste, which left her remote from Cedarville. It was to be inhabited by a circle of gifted and brilliant friends. But it was to be firmly rooted in an American past by being directed toward doing good. Hull-House became an intellectual center in Chicago, justified in an anti-intellectual society by its dedication to social work. Life there was beautiful, graceful and convivial; since it was American, it was also incredibly responsible, hardworking and idealistic. By day the residents slaved at remedying social problems—garbage collection, aid to unwed mothers and political reform amongst immigrant groups. At night they came home to a house where everyone of intellect and repute in the United States and every important foreign traveler visited. Actresses, authors, musicians, royalty, heads of state all came to Hull-House and dined and talked. In the summer no one visited Chicago voluntarily, and the spirit went out of it all. Miss Addams had believed in the foundation of Hull-House that perceptions of reality were to be found only in the sordid reality of the urban slum world. This was how she had justified her return—she was to live and act on the "new urban frontier" of American experience. Yet in this she was the prisoner of an American mystique, and soon she began to retire thankfully in the summers to the homes of friends on the East Coast. For she began to realize that it was not the slums and the unwed mothers which represented reality for her, but a society which would permit her to write and think about them.

She was an intellectual captured by the activism of American life. In Hull-House she had found a way of life which allowed some reconciliation of action and contemplation, but she paid a price. Summers in Bar Harbor allowed her to recapitulate her experience, to sum up contemporary philosophy, to survey pressing social issues, but not the literary and intellectual achievement which another society might have allowed her. A biographer is left with the distressing sense that she had the qualities of mind and spirit to transcend her society; instead she became its model.

The one European import which could not travel to her Chicago salon was a sense of humor. She and her companions were relentlessly serious about what they did, and any kind of frivolity was totally alien to their temperaments. A sense of the comic escaped them because they perceived no gap between the reality of what they achieved and the greatness of their aspirations. They believed their dedication to a life of the mind and a career of social reform was to an end totally achievable. The good society was within their grasp. Freedom for women, which they were in the process of defining, although its definition temporarily escaped them, was perfectly possible and merely waited to be discovered. Hence their high seriousness and their inability to perceive the absurd. This made them high-spirited but not witty, happy but never gay, and curiously one-dimensional. Like characters in a Dickens novel, one always knows what they are going to say.

So much for what Jane Addams did. What was she like? Obsessively devoted to her father, she remained emotionally frozen after his death in her twenty-first year. She had innocent, intense and shatteringly emotional relationships with several women friends. Outside these she was a sad and aloof personality. Kindly, but essentially unknowable to many of her closest co-workers, she directed all of her formidable energies into her public role. It was this regal but unglamorous personality which evoked a fan mail during her lifetime similar to that of a twentieth-century film star. A day's correspondence could bring a letter from a German nun who found *The First Twenty Years at Hull-House* inspirational reading, notes from small children requiring advice on all aspects of life, and emotional thanks from bereft people whose dying relatives had been comforted by reading her ideas on human experience.

This response occurred because she exemplified in her person a philosophy of extreme individualism, which during her active public life was not confronted by insoluble problems, and to which two generations of Americans had a profound commitment. Her principal belief was in an inevitable evolutionary progress of which man's will and intellect were the motive force. This was a kind of intellectual Darwinism which involved a Puritan evolutionary ethic. Man was predestined to rise, but by means of a driving intellectual effort amongst the chosen. Work and the calling were merely thereby transposed to the evolutionary notion of man. All the problems of urban industrial America could be solved, she believed, by the combined efforts of individual intellects and wills. This belief was immensely attractive to her generation because it had the advantage of being neither conservative nor radical. It allowed her to define social problems while pointing to a comfortable solution, and to make these problems seem less anguishing since in evolutionary terms they were preconditions of a developing "good society." Her impact on her contemporaries was so great because she seemed to validate this view of society in her own career. The effort of her own will and intellect had created a new kind of role for women during her own life, and her individual efforts as a social worker had had phenomenal success which was visible to contemporaries.

Her career was edifying in another sense to a generation plagued by religious uncertainty and repelled by the materialism of the gilded age. Her concept of the settlement house and a life of service to society offered contemporaries an ideal of personal commitment to a demanding but simple discipline. In Europe or Asia this might mean vows of poverty or silence. She brought the intensity of discipline and devotion of the mendicant order to busy winters of administrative social work in Chicago and to quiet contemplative summers in Maine, supplying as she always did a specifically American version of a universal desire for a life of discipline. It was one built about comfort, utility and success, but it was nonetheless a life of discipline.

In all areas of deep sensitivity in American culture during these years, she was a kind of apostle, preaching a gospel of comfortable adjustment to things. To a society perplexed by the violent disruption of rural life and the equally undisciplined growth of cities, she preached the acceptance of change. She had a real and creative vision of urban life based on profound disillusionment with her own small-town origins, and she wrote about cities and their growth in an edifying and comforting way. Urban life was the new decree of an evolutionary providence and was not to be decried or feared, but defined and understood. The city was an exciting and creative event in man's evolution, not a tragic falling off from an idyllic rural past. It was exciting because for the first time, in an urban world, man created his own environment. Man was therefore no longer dimly striving to understand God's creation but could control and direct a world which he had created for himself. This was a heady prospect, for in Darwinian terms control of the environment conjured up a vision of infinite and rapid progress directed toward rationally conceived ends. The urban world, moreover, was one in which the true meaning of democracy could be found. Jane Addams had an ideal vision of the Greek city-state which she transposed without any apparent feeling of incongruity to Chicago and to American urban life. Rural life was necessarily imprisoning because it placed a special value on certain kinds of strengths and skills. The modern city and technology offered man an infinite variety of occupations in which his creative instincts could be fulfilled and created leisure unknown in the backbreaking routine of the farm. Here was freedom for humanity impossible in the past. Many of her friends were doctrinaire socialists, and she knew a great deal about Marx, though it is not clear whether she read his writings. She shared his vision of a society transformed by technology, but for her the transformation was happy and harmonious. Industry set the individual free by releasing him from the extended family of his rural past. Young men were no longer dominated by past generations. They need not wait patiently to inherit land and livelihood. They could dispose of their intellect and skills as they chose in the great factories of the new society.

Women were freed by the city in even more exciting ways. They were free to support themselves and to live alone. The maiden aunt acquired dignity and independence by industrial labor. Men and women acquired anonymity and could direct their lives in relation to themselves alone. Fulfillment was to be found here by the individual. Jane Addams saw such isolation as desirable freedom. For her it bore no hint of loneliness, nor did it suggest destruction of human relationships which might have value above those of the individual. The freeing of youth from the limitations of the past was of enormous value in evolutionary terms, for the young of the race carried all its creative impulses, and only if they were free to develop them could progress occur. This was transposing the experience of the frontier to her evolutionary view of life. The young were free to respond to a new environment where outmoded skills might be a positive hindrance.

All this optimism was not made bland by a refusal to recognize the cost in human terms of the creation of an industrial society. Her notion of pain and human suffering was very real, but it was Greek. She wished for no personal resolution of the problems it presented. It was enough that the race should rise. This was a convenient postponement of the problem of evil. It was also a satisfactory externalization of the personal difficulties which freed one's energies for the busy pursuit of social problems and allowed one to compromise about them now in terms of a belief about their resolution in the future. It was thus possible to be a ruthless individualist without ever paying the price, for one always gracefully avoided the confrontation of absolute and insoluble problems. This solution to the dilemmas of the post-Civil War era in the United States answered to a need felt as powerfully in rural Illinois as in Boston, Washington or New York, for it made the change from the rural America of Jefferson and Lincoln to that of a great urban society possible without a major disturbance in the simple individualism of an agricultural world.

To make change acceptable was one thing; to make it edifying answered to a nation-wide reform impulse. The ghettos of immigrant labor in the growing cities were merely scars imported from another world, and Americans must not reject but strive to heal them. The healing process, however politely put, was Americanization. Immigrants at Hull-House practiced their folk arts as a kind of therapeutic release, not because they were felt to be a folk. They attended lectures in sociology and economics and American government and were encouraged to practice thrift and industry. Their language and their culture were understood and respected, but they were taught to see themselves as part of the inevitable evolutionary process which demanded adaptation above all things. This was an exceptional response in an American world which saw immigrants either as a threat to American values or as a labor force to be exploited. Its kindness and generosity cannot be too strongly stressed. Philosophically, nonetheless, it was based on an evolutionary view within which all differences could be resolved in the name of progress, and as such it was merely a broader application of an already dominant philosophy.

This philosophy was one bound to appeal to post-Civil War Americans. In a curious way, however, its appeal was integrally related to the person of the philosopher. As a reformer wishing to change and understand society, Jane Addams also wished to change and understand herself. Her career was a great success story in terms which every American understood. She had come from a small town to the city and achieved mythical success. Unlike Theodore Dreiser's heroines, she had done it in a socially acceptable fashion. As a good Sister Carrie she had stormed to the top of Mrs. Potter Palmer's Chicago and thus participated in the gilded age without becoming besmirched by it. In the process, because of her profound commitment to an intellectual life, she had paused to write and reflect about what she was doing. She wrote with the simple directness of someone who had personally confronted the problems which concerned her. Hers was not an abstract or doctrinaire position in one sense, for she wrote from experience. In a society confused and puzzled about ideas and experience, she wrote about her own confusion and puzzlement, and their resolution. A social reformer in a class society possesses an unquestioned identity, outside of which he wishes to operate to change the social order. In a world of ceaseless social mobility such is not the case. The identity of the reformer is established by the process of reform, while society as a whole rightly comes to estimate his ideas by his person as much as by his policies. Hence for Americans the personality of Lincoln is the subject of as much, or possibly more, debate than his policies, while a British historian devotes much less time to the personalities of Lord Shaftesbury or Sydney and Beatrice Webb. Jane Addams as a person became the final test for her ideas, for she embodied her own solution to the problems of contemporary society.

The society which responded to her was one perplexed by the creation of wealth and leisure, while its predominant values were those of frontier activism and the Puritan ethic. The Spencerian adaptation of Darwinian biology was accepted as explanation of the social process. It served to justify the untrammeled individualism of industrial entrepreneurs which had created the problems of urban poverty and brought about the appearance of what seemed to be real social divisions in a society whose identity lay in its acceptance of the democratic ideal. This identity was threatened in another direction by the "new" immigration of the post-Civil War era. Its size and composition resulted in the great ghettos of exploited urban labor whose existence seemed to challenge the notion of a democratic society on the one hand and to threaten the health of a society which believed it progressed by evolution on the other. In the 1890's these anxieties were intensified because it seemed that with the closing of the frontier, the actual time left for the fulfillment of the American dream might be running out. Some Americans found an escape from this dilemma in imperialism and the entry of the United States into world politics. Others, clinging more closely to a native American ideal, rejected the outside world and looked for the resolution of the problem at home. Imperialism itself was a threat to democratic values, and Americans searched restlessly for moral equivalents to war now that expansion on the North American continent was drawing to a close and the happy aggressiveness of a frontier world must disappear forever. The early 1900's saw ever increasing attempts to redefine democracy and to accommodate to the fact that American economic development lay no longer with an expanding frontier but with the development of urban industry. This was a serious problem, for the mystique surrounding American democratic notions was that of the rural eighteenth-century world and a new one had to be provided to release American energies in this new situation. The creation of a national economy in the great industrial empires brought with it a new concern with federal-state relations, and the emergence of the modern city brought with it the novel problem of city government in what appeared to be a stratified society. This was a particularly distressing problem, appearing as it did for the first time in American experience, and so it seemed natural that the city was the world in which a redefinition of the classic belief was to be achieved. Artistic and intellectual life also faced this dilemma of the American identity in terms of the city. It occurred to no one to search for it any longer at Walden Pond. In these years the problem of poverty on a massive scale was also faced for the first time. It seemed to raise moral problems which went to the very roots of the American consciousness. The classic virtues of thrift and industry were enough for the simple serenity of the New England frame house. They were meaningless in an industrial slum. Charity now became the central problem of an essentially moral people. It too was ridden with disturbing ambiguities, for in evolutionary terms it seemed to threaten the fit with endless labor to preserve the unfit who would weigh down and weaken the race. Charity needed redefinition in an increasingly complex society.

These were all national problems. There were sectional ones as well. A national economy made people aware for the first time of the exploitation of the South. A new concern with democracy raised again the haunting problem of the Negro just as the first signs of his migration North brought a fresh awareness of guilt to perceptive Northerners. There were special problems too, and of these none was more perplexing and disturbing to Americans than that of the role of women. It was a problem of enormous intensity. There was no national or sectional problem which was not in some aspect part of the difficulty in defining the role of women. Wealth and leisure for the urban middle class raised anguishing problems for women unused to seeking public roles, and unable because of America's predominantly frontier culture to conceive of nonactivist roles for women. A Puritan ethic made leisure for these unhappy ladies an object of restless guilt; hence the frenetic and pathetic search of urban leisured women for release from their privileged inutility. Spencer was a torment to them. Reality lay in participation as an individual unit in the struggle for survival. Fulfillment could be found only in an individualism as untrammeled as that of the industrial entrepreneur. Nothing is more universal than the cry of privileged American women of this generation that their wealth, education and social status cut them off from *reality*. The problem of wealth in a society of democratic belief had even wider implications. For women it was *unearned* wealth and carried with it guilt and feelings of obligation to society which must be reconciled.

The national problem of identity was also a feminine one. The genteel society which was emerging in the late nineteenth century did not set much store by simple childbearing. Rather it strove to limit families. Nor did it value the practical helpmate, for hers were not the skills of the new economy. Feminine skills in the rural frontier tradition offered little in the new apartment hotels of the big cities; labor-saving devices ate endlessly into the realm in which old-style feminine efficiency could operate. Since one defines oneself in a mobile society by what one does, the question of identity was desperate and, from the accounts of those who lived through it, a searing experience. The new immigrants exacerbated feminine problems in two ways. They provided cheap domestic labor and thus increased the leisure of the merely comfortably wealthy. In another sense, they helped to dramatize the erosion of old feminine values. Because of their economic position women were drawn into the factories of urban industry, and because they were exploited they worked until there was no energy left for homes and children. Contemporaries barely sensed their tragedy and instead saw them as the new type of womanhood, the creation of the city. The close of the frontier meant the release of women from the old ideal of the self-sufficient household which had hitherto held unquestioned moral value.

The new environment of urban life also suggested congeniality for feminine endeavor. Perhaps nothing was more stimulating to this expectation than the appearance of imperialistic aspirations in the American people. The notion of the acuteness of feminine moral perceptions came into its own. In the city, women, exempt as they were from masculine aggressiveness, could band together to create a better world. Here was a real issue and a noble task, and they seized it joyfully, as any scrutiny of membership of anti-imperialist leagues will show. Attempts to redefine democracy raised the question of female suffrage in the larger context of the whole democratic mystique. Curiously, it was never argued with the violence and bitterness which accompanied the issue in Great Britain, for it was genuinely seen by all parties to the debate to be part of a much larger problem which all Americans shared in common. Women suffragists encountered the perennial problems of the Constitution and probably no campaign aroused such prolonged discussion of constitutional issues as did the long-drawn-out but remarkably amiable one to secure ratification of the Equal Rights Amendment. By the late 1890's it was not merely the problems of cultivated women of leisure which attracted attention, but the phenomenon of the working-class woman, who was by then a significant part of the labor force. The most exploited laborers in the immigrant ghettos were women and children, and in the process of redefining democracy it seemed as if the role of the state might have to be redefined to protect them. City government, said women of these generations, was "housekeeping on a large scale,"[4] and it was in civic reform that they first found an outlet for their energy and reforming zeal. Education at the college and graduate level brought women in significant numbers into national intellectual life and this fostered a new awareness of feminine problems. Harriet Monroe and Willa Cather were pioneers of their generation in the assertion that feminine insights provided new and necessary views of experience. The major fields of attraction for feminine endeavor were sociology, medicine, law and government, for these in one fashion or another offered an explanation of the predicament of American women and provided possible avenues toward its resolution. They were all avenues toward an urban existence and led to unquestioning acceptance of the goodness of urban life. The problem of charity touched women very deeply. Protestant, Catholic or Jew, they came from traditions in which femininity was equated with caring for the sick and aiding the poor and sheltering the child. Southern child labor in the canning factories, therefore, touched a nerve of conscience, and problems of urban poverty seemed to be especially delicate for the refined moral perceptions of literate and privileged women. In exceptional cases the logic of their belief in the special intensity of women's moral perceptions made women such as Florence Kelley and Jane Addams confront the problems of the Negroes in American society and attempt to formulate some definition of a democratic belief which would encompass them generations before the issue was faced more generally.

It was the essence of Jane Addams' greatness that she perceived, defined and reflected about every one of these issues. The limitations of her milieu are reflected in her intellectual history. It is not one of the progression of an individual intellect, but one which reflects and redefines a culture. Her reflections on contemporary problems are often a perfect image of the intellectual world of her time. She was captivated by Darwin and Spencer at a time when all her contemporaries were captivated. She abandoned them as philosophers of philanthropy when all her fellow philanthropists did after the great depression of 1893–1894. Her notion of a settlement house was conventional in terms of the social theory of her time, and her view of urban life and the role of women in it was one endlessly discussed at the University of Chicago from the time of its foundation to the outbreak of the First World War. She thought of culture, art and education in John Dewey's terms and her acceptance of pragmatism was never questioned during a long lifetime of disconcerting questioning of the meaning of experience. Yet despite these qualifications, hers was one of the most creative and influential minds in late nineteenth- and early twentieth-century America. Her genius was twofold: first, the gift of organization which created Hull-House, combined with an instinctive search for intellectual excellence which brought to it the collection of gifted residents and visitors who helped to make it what it was—a center of endless experiment and discussion of social problems, and a place where gifted young men and women could discover and develop their gifts in relation to the newly developing urban industrial society. Second, in her literary and reflective capacity, she was the exponent of a positive social morality which served to humanize the predominant Puritan ethic. She strove to articulate the problems of her society and to suggest an ethical response to them in terms of a life of public service. Her life was a model of democratic ethics in terms of positive achievement. It was for this reason that she became a legend in her lifetime, and that her

writings were received with pietistic reverence. They had something
of the character of revelation for their readers, for they cast light on
confusion. They made aspirations guiltily suppressed seem valid;
they brought hope for the resolution of anxieties half understood,
and they did so in terms of unswerving adherence to the American
democratic ideal, redefined but comfortingly recognizable. With the
revelation came the charismatic figure. She was the model of
feminine virtue which answered to every need of American women
of her day. She embodied in her person a solution to the problem of
the role of women which was acceptable for both men and women,
for her active public career carried with it no threat to the accepted
fabric of society. It was a model of respectability. Her innovations as
a moralist were concerned with the nature of charity and economic
morality in a democracy dedicated to free enterprise. On other issues
she re-enforced convention rather than attacking it. It was her good
fortune to attempt to redefine the role of women in a democratic
society without reference to sexual mores in a world which was as
reticent as she herself upon the subject. For her readers, as for her,
all sexual liberty was licence. It was a dimension of liberty which
no one was anxious to explore publicly.

In one respect only did she offend the popular consciousness, and
this was in a characteristically American vein. Her commitment to
pragmatism was so complete and her notion of human perfectibility
so unqualified that she could not conceive of absolute problems
insoluble by redefinition or negotiation. Hence her pacifism. She
accepted the notion of man's innate aggressiveness, but believed that
in an evolving world man should learn to direct his aggressions
positively. She applied the notion of woman's finer moral perceptions
to the problem of war and developed the belief that it was the
natural role of educated women to lead the world in the eradication
of violence. Her preoccupation with the control of violence was an
aspect of her concern with the freeing of women from the inferior
status of the past. A world which still resorted to violence to settle
disputes would, she felt, always impose burdens on women, for they
would be penalized for their inferior strength. Thus the outbreak
of war in 1914 seemed to her to threaten the position of women
throughout the world. She directed her amazing talents as an or-
ganizer and publicist to the peace movement and continued to do so
unflinchingly after the entry of the United States into the war in
1917. Her popularity suffered enormously and as a consequence her
leadership of welfare and charitable movements was questioned

violently until the late twenties. No matter how strongly asserted, her pacifism was still that of the extreme individualist believer in progress. It was a matter of converting individual wills to the creed of nonviolence; she never envisioned a planned society where conflicts of interest might not arise. Characteristically, her political hero during the twenties and until her death in 1935 was Herbert Hoover. They both shared a faith in a kind of individualism which a world war and an economic crisis of catastrophic proportions could not dim.

The high fervor for the creation of a better world and a more just social order which swept the nation during the New Deal reinstated Jane Addams as the national heroine and shortly before her death she was feted in Washington on the occasion of her seventy-fifth birthday as no other woman has been in this country. The myth remains unmarred and the one deviation from popular opinion is more sympathetic to a later generation. Today no woman aspires to such a role, nor do the conditions of our world seem likely to permit such achievement. It is not that there are no crises of feminine identity or that their pain is any less acute. Rather, their solutions are found elsewhere. Public roles for women abound in many professional spheres and entry into them is clear and unambiguous. The acquisition of a professional discipline is now such a routine business that it no longer serves to define the identity of any educated woman. This has happened for two reasons. The romantic notion of the special moral character of women has disappeared, dispelled by the cool analysis of a feminine unconscious fully as given to dark urges as is its masculine counterpart. Eugene O'Neill's Anna Christie was the victim of a wicked masculine world; today she would be a statistic in a Kinsey Report. A feminine career exempt from this notion of mission must be justified in less exalted terms and no longer serves as a total explanation of what one is or seeks to achieve as a woman. Second, the philosophy of extreme individualism which led women of Jane Addams' generation to see achievement only as individual achievement has gone because two generations of Americans have confronted problems too massive for any individual solution. Jane Addams' joyful recognition of the personal isolation possible in an urban world has been replaced by the recognition that such epic loneliness may be destructive. Both the aspiration to achieve alone, then, and the certainty of success are gone. Most of the spheres in which women of Jane Addams' generation found impressive public careers are now controlled by agencies of federal and state governments guided by experts and subject to bureaucratic control in which none but the most naïve would seek total personal fulfillment.

The generation which succeeded Jane Addams discovered Freud, gained the knowledge necessary to control conception and replaced her notion of freedom for women to participate in public life with a concern for freedom from sexual restraint. In the post-Freudian world it was less possible to externalize problems of emotional adjustment and to channel psychic energy into a public role. A woman of Jane Addams' emotional difficulties born into this generation would have sought psychiatric assistance instead of founding Hull-House; she would have sought the answers to her problems in self-awareness rather than in activism; and she would have expected to find their resolution in personal relationships.

Today the problem which remains to perplex American women is the absence of an ideal which is both specifically feminine and unmistakably intellectual. Knowledge, as in Jane Addams' day, is still justified in terms of utility. For Jane Addams, achievement for a woman was clear. It was defined in terms of the militant feminism of her day, and it meant entering into any activity in public life, for that had hitherto been a masculine preserve. She was fortunate that she could turn her remarkable intellectual powers to a task that was both socially necessary and yet in many ways distinctively feminine. Hull-House, and the values which it symbolized, was feminine, activist and magnificently public. Today it is a monument, not a necessity. The intellectual bases of the old self-confident feminism are gone, and with them the kind of life which it inspired. Intellect, utility, femininity—these are harmonized no longer by any militant faith. There is instead an emerging idea of femininity which asserts the value of early marriage, large families and the importance of the skills of the home, but it does not define an ideal of intellectual excellence appropriate to such a role. Since discipline of the mind must still be directed toward some utilitarian end, the young woman graduate retains the expectation that her education is the preliminary to some useful activity. She no longer seeks fulfillment in a public role, for she is aware that fulfillment is to be found in marriage and the home, but she is oppressed by the need to prove the utility of her intellect. The notion of knowledge as an end in itself, a notion which can produce either a salon or the contemplative life, is foreign to the American temper outside purely academic circles. The American woman of intellect instead seeks to justify herself by achievement in professional or business life, and to achieve in these she must conform herself to a masculine ideal of excellence. A pleasure in knowledge for its own sake, so typical of European women of the same background and education, is not possible for the American woman, and hence to devote herself to her home and family is to accept a life devoid of intellectual significance. Popular culture provides many instances of acceptance of such a belief. Film heroines who are clever are formidably unfeminine, and conquest by the hero inevitably means not a realization of their gifts, but an abandonment of them for unreflecting domesticity.

The educated American woman today cannot be inspired to achievement in Jane Addams' terms, for she has no Utopian vision of feminine equality to be gained in a better society, nor would she value such a society could she believe in its possibility. She would like her intellect and femininity to place her in a harmonious relation to society, not outside it. The young woman in search of the vivid intellectual experience which took Jane Addams to Hull-House and her salon would today search for it in graduate school. This is often not because she has a vocation for a life of learning and scholarship, but because her society does not offer her any but a professional life of independent intellectual pursuits. Here her problems are simply exacerbated. American institutions of higher learning exemplify in the most spirited fashion the notions of competition which permeate American life, and despite herself the young scholar assumes the dogged belligerence of graduate life. She is further than ever from her ideal of informed and harmonious femininity, and she has been forced to adopt a public stance which seems ludicrously opposed to it. She is not a model of anything which her society values, nor does she often have the satisfaction of personal fulfillment, for she must repress many feminine desires to retain her position in a rulthlessly competitive world.

A special set of circumstances and a brilliant insight allowed Jane Addams her salon in a form which allowed her to express and embody all the best values and aspirations of her world. Her insight was a reconciliation of feminine intellect and public life. Today our need is for a similar insight, reconciling intellect and private life. What is feminine intellect about? What is achievement for an intelligent and gifted woman today? What is the feminine liberty so passionately sought by Miss Addams' generation? Is it simply freedom to adopt a masculine notion of excellence? These are our problems today, unsolved, and as yet too little thought about.

REFERENCES

1. Caroline F. Urie to Ellen G. Starr, West Roxbury, Massachusetts, May 25, 1935, Ellen G. Starr Papers, Sophia Smith Collection, Smith College Library, Northampton, Massachusetts.

2. Jane Addams, "My Experiences as a Progressive Delegate," *McLures Magazine,* November, 1912, pp. 12–15.

3. William James to Jane Addams, Cambridge, Massachusetts, December 13, 1909, Jane Addams Correspondence, Jane Addams Papers, Swarthmore College Peace Collection, Swarthmore, Pennsylvania.

4. Jane Addams, "The Modern City and Municipal Franchise for Women," Address to the National American Woman Suffrage Association, Baltimore, Maryland, February, 1906. Seven-page leaflet, Jane Addams Papers, Swarthmore College Peace Collection, Swarthmore, Pennsylvania.

JOAN M. ERIKSON

Nothing to Fear: Notes on the Life of Eleanor Roosevelt

THE FOREIGN visitor to this country in the 1930's might well have been astounded by the portrayal in newspapers and magazines of the First Lady of the land. Eleanor Roosevelt was featured prominently in the press as the butt of jokes and anecdotes. Much of this humor was kindly, some of it was cruel, and upon occasions it became vicious. Cartoonests were never at a loss with the assignment of portraying Mrs. Roosevelt. She smiled often and broadly, displaying prominent front teeth. The caricatures were cruel and repetitious, combined with such taunting remarks as, "Eleanor can bite an apple through a picket fence." That she continued to smile frequently, broadly and unaffectedly in spite of consistent lampooning attests to unusual fortitude, perhaps especially in a woman.

What were the characteristics which offered themselves for this ridicule? The more kindly humor focused on her soft-hearted and sometimes deep involvement in any cause which supported the improvement of conditions for the underprivileged. She was moved by any tale of woe, often using private funds to alleviate an individual financial problem, but she also espoused wholeheartedly and without cautionary hesitation the more debatable large-scale official measures for dealing with employment.

But the most savage ridicule was focused on her phenomenal energy. This ability of Eleanor Roosevelt to go on when all companions were falling by the wayside, to travel extensively, to write reams about seemingly insignificant daily affairs, to talk enthusiastically about the issues that concerned her, to entertain in the White House as if it were a public museum—all exposed her constantly to the suspicion of others less endowed. Her critics suggested that this drive could be maintained only in the service of an extraordinary hunger for power and that she was a flagrant busybody on the national scale; that she was in love with the sound of her own voice and the sight of her own words in print. This kind of energy might be admirable in a man. It was applauded among the qualities of her uncle, Theodore Roosevelt, whom in some ways she was said to resemble. But it was said to be unseemly in a woman who after all belonged at home, even if home happened to be the White House and her children for that very good reason were all away in school or college. Moreover, these activities were the more disconcerting to her critics because it gradually became evident that they were not merely a kind of innocuous busywork on the part of the President's wife. She was, in fact, unquestionably effective as a voice urgently enlisting the responsible participation of women in public affairs and in the support of the various humanitarian causes which she promoted; and she was a successful ambassadress to the countries that she visited. Perhaps the only weapon against such formidable enterprise was ridicule.

How does a person, especially a woman, who is kept prominently in the public eye, survive such attack? Close friends of Mrs. Roosevelt report that she deliberately avoided reading what the papers printed about her. When her attention was called to particularly ugly criticism she would reply, "They mean my husband; they are only getting at him through me." On a trip to Puerto Rico a cartoonist in a local paper produced a cruel cartoon featuring her teeth and expression. When her friends objected and clamored that he be fired, she defended his right to draw her as he wished and invited him to tea. Westbrook Pegler, in his column, often attacked her viciously. When this was pointed out to her, she said, "I think he must be a very unhappy man."

But avoid what she might, the venom must to some degree have penetrated through her defenses. She made no effort, however, to fend off the negative reaction and to make her image more effective. She smiled as usual, her daily schedule remained a source of wonder to friend and foe alike, and she continued to plunge with earnest enthusiasm into the causes which interested her. Her name was a byword for the soft touch. (The number of daily requests for personal help which came to her by mail are legendary.) In fact, instead of reacting to personal criticism by letting it interfere with the work at hand, she seemed to open herself to it with apparently naïve abandon.

Her first book of memoirs is a touchingly self-revealing story of the little girl who grew up to be Eleanor Roosevelt. She wrote in the conclusion that her purpose was to give "as truthful a picture as possible of a human being." This she tried to do in the honest, straightforward prose of a schoolgirl. In her "My Day" column, she continued this self-exposure of her actions and thoughts. Perhaps she felt that in this kind of intimate sharing of the banal elements of a woman's life she could reach more women and draw them into sympathetic support of the causes she sponsored. Perhaps, too, she hoped to impart some of her discipline and her energy into lives grown sluggish in the constant coping with household chores.

Her memoirs reveal, I think, the sources of her courage and her discipline, her enthusiasm and her serenity. One of her favorite quotations was "Back of tranquillity lies always conquered unhappiness," and her unassuming autobiographic writings offer a better and more intuitive account of such conquest than do many more ambitious self-revelations. She records her memories with a feminine concreteness and closeness to people, reminiscing with critical sympathy about the little girl and the young woman whose life is being described. Her later writings lose some of this quality. They read as though the events reported had initially been more self-consciously recorded in a diary and later assembled to continue a history. There is little self-observation. In them we find Mrs. Roosevelt in action and history taking form around her, but we are given few glimpses of the inner development of the maturing woman.

This account, then, will follow her life only as far as she reveals some hints of her inner experience of growth to us. It will attempt to let Eleanor Roosevelt speak, underlining with commentary only such insights as may otherwise escape the reader. Her own words are, in fact, often so naïve and without humor that the dynamic truths they express can be overlooked in what might be considered an amateurish and superficial style. Let us review briefly some of the most critical and telling experiences of her childhood as she has recorded them, seeking possible sources for her outstanding qualities —for she was no stranger to adversity.

Anna Eleanor Roosevelt was born in 1884 in New York. Her mother was Anna Hall Roosevelt, then twenty-one years old and according to the *New York Times*, "one of the most beautiful and popular women in New York Society." Her father was Elliot Roosevelt, aged twenty-four, at the time of her birth a dashing, handsome and adventurous man, brother of Theodore Roosevelt and also a member of one of New York's socially elite families.

Eleanor was not a pretty baby. As she grew older it became apparent that she would be an unattractive little girl and that she had inherited none of the acclaimed charm and good looks of the women in her mother's family. This seems to have estranged her from Anna, who lavished her affection on the two sons who followed Eleanor. "I felt a curious barrier between myself and these three," she writes.

. . . and still I can remember standing in the door, very often with my finger in my mouth—which was, of course, forbidden—and I can see the look in her eyes and hear the tone of her voice as she said: "Come in, Granny." If a visitor was there she might turn and say: "She is such a funny child, so old-fashioned, that we always call her 'Granny.'" I wanted to sink through the floor in shame, and I felt I was apart from the boys.

And again,

I must have been very sensitive, with an inordinate desire for affection and praise—perhaps brought on by the fact that I was fully conscious of my plain looks and lack of manners. My mother was always a little troubled by my lack of beauty, and I knew it as a child senses those things. She tried very hard to bring me up well so my manners would in some way compensate for my looks, but her efforts only made me more keenly conscious of my shortcomings.

But if the little girl Eleanor's relationship with her mother was uncomfortable and cool, her delight in and closeness to her father provided warmth and tenderness to grow on. He had welcomed her as "a miracle from Heaven," later nicknaming her "Little Nell," and he seemed to find her in all ways charming, amusing and companionable.

I remember my father acting as gondolier, taking me out on the Venice canals, singing with the other boatmen, to my intense joy. I think there never was a child who was less able to carry a tune and had less gift for music than I. I loved his voice, however, and above all, I loved the way he treated me. He called me "Little Nell," after the Little Nell in Dickens' "Old Curiosity Shop." Later he made me read the book, but at that time I only knew it was a term of affection, and I never doubted that I stood first in his heart.

One senses that Eleanor's relationship to her father was never as uncomplicated as she describes it, and soon one stark complication became critical: this delightful father began to drink heavily and later became a confirmed alcoholic. He was banished from the family to visit European spas in search of a cure, and later to live in a small Virginia town. The little girl, then eight years old, was told that her father was sick, which puzzled her, for sick people need to be taken care of, not to be exiled.

In simple terms Eleanor Roosevelt then described a series of traumatic events. The year after her father's departure, her mother died very suddenly of diphtheria, and very shortly afterward Elliot, Jr., also died. Eleanor and her younger brother Hall were moved into their Grandmother Hall's house, and it was in this household and in their summer residence at Tivoli that she grew up.

After we were installed, my father came to see me, and I remember going down into the high ceilinged, dim library on the first floor of the house in West 37th Street. He sat in a big chair. He was dressed all in black, looking very sad. He held out his arms and gathered me to him. In a little while he began to talk, to explain to me that my mother was gone, that she had been all the world to him, and now he had only my brothers and myself, that my brothers were very young, and that he and I must keep close together. Some day I would make a home for him again, we would travel together and do many things which he painted as interesting and pleasant, to be looked forward to in the future together.

This experience remained etched on her memory and guided her life through many years. The following statement, however, could have been written only by an individual of remarkable psychological innocence:

Somehow it was always he and I. I did not understand whether my brothers were to be our children or whether he felt that they would be at school and college and later independent.

There started that day a feeling which never left me—that he and I were very close together, and some day would have a life of our own together. He told me to write to him often, to be a good girl, not to give any trouble, to study hard, to grow up into a woman he could be proud of, and he would come to see me whenever it was possible.

When he left, I was all alone to keep our secret of mutual understanding and to adjust myself to my new existence.

He came occasionally to see his children that year in New York, and these visits were joyous ones for his lonely little daughter.

Though he was so little with us, my father dominated all this period of my life. Subconsciously I must have been waiting always for his visits. They were irregular, and he rarely sent word before he arrived, but never was I in the house, even in my room two long flights of stairs above the entrance door, that I did not hear his voice the minute he entered the front door. Walking down stairs was far too slow. I slid down the banisters and usually catapulted into his arms before his hat was hung up.

But Eleanor was to learn that no happiness was secure, and that security itself was an illusion. Even this period of existing hopefully from one visit to the next was short-lived, for within the year her father was killed in a riding accident.

On August 14, 1894, just before I was ten years old, word came that my father had died. My aunts told me, but I simply refused to believe it, and while I wept long and went to bed still weeping, I finally went to sleep and began the next day living in my dream world as usual.

My grandmother decided that we children should not go to the funeral, and so I had no tangible thing to make death real to me. From that time on I knew in my mind that my father was dead, and yet I lived with him more closely, probably, than I had when he was alive.

The years in Grandmother Hall's New York house and in Tivoli with her aunts and uncles must have been dreary ones by any standard. Granted that one has a tendency to remember injustices and sorrows more vividly than pleasures, the list of Eleanor's deprivations and discomforts is still unnerving. She was forbidden sweets and therefore stole them, lied, got caught and was disgraced and shamed. She was made to wear a steel brace to improve her posture which was "vastly uncomfortable and prevented my bending over." To keep her from catching colds, she alone of the family was obliged to take a cold bath every morning. Her clothes were a source of constant embarrassment to her. She was tall, thin and shy and was dressed in skirts which were above her knees while other girls of her size wore them half way down their legs. Grandmother believed in warm clothing, and long thick underwear was prescribed and worn according to set dates in the calendar rather than as made reasonable by the temperature. Mrs. Roosevelt later recalls, "All my clothes seem to me now to have been incredibly uncomfortable." In addition to these physical discomforts and deprivations, this young girl was kept very much to herself under the surveillance of governesses and maids.

They always tried to talk to me, and I wished to be left alone to live in a dream world in which I was the heroine and my father the hero. Into this world I retired as soon as I went to bed and as soon as I woke in the morning, and all the time I was walking or when anyone bored me.

The companionship of children her own age was also denied her during the long summers at Tivoli because her Uncle Vallie had also become alcoholic and no guests were welcome at the house. Her grandmother, who was strict with her in every way, also refused to let her visit her Roosevelt relations with any frequency and denied her the opportunity to travel with a young friend and her family.

My grandmother was adamant and would not allow me to go. She gave me no reasons, either. It was sufficient that she did not think it wise. She so often said "no" that I built up the defense of saying I did not want things in order to forestall her refusals and keep down my disappointments.

Yet life was not all black. Her aunts and uncles led interesting, even somewhat wild lives, in spite of Grandmother's efforts at restraint, and Eleanor took vicarious pleasure in their exploits. And there was always time for reading, for walking and for dreaming— these three lonely occupations which she loved.

When she was fifteen, however, a friend and mentor came into her life from outside the family, a woman who was destined to sponsor what was strongest and most forward-looking in Eleanor. Grandmother Hall decided to send her to England to a private school for girls under an excellent headmistress. Intellectually, Mlle. Souvestre "shocked me into thinking," she writes. She had "an active keen mind" and she conveyed her vital interest in public affairs to her pupils. She expressed indignation at the judgment against Dreyfus, announced her total lack of sympathy with Britain during the Boer War, in fact taking the position that war was no solution to international problems—certainly a bold opinion to hold in the early 1900's. Beyond stimulating young Eleanor to independent thinking, she also undertook to increase her limited knowledge of the world by traveling with her on the continent during the holidays. They traveled widely, off the more beaten paths, Eleanor finding both advantage and enrichment in learning languages. She did learn French, German and Italian. She was allowed to remain three years under the tutelage of this gifted and inspiring teacher. Then, after having glimpsed new vistas of freedom, she was called home to be introduced to New York society. She was eighteen.

In decisive and "formative" years, then, Eleanor learned that the spirit can count for more than appearance and social form. However, she was as yet too young to sustain such insight, and the ways of her social class decreed that she must try to conform. Coming out was a gruelling experience for this shy, still rather awkward girl, and she gives us this account of her misery:

My aunt, Mrs. Mortimer, had bought my clothes in Paris, and I imagine that I was well dressed, but there was absolutely nothing about me to attract anybody's attention. . . . I do not think I quite realized beforehand what utter agony it was going to be or I would never have had the courage to go. . . . I knew I was the first girl in my mother's family who was not a belle, and though I never acknowledged it to any of them at the time, I was deeply ashamed. . . . Gradually I acquired a few friends . . . and finally going out lost some of its terrors; but that first winter, when my sole object in life was society, nearly brought me to a state of nervous collapse.

Whatever tensions contributed to Eleanor's nervous state, it is clear that she suffered not only from strenuous and incompatible activity, but also from an inner conflict between socially approved goals and her own aspirations and emerging potentialities. The rules of her class, however, aligned her activities at first with the customary contribution of a lady to social problems: charity.

During this period of her life in New York with her Aunt Pussie she turned her attention to all kinds of charitable endeavors. From her childhood on she had been taught that people of wealth and social standing should engage in philanthropy. There was an obligation to be kind to the poor and to give to those who had less, she had always been told. Therefore, she could remember that when she was still quite a little girl she had played her part in fulfilling this obligation by aiding her father in serving Thanksgiving dinner to the poor little boys at the Newsboys Club, and he had told her of the hard life they led. And she had spread the season's cheer by helping her grandmother decorate a Christmas tree for a children's ward in the hospital. She had visited the Orthopaedic Hospital with Auntie Grace and The Bowery Mission with Aunt Maud and Aunt Pussie. So it seemed appropriate that at nineteen she should offer her services to teach fancy dancing and calisthenics at the Rivington Street Settlement House and to investigate working conditions in garment factories and department stores for the Consumers League. Later she would turn indignantly against a system that offered mere charity where it should provide the underprivileged with the right of equal opportunity to help themselves. For the time being, however, she learned to work and to care deeply.

I had painfully high ideals and a tremendous sense of duty at that time, entirely unrelieved by any sense of humor or any appreciation of the weaknesses of human nature. Things were either right or wrong to me with very few shades, and I had had too little experience to know as yet how very fallible human judgments are.

In 1903 she became engaged to her distant cousin Franklin Roosevelt. There must have been general astonishment then, even as this betrothal now in retrospect astonishes. Franklin expressed himself in a letter to his mother as being "the happiest man just now in the world; likewise the luckiest." Mrs. Roosevelt, Sr. promptly sent him off on a Caribbean tour. Eleanor later wrote about her engagement with touching candor:

I had a great curiosity about life and a desire to participate in every experience that might be the lot of woman. There seemed to me to be a necessity for hurry; without rhyme or reason I felt the urge to be a part of the stream of life, and so in the autumn of 1903 when Franklin Roosevelt, my fifth cousin once removed, asked me to marry him, though I was only nineteen, it seemed an entirely natural thing and I never even thought that we were both rather young and inexperienced. I came back from Groton, where I had spent the weekend, and asked Cousin Susie whether she thought I cared enough, and my grandmother, when I told her, asked me if I was sure I was really in love. I solemnly answered "yes" and yet I know now that it was years later before I understood what being in love was or what loving really meant.

A year later, after Eleanor had met Franklin's side of the family, the engagement was announced and the wedding set for March 17. Theodore Roosevelt had been elected President. He was, in fact, inaugurated on March 4, and his first visit to New York following this ceremony was made in order to give his niece away in marriage. It followed naturally that he became the star of the festivities, with crowds forming to catch a glimpse of the President and large groups gathering around him at the reception. It was a memorable wedding and it should have warned Eleanor that her life would not be her own—until she would eventually make it her own.

For their honeymoon the young couple went to Hyde Park and thus a new era began for the bride, of a kind of upper-class captivity. Holidays would be spent at Hyde Park with mother-in-law; in summer they would move to Campobello with her and in winter they would live in a house bought for them, furnished for them, staffed with servants for them by her, and right next door to her.

Sarah Delano Roosevelt was a domineering woman who had devoted years of widowhood to the upbringing of her only son. His marriage in no way decreased her sense of responsibility and she took over the training and management of her daughter-in-law with a conviction and dedication which trapped the young wife in a sense of helplessness. Upon moving into the newly built, furnished and staffed house on East 65th Street, Eleanor felt so submerged in the strong personalities of her husband and mother-in-law that she at one point burst into tears, a self-indulgence she permitted herself only twice throughout her adult life. When Franklin asked her what might be the matter she confessed that she did not like living in a house which was not in any way hers, one that she had in no way planned and which did not represent the way she wanted to live. But her young husband, who was also a devoted son, just teased her and told her not to be silly.

Since Eleanor, during these years, was going through one pregnancy after another—Anna, 1906; James, 1907; Franklin, Jr., 1908 (died at eight months); Elliot, 1910; Franklin, Jr., II, 1914; John, 1916—and was very occupied with her unsuccessful efforts to manage the nurses and servants who were the experts called in to care for her babies, she could do little to express her own wishes, nor did she have the physical strength to combat the formidable team of husband and mother-in-law. Although she was for ten years "always just getting over having a baby or about to have one," she was not unaware of what was happening to her own personality. She recognized that she was in danger of developing "into a completely colorless echo," that she "was not developing any individual taste or initiative," and that something within her craved to be an independent individual.

As F. D. R. became involved in politics and was sent first to Albany and then to Washington, Eleanor undertook the duties appropriate to the wife of a New York senator and later those incumbent on her when he became the Assistant Secretary of the Navy. The social round of duties in Washington was strenuous but she had the advantage of the advice of her practiced Auntie Bye, who had advised Theodore Roosevelt when he held the same post, regarding the complications of procedure and protocol. During the war years she plunged into activities with other women in the Navy League providing comforts for seamen or visiting naval hospitals, talking to sick and wounded men and cooking in a Red Cross canteen.

The war years in Washington were hectic and demanding for the Roosevelts. Probably it was during this period that Eleanor's capacity for discipline, endurance and energetic undertaking were first really challenged and confirmed. She says of this experience, too, that the exposure to all kinds of people and to the confidences of the boys in the naval hospitals provided her with "a liberal education." Out of these contacts with human beings, she writes, "I became a more tolerant person—far less sure of my own beliefs and methods of action, but I think more determined to try for certain ultimate objectives." Then, once again, her horizon was widened by travel. The trip with President and Mrs. Wilson to the Paris Peace Conference, where she could feel herself a part of historic decision-making, no doubt also added to her status as a mature woman. During F. D. R.'s unsuccessful campaign for the Vice-Presidency in 1920 she had her first taste of traveling around the country on the campaign train, and she later referred to this experience as "the start of my political education."

Then a crisis occured which threatened to contract her life space and that of her husband and to preshadow a future of severe restriction. In the summer of 1921, F. D. R. contracted infantile paralysis at Campobello. Eleanor became his day and night attendant and nursed him with efficient dedication.

Almost everything we have noted about Eleanor Roosevelt's development up to this point would seem to suggest that she was now offered a potentially absorbing role. Needing to be needed, eager to please, dedicated to service—how appropriate that she should now devote herself to an invalid husband's care. An amazing transformation, however, took place slowly but irrevocably, for it was at this point in her life that the woman who as a girl had bowed to domination by mother, grandmother, husband and mother-in-law, firmly stood her full height and took over the responsibility not only for her husband's care and her family's well-being, but also for their joint right to manage their own future. Mrs. Roosevelt, Sr., was the first to record the change. In a letter to her brother about the sickroom at Campobello, she wrote the simple truth. "Eleanor is in the lead."

How true this was she perhaps did not quite realize at the time. When it became clear that F. D. R. would not recover the use of his legs and that he would be permanently crippled, his mother demanded that he be brought to Hyde Park, where he could have rest and complete quiet. There, she said, he could write as he always wanted to and "he can keep busy doing that or reading books or collecting stamps." But she had not counted with her daughter-in-law. "That's the last thing he should do," Eleanor told her. "And I won't let him."

This was the beginning of a determined struggle between the two women, between two generations who "knew what was best" for a stricken man. Eleanor by then had found a firm ally in the person of F. D. R.'s friend Louis Howe, who was also intent on not allowing him to become a dispirited invalid. Together they contrived to bring rewarding activities, interesting people and stimulating ideas to F. D. R. Howe searched the bookstores for rare old books and studied stamps so that he could talk intelligently about them. But Eleanor and Howe agreed that hobbies would not be enough for their charge, and even when he added a work schedule it was clear to them that his real interest was politics. So it was decided that Eleanor should become active in politics and in this way involve F. D. R. in current issues. She turned her attention and amazing energy to the work of the Women's Trade Union League and brought some of her co-workers home with her to meet her husband. She joined the Women's Division of the Democratic State Committee and began a round of public speaking, which, though frightening for her initially, proved most successful. (She had a habit of giggling which infuriated Louis Howe, and he reproved her severely.) And she traveled extensively all over the state organizing women voters into the Democratic party.

All of this activity came to a head when Al Smith, in 1924, asked F. D. R. to take charge of his preconvention campaign and to nominate him as presidential nominee for the Democratic party. F. D. R. agreed, and though his candidate ran unsuccessfully, he showed a triumphant courage by facing the Democratic convention on his own feet, even though his legs had to be supported by braces, and by giving his now famous "Happy Warrior" speech. F. D. R. was back in the public eye. He was back in politics.

The rest is well known. From the childhood and young womanhood sketched here, the woman emerged who more than any other woman in American history played a leading role in public affairs, the woman who gave to the position of the President's wife an entirely new force, the woman who was to become chairman of the committee which drew up the United Nations Declaration of Human Rights. We shall not here discuss in any detail these later developments which proved that the time was ripe for the emergence of a woman like Eleanor Roosevelt, even as she had now become adequate to and ready for her historical role. But let us ask ourselves whether it is possible to trace any inner logic in this story.

Eleanor Roosevelt's account of her early life highlights a lesson often lost in the study of biographies. This record of her childhood experiences could, if it were offered as a case history, account for a total failure to accept the challenge of participation in an active and productive life. Such documentation could be used trauma for trauma to "explain" failure. Yet Eleanor Roosevelt "succeeded," in many ways triumphantly, in other ways not without tragic overtones. Victory of this caliber should be kept before us to contribute to a better understanding of the intimate history accompanying great events.

Reviewing, then, the traumatic aspects of her childhood, can we bring into focus the qualities, the strengths that were pitted against failure—and that won? What became of the shame of "Granny," the deep sadness of "Little Nell," the pervading sense of inferiority and fear of the small girl Eleanor? The inner tranquillity of the Mrs. Roosevelt that the world knew and honored was indeed the fruit of actively "conquered unhappiness," of deprivation transcended. But, in addition, she became an individual who manifested such transcendance in what Woodrow Wilson called "activity on a large scale."

She seems to have settled her account with her unlucky childhood by a determined rebalancing of the scales and by projecting this shift onto an almost global screen. Once deeply ashamed of her own unattractiveness, she spent her entire life developing her capacity for empathizing with people. She listened with compassion. Her response to any demonstrable need was immediate and generous to a fault. Indignation was by no means foreign to her, but she transformed it into strong feelings in the service of causes. Such empathizing requires the capacity to be self-effacing. Having set her own needs aside, as it were, her relationships with others could be immediate and warm. She became one of the most attractive and charming women in public life.

The little girl Eleanor had been ashamed about her physical cowardice. She had been afraid of the dark and of burglars, of water, of horses, of physical exploits of many kinds. Her reckless and dashing father had chided her about this and had tried to encourage his timid daughter. Her Uncle Ted had teased her, and her Hall aunts and uncles had made fun of her fears. This same child became renowned as a grown woman for her endurance and her fearlessness in meeting danger. It was not a courage lightly won. Perhaps it grew out of her determination to accept all challenges actively in order to avoid that fate worse than death—public shaming. Green with seasickness on a battleship one day, the suggestion was made to her that she climb the 100-foot ladder of the skeleton mask. She did, and in time she slowly overcame her fear of height and of seasickness.

Even more than physical apprehension of danger she suffered from fear of the disapproval of those from whom she needed love. In her loneliness and perplexity she lied and she stole.

I could bear with swift punishment of any kind far better than long scoldings. I could cheerfully lie anytime to escape a scolding, whereas if I had known that I would simply be put to bed or be spanked I probably would have told the truth. This habit of lying stayed with me for a number of years. I now realize I was a great trial to my mother. She did not understand that a child may lie from fear; I myself never understood it until I reached the age when I suddenly realized that there was nothing to fear.

One may note here that this realization came to her only when she left her grandmother's house for school in England, for she writes, "this was the first time in all my life that all my fears left me."

She did later lead a fearless public life, disregarding petty criticism and caricature and striking out boldly for charity in issues both big and small. And it was she who selected for her husband's tombstone the depression-conquering slogan, "The only thing we have to fear is fear itself."

Having suffered from certain psychological deprivations as a child, she responded with immediate concern to the support of any oppressed group. She championed the cause of educating and freeing women so that they might become responsible citizens. She did not address herself to this problem by joining groups working explicitly for women's rights. Instead she set herself the task of demonstrating in her own person how the rights already gained could be made use of to greatest advantage. She wasted no breath on battle-cries—she simply rearranged the furniture, as it were, placing her desk in an advantageous position in the living room and getting up an hour earlier to make time for her correspondence. Her devotion to the cause of the underprivileged found its crowning achievement in her magnificent work for the Committee on Human Rights of the United Nations.

Deprived in her childhood of the people she loved most, of the possibly compensatory sweets, of trips and of friends, and being exposed so often to "no" as the answer to her requests, she learned early not to ask for things, and better still not to want or hope for them, in order to avoid disappointment. But she was an observant child and noted that the grandmother who disciplined her so sternly had no discipline whatsoever where her own children were concerned. She spoiled them unrestrainedly and was helplessly outraged with their misbehavior, especially when her sons began their heavy drinking. Mrs. Roosevelt speaks of this drinking as having made a deep impression on her:

This was my first [really her second] contact with anyone who had completely lost power of self-control and I think it began to develop in me an almost exaggerated idea of the necessity of keeping all of one's desires under complete subjugation.

Actively then she began to impose on herself the controls, the discipline to which she had been passively subjected as a little girl. She became extraordinarily self-disciplined. Her workday was strenuous, but organized to the minute, for with the proverbial energy went control, the capacity both for renunciation and for complete relaxation. She exercised every morning without fail and she could sleep anywhere sitting up in a chair.

This life-sustaining strength came somehow from the few people whom she loved and admired and with whom she identified. Who were these important people? Her relationship with her mother, at least in later childhood, was certainly not one of loving mutuality. The little Eleanor admired this glamorous mother and loved to watch her as she dressed to go out in the evening, and she was content to rub her mother's head by the hour when she complained of a headache. However, she also knew her as a stern judge who found a child who could lie despicable, but who nevertheless "made a great effort for me" obviously out of a sense of duty. One is tempted to wonder how much of the onus of this mother's disappointment in her "uncontrolled" husband was projected onto the little daughter who looked so much like him.

Be that as it may, the daughter could not learn from this mother how to become the loving and caring mother of her own children. She writes of her own mothering, "I never had any interest in dolls or in little children and I knew absolutely nothing about handling or feeding a baby." No wonder, then, that she felt incompetent and awkward with her own babies and turned them over to nurses and governesses. Writing later in life, she deplores this lack of training and understanding and expresses the wish that she had taken over the upbringing of her children herself. "Had I done this," she says,

. . . my subsequent troubles would have been avoided and my children would have had far happier childhoods. As it was, for years I was afraid of my nurses, who from this time on were usually trained English nurses who ordered me around quite as much as they ordered the children.

Eleanor Roosevelt's role as a mother is both fascinating and disturbing. Motherhood seems to have happened to her as an inexorable fate, before she could grasp its meaning. In her story she emphasizes how strongly she felt her responsibility for her children's welfare, how dutifully she cared for them when ill or injured, but little joy or even satisfaction in mothering shines through.

The mother surrogate appointed by Anna Hall to take over the upbringing of her children was also unable to provide the little Eleanor with warm mothering. Grandmother Hall, according to the story we are told, apparently had just decided to mend her previously all too permissive ways with children when it devolved on her to bring up her daughter's child. No doubt this responsibility was unwelcome. She had already brought up a family of five children, widowed as she was, with rather questionable success. Perhaps she also saw in her granddaughter the child of her tragically intemperate son-in-law, and determined to control her with a firm hand. She is mentioned with sympathy and understanding in Mrs. Roosevelt's account of her life with her, but with neither admiration nor love. She speaks of one lesson, however, which she took to heart:

My grandmother's life had a considerable effect on me, for even when I was young I determined that I would never be dependent on my children by allowing all my interests to center in them. The conviction has grown through the years. In watching the lives of those around her, I have felt that it might have been well in their youth if they had not been able to count on her devotion and her presence whenever they needed her. . . . it might have been far better . . . had she insisted on bringing more discipline into their lives simply by having a life of her own.

Whether or not, in the end, Eleanor Roosevelt's "life of her own" benefited her children is not a matter to be discussed here, although the hostile press during her lifetime did not shirk suggestive remarks. What must be said, however, is that this whole question of a mother's "life of her own" and her children's lives is a matter demanding concrete study free from prejudice and from unpleasant eagerness to draw general (and negative) conclusions from the lives of pioneers and innovators.

One figure stands out in the story of young Eleanor who is described by her in only the happiest and most admiring terms. This was Mlle. Souvestre, the principal of the English school where she spent three wonderfully happy years. Mlle. Souvestre was apparently the epitome of what a fine teacher should be, both intelligent and wise, dignified and motherly, disciplined in her thinking but independent. Though she did not flout convention, she remained honest and nonconforming in her attitudes. She must also have been a fine judge of character, for she took the shy awkward American girl under her wing, called her "ma chère petite" and set herself the task of developing in her pupil a sense of self-confidence and also of opening her mind to intellectual interests. She discovered Eleanor's remarkable capacity to memorize, to listen to and remember conversation, and she gave her ample opportunity to use and develop this gift, of which she made such admirable use in later life.

In her Eleanor found a thoughtful and intelligent woman of strong convictions, who was unafraid to represent what she believed. Under the tutelage of this devoted teacher, then, Eleanor absorbed principles which could give her commitment to her American heritage new impetus and later enlist her uncompromising involvement in the struggle for human dignity. Here was a woman to love, admire and deeply respect, and Eleanor writes of her that she "exerted the greatest influence, after my father, on this period of my life."

"After my father." What influence did her father have on the life of Eleanor Roosevelt? For the little girl who loved him so devotedly it would be almost impossible to exaggerate his role. He was her life, her *raison d'être*. Her life was dominated by his presence even after his death, and his wish became her will. When she went off to school she took the "letters of my father's which I always carried with me" and these were read and reread. She habitually bit her fingernails, but one day "I came across one in which he spoke of always making the most of one's personal appearance, and from that day forward my nails were allowed to grow."

When she was forty years old and the wife of the President of the United States, she wrote:

On the other side of my family, of course, many people whom I have mentioned will be described far better and more fully by other people, except in the case of my father, whose short and happy life was so tragically ended. With him I have a curious feeling that as long as he remains to me the vivid, living person that he is, he will, after the manner of the people in the "Blue Bird," be alive and continue to exert his influence which was always a very gentle, kindly one.

Could one not say that the young Eleanor and the mature woman she became were the product of an act of will—the will to be the daughter that her father had lovingly preordained, the daughter that would make him proud? This deep love for her father and her conviction that she was beloved and that much was expected of her was surely the source of the inner strength which upheld her and made it possible for her to transcend her misfortunes.

And she married Franklin Roosevelt. It is impossible to judge what mixture of conventionality and of affection marked the beginnings of this relationship. One has the impression that in this instance two emotionally immature people found one another whose needs for intimacy may have remained atuned to the demands of a more remote destiny. Hindsight, at any rate, makes it seem probable that these two people sensed potentialities which in each could only be realized with the help that each could offer the other.

In her autobiography Eleanor Roosevelt gives us little information and only few hints about her relationship with her husband. Perhaps this is just reticence, but one is tempted to conjecture that only by deliberately barring this scene-stealing actor from the stage could she highlight herself in the setting of her early married life. There are known facts, however, and her own words to consider. At eighteen years of age Eleanor was not a promising and popular debutante. To become at nineteen the fiancée of one of the socially most outstanding young bachelors of New York must have been in itself both a pleasant development and one which promoted her personal and social security. To be chosen, to be wanted in spite of Mrs. Roosevelt, Sr.'s obvious reluctance to give her approval, surely must have warmed her heart and supported her wavering self-confidence. And his name was Roosevelt, a loved name for the daughter of a Roosevelt who had grown up in a family of Halls. He was also her own father's godson.*

What does Eleanor's story tell us of F. D. R.'s role in her development? Speaking of an annoying fault in her character, Eleanor describes how as a young wife she was given to moods and would retreat into wordless martyrdom and limelight self-effacement: "my Griselda mood," she called it. Franklin was the antidote for this. He could tease her out of her gloom, and she was grateful. She was also very inept as a housekeeper and knew little about wifely duties, and she writes appreciatively, "I marvel now at my husband's patience, for I realize how trying I must have been in many ways." She mentions too that he talked history endlessly on their honeymoon, that he was informed about the government of his country (which she was not and vowed to become) and that he taught her how to keep track of money; "my husband educated me in the question of accounts." And she learned things because it

---

* The Roosevelts had met Elliot on a world cruise and had become so devoted to him that they had asked him to be their son's godfather.

is a wife's duty to be interested in whatever interests her husband. "You so obviously must want that which you ought to do," she wrote. "So I took an interest in politics."

She also made a heroic effort to take part in the sports which he loved, golf, sailing and swimming; but she was inept and he finally discouraged her efforts. He was a collector of books, stamps and anything pertaining to the American Navy. Of these interests she says only that she wasted time trying to restrain him.

In a remark evaluating her own development at the time of the First World War, she makes an astonishing statement—astonishing because the tribute to her husband is so casual. She describes an argument with her grandmother about her brother Hall's enlistment and adds: "This was my first outspoken declaration against the accepted standards of the surroundings in which I had spent my childhood, and marked the fact that either my husband, or an increasing ability to think for myself, was changing my point of view." Perhaps F. D. R.'s outstanding contribution to Eleanor's development was to foster that "increasing ability to think for myself."

From these sources, then, and undoubtedly from other interesting and exemplary figures of her wider family and her time, such as Uncle Ted and Auntie Bye, Eleanor gradually built up that personality which was to become the legendary figure—the "Great Lady" of our country and the world. This slow unfolding withstood a number of crises. The self-confidence that had been nourished at school abroad apparently suffered a considerable set-back when she became a debutante. A constant round of gaieties and parties was inconsistent with any of the goals for which her education had prepared her, and surely her image of herself was not that of a social butterfly. Her early engagement to F. D. R. seems to have been a relationship that she almost drifted into; and her first years of married life, with the problems of getting along with mother-in-law and the perplexities of bearing and caring for children, seem almost to have inundated her with demands. Obviously these were years of tremendous importance in her development— obviously she grew in stature and gained poise through her experience.

But a moment came in her life which again brought near tragedy —her husband's serious illness. Once before, as a little girl, she had been the helpless observer of the tragic destruction of a beloved person. This time she was not helpless. This time she responded with a will of iron, the patience and endurance, the love necessary to rehabilitate the man, now stricken, whom she had married. An extraordinary consolidation of her capacities seems to have taken place so that she could even take a firm stand against the pronouncements of the overprotective mother-in-law who had always dominated her. She became F. D. R.'s champion against invalidism and resignation, thereby actively redeeming her own father's tragedy. She became Eleanor Roosevelt.

For almost twelve years Eleanor Roosevelt was the First Lady of the land, the wife of the President of the United States. In truly growing into the role of her great husband's wife, she found her stature as a citizen and a leader. History had called her husband to a high office, and although she had undertaken her role as mistress of the White House with misgiving and reluctance, she nevertheless became the most outstanding wife of a President that this country has produced. The historical setting both challenged and supported the development of her unusual potentialities, and her position gave her scope to fulfill them in a grand manner.

This is our image of Mrs. Roosevelt during her years in the White House. But how does she herself describe this period of her life? "I think I lived those years very impersonally. It was almost as though I had erected someone a little outside of myself who was the president's wife. I was lost somewhere deep down inside myself." Briefly but poignantly reviewing her life when she was sixty-four years of age, she summarized: "In my early married years the pattern of my life had been largely my mother-in-law's pattern. Later it was the children and Franklin who made the pattern. When the last child went to boarding school I began to want to do things on my own, to use my own mind and abilities for my own aims. When I went to Washington I felt sure that I would be able to use opportunities which came to me to help Franklin gain the objectives he cared about—but the work would be his work and the pattern his pattern. . . . I was one of those who served his purposes."

The final volume of her autobiography is entitled "On My Own." What were her "own aims"? Though warmly supporting many causes, essentially she was dedicated to two utopian ideals—Equality: equality of women in their responsible involvement in public affairs; human equality between individuals in a classless society; equality of rights and opportunities for all races, classes and creeds—for all mankind—these to be won in the service of human dignity; and Peace: a precept learned in her youth remained her conviction—that war is no solution to problems between nations or between people. Her appointment to the United Nations after F. D. R.'s death provided an ideal setting for activities directed toward these aims. She believed deeply in world government and she was eminently fitted to become the chairman of the Committee on Human Rights.

Transcendence of the human condition through activity on a large scale, then, could characterize Eleanor Roosevelt's career. In the final paragraph of her book, written when she was seventy-four years old, however, we can still hear the voice of a younger Eleanor, an echo from the past:

It seems to me that we must have the courage to face ourselves in this crisis. We must regain a vision of ourselves as leaders of the world. We must join in an effort to use all knowledge for the good of all human beings.

When we do that, we shall have nothing to fear.

Notes on Contributors

LOTTE BAILYN, born in 1930 in Vienna, Austria, combines an academic role as lecturer on social psychology in the Department of Social Relations at Harvard University with that of wife and mother. Her publications include *Mass Media and Children: A Study of Exposure Habits and Cognitive Effects*, Psychological Monograph No. 471 (1959), and, with Bernard Bailyn, *Massachusetts Shipping, 1697–1714: A Statistical Study* (1960), as well as studies, with Hebert C. Kelman, in professional journals.

JILL CONWAY, born in Hillston, New South Wales, Australia, in 1934, was graduated from the University of Sydney in 1958. In 1960 she came to Radcliffe College to enter Graduate School. At present in Europe with her husband, she is completing a doctoral dissertation, of which her contribution to this issue is a part, on the relation between development of the field of social work in America and the changing rôle of women. Her publications in Australia include articles and reviews on Australian colonial history.

CARL N. DEGLER, born in 1921, is presently professor of history at Vassar College. During the academic year 1963–1964, he was also visiting professor of history at Columbia University. He is the author of *Out of Our Past: the Forces that Shaped Modern America* (1959), "Charlotte Perkins Gilman on the Theory and Practice of Feminism," *American Quarterly* (1956), and is a contributor to *Notable American Women*, a biographical dictionary now in process of compilation.

ERIK H. ERIKSON, born in Germany in 1902 of Danish parentage, has, since 1960, been professor of human development and lecturer on psychiatry at Harvard University, following upon a distinguished career as psychoanalyst and training psychoanalyst. His many publications include *Childhood and Society* (1950), *Young Man Luther* (1958), *Insight and Responsibility* (1964), as well as many monographs and papers. His essay, "Youth: Fidelity and Diversity," appeared in the Winter, 1962 issue of *Dædalus*.

JOAN M. ERIKSON, born in Canada in 1903, is an artist in many fields. Trained as a dancer in Vienna while her husband was working with Sigmund Freud, she is also skilled in jewelry making, and her jewelry has been widely exhibited. At present she is engaged on a book on the history of beads. Her interest in arts and crafts has, in addition, led her to work with psychiatric patients in crafts.

ROBERT JAY LIFTON, born in 1926, is Foundations' Fund for Research in Psychiatry Associate Professor at Yale University. His main research interest is the interrelationship between individual psychology and historical change, and he recently completed two and one half years of work in Japan. His book, *Thought Reform and the Psychology of Totalism,* is based on research in Hong Kong in 1954–55. Dr. Lifton's latest contribution to *Dædalus* was an article on "Psychological Effects of the Atomic Bomb in Hiroshima—The Theme of Death," which appeared in the Summer 1963 issue. He is currently working on a book dealing with his Hiroshima study.

DAVID C. McCLELLAND, born in Mount Vernon, New York, in 1917, is professor of psychology and chairman of the Department of Social Relations at Harvard University. He has served in various administrative capacities on governmental and foundation projects studying the motivation for achievement and the early identification of talent. His most recent publications are *Talent and Society* (with others); three chapters in *Motives in Fantasy, Action, and Society* (edited by John W. Atkinson); *The Achieving Society;* and *The Roots of Consciousness.*

ESTHER PETERSON, born in 1906 in Provo, Utah, has been, since August, 1961, Assistant Secretary of Labor. She retains her appointment previously held as Director of the Women's Bureau, and has recently been named Special Assistant to the President for Consumer Affairs. Such multiple responsibility has characterized her career; for several years after her marriage she alternated teaching with her duties as housewife and mother. She was Executive Vice-Chairman of the President's Commission on the Status of Women. The Commission, under the chairmanship of Mrs. Eleanor Roosevelt, was assigned by President Kennedy, "to develop plans for advancing the full partnership of men and women in our national life." The Commission completed its assignment and presented its report to the President October 11, 1963.

DAVID RIESMAN, born in Philadelphia in 1909, began his career as a lawyer. After the war he turned to the field of the social sciences, and was for several years a professor at the University of Chicago. In 1958 he came to Harvard University as Henry Ford II Professor of the Social Sciences. He is the author of *The Lonely Crowd* (1950), *Faces in the Crowd* (1952), *Thorstein Veblen: A Critical Interpretation* (1953), *Constraint and Variety in American Education* (1956), and *Abundance for What? and Other Essays* (1964). He is at present working under a Carnegie Corporation grant on studies of higher education in America.

ALICE S. ROSSI, born in 1922, is a research Associate in the Department of Sociology at the University of Chicago, where she is engaged in writing a book on middle-class kinship, and is preparing a monograph on a special commission from the Carnegie Corporation on influences on women's occupational choices. Her own choice having combined children and scholarship, she has carried on her studies at Cornell, at

Harvard, and now at Chicago. She is the author of *Generational Differences in the Soviet Union*, 2 vols. (mimeo.), Russian Research Center Series, Cambridge (1954), various articles, and, with her husband Peter H. Rossi, of "Some Effects of Parochial School Education in America," *Dædalus*, Spring, 1961.

EDNA G. ROSTOW, whose training has included psychoanalysis, social work, and social administration in London and in this country, is a consultant in psychiatry in the Department of University Health, Yale University. Her publications include "Feminism and Femininity," *Yale Review*, Spring, 1962; with Clement C. Fry, M.D., *College Mental Hygiene* (1942); and, with Eugene V. Rostow, "Law, City Planning and Social Action," in *The Urban Condition*, ed. L. J. Duhl, M.D. (1963). Throughout her career, she has balanced her professional experience as a member of the university staff with the active social life of a faculty wife.

DIANA TRILLING, born in New York City, is a major critic and free lance writer on literary, social, and political subjects. Her articles have appeared in many magazines including *Partisan Review, Nation, American Scholar,* and *Encounter.* Her most recent book, *Claremont Essays,* appeared in 1964. In addition, she edited and wrote the introductions for the *Viking Portable D. H. Lawrence* and *Letters of D. H. Lawrence.*

INDEX

Abbott, Grace and Edith, 249, 250
"Adaptive ego," 26
Addams, Jane, 196, 247–266
Adolescence, *see* Youth
Adoption, 87
Aggression, 175
Allport–Vernon–Lindzey tests, 176–177
Apprentices, 151
Atomistic thinking, 13–14
Autonomy, sense of, 55

Baboon behavior, 16–17
Baldwin, James, 60
Beauvoir, Simone de, 20, 33, 34, 94
Bennett's Mechanical Comprehension Test, 178
Bettelheim, Bruno, 4
Birth control, 206, 207
Bolívar, Simón, 23
Bowlby, John, 47, 48
Bureau of Labor Statistics, 161

Camus, Albert, 38
Careers, 88–89, 91–94, 115–119, 129–130, 134, 238–245; seriatim approach to, 243–245
Caribbean family life, 22–24
Castration phantasy, 63
Cather, Willa, 260
Child care, 78–81, 106–115, 119–121; jobs in, 121–122; centers for, 122–125, 209
Children's Bureau, 249
Citizenship, 24–25
Clothing of women, 67–68, 197
Coleman, James, 81
Collier, Virginia, 208–209
Commission on the Status of Women, 158, 161, 162, 167–168

Committee on Social Insurance and taxes, 162
Counseling, 168
Counterfeit nurturance, 45–46
Cummings, E. E., 18

Daedalus Youth issue, 4
Dating in school and college, 81–82
Deutsch, Helena, 13
Divorce, 198–199

Economic pressures, 151–153
Educated women, 89–97, 149–150, 159, 168, 193–194, 202–203, 216–225, 233–234, 264–265
Ego-organization, 25–26
Emotional isolation, 61–65, 69–70
"Emotional-symbolic substrate," 39
Equal Pay Act, 164–166
Equality of the sexes, 2–3, 98–140; reasons for, 105–106, 114–115; effect on children, 108–110; in employment, 166–167; social forces behind, 197–202
Erikson, Erik, 37
Ethical standards in literature, 54–57
Evolutionary philosophy, 254, 257

Fair Labor Standards Act, 160–161
Family, 87, 106–115, 240–242; *see also* Home
Father's role in home, 125–126, 132–133, 148–149, 195, 224, 226–227
Feminism, 41, 98–104, 193–194, 203–204, 206, 221; ideology of, 247–248
Fleming, Ian, 178
Food preparation in the home, 79–80
Freedom for women, 89, 197–199, 222–223, 255, 260

291

Index

WS

Lifton, Rob

THE WOMAN I

Boston :

293 pages